Radical Street Performance

Radical Street Performance is the first volume to collect together an extensive array of writings by scholars, activists, performers, directors, critics and journalists.

The more than thirty essays in this anthology explore the myriad forms this most public of performances can take:

- agit-prop
- invisible theatre
- demonstrations and rallies
- direct action
- puppetry
- parades and pageants
- performance art
- guerrilla theatre
- circuses

These essays look at performance in Europe, Africa, China, India and both the Americas. They describe engagement with issues as diverse as abortion, colonialism, the environment and homophobia, to name only a few. Editor Jan Cohen-Cruz has introduced and organized them into thematic sections: Agit-prop, Witness, Integration, Utopia and Tradition.

Radical Street Performance is an inspiring testimony to this international performance phenomenon, and an invaluable record of a form of theatre which continues to flourish in a televisual age.

Including contributions by: Eugenio Barba, Augusto Boal, Yolanda Broyles-González, Dwight Conquergood, Abbie Hoffman, Baz Kershaw, Adrian Piper, Nellie Richard, Richard Schechner, Diana Taylor, Ngũgĩ wa Thiong'o and David Welch.

Jan Cohen-Cruz is Associate Professor of Drama at New York University. A one-time member of the NYC Street Theatre, Jan has facilitated theatre workshops at prisons, psychiatric facilities and schools.

Radical

Street

Performance

An International Anthology

Edited and with introductions
by

Jan Cohen-Cruz

London and New York

First published 1998
by Routledge
2 Park Square, Milton Park, Abingdon, Oxon, OX14 4RN

Transferred to Digital Printing 2005

Simultaneously published in the USA and Canada
by Routledge
270 Madison Ave, New York NY 10016

Typeset in Perpetua by Florencetype, Stoodleigh, Devon

British Library Cataloguing in Publication Data
A catalogue record for this book is available from the British Library

Library of Congress Cataloging in Publication Data
A catalogue record for this book has been requested

ISBN 0–415–15230–5 (hbk)
ISBN 0–415–15231–3 (pbk)

Printed and bound by Antony Rowe Ltd, Eastbourne

Contents

CONTENTS

PART TWO
Witness

PART THREE
Integration

CONTENTS

Illustrations

Acknowledgements

I want to thank those who dialogued with me about these essays, especially Dionisio Cruz, Susie Ingalls, Katherine Linton, Lucy Winner, Todd London, John Bell and Steve Wangh. I am indebted to Eugene van Erven for contacts in the Philippines, Lisa James for facilitating the Belgrade connection and Jackson Vena in South Africa. New York University Department of Drama Chair Una Chaudhuri has provided on-going support. Aleksandra Jovicevic made valiant but inconclusive efforts to research a site-specific Italian street performance. Scott Walden assisted above and beyond with Adrian Piper's contribution. Lorie Novak and Krishna Dunston aided me technically, as did Irene Zelterman emotionally. Rosie and Daniel cheerfully accompanied me on a research trip to South Africa rather than partaking in a more conventional summer vacation. Dan Bacalzo was an active assistant, wildly competent and knowledgeable, thoughtful, reliable, calm, involved intellectually and energetically throughout. This project was supported in part by a New York University Research Challenge Fund Grant.

I heartily thank all those who contributed original essays to this collection. I am also grateful for permission to reprint the following essays, and acknowledge here their sources:

Peter Handke's 'Theater-in-the-Street and Theater-in-Theaters,' originally published as 'Straßentheater und Theatertheater,' from *Prosa. Gedichte. Theaterstücke. Hörspiel. Aufsätze.* © Suhrkamp Verlag Frankfurt am Main 1969.

Vladimir Tolstoy's 'Introduction' and documents on Russian revolutionary theatre from *Street Art of the Revolution*, ed. Vladimir Tolstoy, Irina Bibikova and Catherine Cooke. © 1990 by Thames & Hudson.

Edgar Snow's 'Red Theater,' from his book *Red Star Over China*. © 1938, 1944 by Random House, Inc. © 1968 by Edgar Snow. Used by permission of Grove Atlantic.

ACKNOWLEDGEMENTS

The longer versions of Safdar Hashmi's essays 'Jana Natya Manch' and 'Concept of People's Theatre' appear in *The Right to Perform: Selected Writings of Safdar Hashmi*. © 1989 by SAHMAT.

The full text of Suzanne Lacy and Leslie Labowitz, 'Feminist Media Strategies for Political Performance,' © 1980 Leslie Labowitz. From Douglas Kahn and Diane Neumaier, eds., *Cultures in Contention*, © 1985 The Real Comet Press, Seattle, WA. Reprinted by permission.

Alisa Solomon's 'AIDS Crusaders ACT UP a Storm' originally published in *American Theatre*, Vol. 6, No. 7. © 1989 by Theatre Communications Group.

Steven Durland's 'Witness: The Guerrilla Theater of Greenpeace' originally published in *High Performance* 40, Vol. 10, No. 4. © 1987 by Steven Durland.

Diana Taylor's 'Making a Spectacle: The Mothers of the Plaza de Mayo' is an abridged version of an essay originally published in *The Politics of Motherhood: Activist Voices from Left to Right*, ed. Alexis Jetter, Annelise Orleck and Diana Taylor. Hanover: University Press of New England, 1997.

The complete text of Marguerite Waller's 'Border *Boda* or Divorce *Fronterizo*?' in *Negotiating Performance*, ed. Diana Taylor and Juan Villegas. © 1994 by Duke University Press, Durham, NC. Reprinted with permission.

Dan Sullivan's 'Theater in East Harlem: The Outdoor Audience Gets Into the Act' originally appeared in the *New York Times*, August 30, 1968. © 1968 by The New York Times Co. Reprinted by permission.

A longer excerpt of Hollis Giammatteo's *On the Line, a Memoir* was published in *Prairie Schooner*, Vol. 64, No. 2, 1990. Reprinted with permission of the author.

Augusto Boal's 'Invisible Theater' from his book, *Theater of the Oppressed*. © 1985 by Theatre Communications Group.

Adrian Piper's 'Xenophobia and the Indexical Present II: Lecture' in her *Out of Order, Out of Sight Volume I: Selected Writings in Meta-Art 1968–1992*, published by the MIT Press. © 1996 by Adrian Piper.

Lauren Berlant and Elizabeth Freeman's 'Queer Nationality' originally published in *Fear of a Queer Planet*, ed. Michael Warner. © 1993 by the University of Minnesota Press.

Nelly Richard's 'The Dimension of Social Exteriority in the Production of Art' first appeared in *Art + Text*, No. 21 Special Issue: *Margins and Institutions: Art in Chile Since 1973*. © 1986 by Nelly Richard.

Alice Cook and Gwyn Kirk's 'Taking Direct Action' excerpt from their book, *Greenham Women Everywhere: Dreams, Ideas and Actions from the Women's Peace Movement*, published in London by Pluto Press Limited. © 1983 by Alice Cook and Gwyn Kirk.

David Welch's 'Triumph of the Will.' © David Welch 1983. Reprinted from *Propaganda and the German Cinema 1933–1945* by David Welch (1983) by permission of Oxford University Press.

Jean-Jacques Lebel's 'Notes on Political Street Theatre, Paris: 1968, 1969' originally appeared in *TDR: The Drama Review* 13.4 (T44) Summer 1969. © 1969 by *TDR*.

The full version of Eugenio Barba's 'Letter from the South of Italy' is in his *Beyond the Floating Islands*, published by PAJ. © 1986 by Eugenio Barba.

Abbie Hoffman's 'America has More Television Sets than Toilets' reprinted by permission of: Abbie Hoffman. From *Soon to Be a Major Motion Picture*, Putnam, 1980. Copyright 1980 by Abbie Hoffman. All rights reserved. Reprinted by permission of The Putnam Publishing Group from *Soon to Be a Major Motion Picture* by Abbie Hoffman. © 1980 by Andy, Amy and america Hoffman.

The longer version of Richard Schechner's 'The Street is the Stage' appears in his book, *The Future of Ritual*, published by Routledge. © 1993 by Routledge.

Baz Kershaw's 'The Celebratory Performance of John Fox and Welfare State International' is taken from his chapter, 'Fragmentation in the 1990s? *The Celebratory Performance of John Fox and Welfare State International*' in his book, *The Politics of Performance: Radical Theatre as Cultural Intervention*. © 1992 by Routledge.

A different version of Dwight Conquergood's 'Health Theatre in a Hmong Refugee Camp: Performance, Communication and Culture' was published in *Refugee Participation Network* 13, June 1992, Oxford University Refugee Studies Programme. © 1992 by Dwight Conquergood.

ACKNOWLEDGEMENTS

'The Language of African Theatre' is reprinted by permission of Ngũgĩ wa Thiong'o, from his *Decolonizing the Mind: The Politics of Language in African Literature*. (Heinemann, A division of Greenwood Publishing Group, Portsmouth, NH, 1986).

'El Teatro Campesino and the Mexican Popular Performance Tradition' is excerpted from Yolanda Broyles-González's book, *El Teatro Campesino: Theater in the Chicano Momement*, published by University of Texas Press. © 1994 by Yolanda Broyles-González.

I also thank the photographers and copyright holders for allowing me to enliven these pages with the following images:

2.1 *Storming the Winter Palace*, 1920. Mass theatrical re-enactment in Petrograd for the Third Anniversary of the Russian Revolution. Reprinted from *Street Art of the Revolution*.

4.1 Jana Natya Manch in Sahibabad after Safdar Hashmi's murder. Photo courtesy of SAHMAT.

5.1 *In Mourning and in Rage*, 1977. Photo by Susan Mogul. From the collection of Suzanne Lacy.

6.1 ACT UP! *Rachael*, San Francisco International Conference on AIDS, June 1990. © Ann P. Meredith, 1990.

7.1 Women in Black. © Vesna Pavlović.

8.1 Greenpeace action at Belgium's largest municipal incinerator to stop waste from being burnt. © Buyse/Greenpeace.

9.1 Las Madres de la Plaza de Mayo. Photo by Cristina Fraire. From the collection of Diana Taylor.

11.1 Church Ladies for Choice with large banner. © Lisa Kahane.

16.1 Catalysis IV © Adrian Piper.

19.1 The Living Theatre's *Six Public Acts*. Ann Arbor, May 1975. Photo by Ron Blanchette. From the collection of The Living Theatre.

21.1 Nuremberg Party Rallies, Labor Service Day 1938. Photo from *Reichstagung in Nürnberg*.

23.1 Odin Teatret actor in Southern Italy. Photo by Tony D'Urso. Courtesy of Odin Teatret.

25.1 Beijing University students dance in Tiananmen Square during demonstrations 1989. © AP/Wide World Photos.

26.1 *Town Hall Tattoo*. Courtesy of Welfare State International.

27.1 The tiger leads the 1985 Rabies Parade. Photo by Dwight Conquergood, from his collection.

30.1 A street performance of El Teatro Campesino's *Las Dos Caras del Patroncito*. © 1976 George Ballis/TAKE STOCK.

31.1 The street theatre group Peryante. Photo by Donato Majia Alvarez, 1984. From the collection of Joi Barrios.

32.1 Circus Amok. © Kathryn Kirk.

33.1 The Bread and Puppet Theater at a demonstration in New York City. © Keith Meyers/NYT Pictures.

Contributors

Eugenio Barba worked with Jerzy Grotowski before founding Odin Teatret in 1964, with actors denied entry to Oslo's Theatre School. He has directed the company in eighteen productions. In 1979 he founded the International School for Theatre Anthropology, another expression of his deep interest in actor training. His writings include *Beyond the Floating Islands, A Dictionary of Theatre Anthropology: The Secret Art of the Performer* and *The Dilated Body*.

Joi Barrios, Assistant Professor at the University of the Philippines, chaired the UP Vaudeville Troupe (aka Peryante), the Alliance of Youth Theater Groups and the Concerned Artists of the Philippines. She has published plays and poetry, received a Palanca Award and been honored by the Cultural Center of the Philippines and the Institute of National Language.

John Bell teaches theatre history, theory and practice at New York University and Rhode Island School of Design. A founding member of Great Small Works theatre company, he has also been part of Bread and Puppet Theater since the mid-1970s.

Lauren Berlant teaches English at the University of Chicago. She is the author of *The Anatomy of National Fantasy: Hawthorne, Utopia, and Everyday Life, The Queen of America Goes to Washington City* and several essays on gender, sexuality, race, capitalism and the public sphere during the nineteenth and twentieth centuries in the United States.

Irina Mikhailovna Bibikova graduated from Moscow State University and wrote her dissertation on Russian wooden reliefs. She has worked at the Museum of Russian Architecture and the Scientific Research Institute of the Academy of Artists of the USSR. She contributed to *Russian Decorative Art* and is the author of *The History of Folk Houses on the Volga*.

Augusto Boal, a director, playwright, theoretician and teacher, is the creator of Theatre of the Oppressed, a body of theatrical techniques that physically activate spectators and empower them to rehearse alternatives to their indi-vidual and collective oppressions. His books include *Theatre of the Oppressed*, *Games for Actors and Non-Actors* and *Rainbow of Desire*.

Yolanda Broyles-González was the first woman of color to receive tenure at the University of California, Santa Barbara. In 1996 she received the lifetime Distinguished Scholar Award from the National Association for Chicana/o Studies. Author of *El Teatro Campesino: Theater in the Chicano Movement*, she has widely published in the areas of cultural studies and minority discourse. A major book on the performer Lydia Mendoza is forthcoming.

L. Dale Byam, adjunct instructor in drama at New York University, is founder/director of Theatre in a New Key (THINK), a professional community theatre company for youth. She adapted Brecht's *Caucasian Chalk Circle* and wrote numerous other plays. Her dissertation, soon to be published, is on community theatre in Zimbabwe. She is producing a video documentary on popular culture in the Caribbean.

Sudipto Chatterjee is a playwright, poet, performer, scholar, translator and filmmaker from Calcutta, India. He is currently completing his PhD in Performance Studies at New York University, where he also teaches drama and cinema. He completed a documentary on Suman Chatterjee, *Free To Sing?*, in 1996. His article '*Mise-en-*(Colonial-)*Scène*: The Theatre of the Bengal Renaissance' appeared in *Imperialism and Theatre*.

Jan Cohen-Cruz was a member of the NYC Street Theatre/Jonah Project in 1971–2. This led to facilitating theatre workshops in prisons, psychiatric facilities, community centers, etc. She is co-editor of *Playing Boal: Theatre, Therapy, Activism* and her articles on activist, community-based performance have appeared in *TDR*, *High Performance*, *American Theatre*, *Urban Resources*, *Women and Performance*, *The Mime Journal* and the anthology *But Is It Art?* Jan is also a practitioner of community-based theatre, most recently guiding the theatre component of an arts-based AmeriCorps project, President Clinton's domestic Peace Corps. She is an Associate Professor in the Drama Department at New York University.

Dwight Conquergood is Charles Deering McCormick Professor of Teaching Excellence and Chair of Performance Studies at Northwestern University. He also is Faculty Associate at the Joint Center for Poverty Research at Northwestern and the University of Chicago. In addition to his academic work, he has consulted for the International Rescue Committee and several state agencies on refugee issues, and currently is consultant for the Office of the Illinois Appellate Defender and the Indiana Public Defenders Council on the defense of death penalty cases.

Alice Cook is a writer who has been involved in the peace movement. In 1983, she gathered stories from participants in the women's peace camp at Greenham Common, England and, with Gwyn Kirk, published *Greenham Women Everywhere: Dreams, Ideas and Actions from the Women's Peace Movement*.

Catherine Cooke trained as an architect at Cambridge and is now a Lecturer in Design in the Technology Faculty of the Open University. She specializes in Russian and Soviet architecture, particularly Constructivism.

Steven Durland is a visual artist, writer, editor and arts administrator. He is co-director of Art in the Public Interest and served as co-editor of *High Performance* magazine from 1986 to 1997.

Elizabeth Freeman did graduate work in English literature and queer/feminist theory at the University of Chicago. She was a member of Chicago's Coalition for Positive Sexuality, an activist group dedicated to guerrilla safe-sex education in the public schools. She is currently teaching at Oberlin College.

Hollis Giammatteo co-founded a theatre in Philadelphia called Wilma, writing scripts, hosting experimental companies and acting in the resident ensemble. She moved west and co-organized an anti-nuclear peace walk, described in her memoir, *On the Line*. It received the 1988 PEN/Jerard Award, was excerpted in literary magazines including the *North American Review* and *Prairie Schooner*, and garnered a National Endowment for the Arts literary fellowship. Her most recent novel is *The People of Good Bye*.

Peter Handke is the German author of numerous plays, novels, books of poetry, short stories and essays. His work has been extensively translated and he is the recipient of awards including the Gerhart Hauptmann Prize and the George Buchner Prize.

Safdar Hashmi was a political activist, playwright, actor and poet in India. He was murdered on 1 January 1989 by a group of hired killers while performing a street play in a working-class area just outside of Delhi. The play (and most of his work) was critical of the establishment, and death transformed Hashmi into a revolutionary martyr.

Abbie Hoffman, co-organizer of the Youth International Party (Yippies), came to prominence in 1968 during the anti-Vietnam War demonstrations that he so exuberantly theatricalized. He went underground in 1973 to avoid a drug-related prison term, remaining active in environmental causes. He later turned himself in and continued to work for ecological and anti-imperialist causes until his death in 1989 from an overdose. His books include *Revolution for the Hell of It* and *Steal This Book*.

Baz Kershaw has had considerable experience in alternative and community theatre, both as a writer and director. He founded England's first mobile rural community arts group and first reminiscence theatre company. He co-authored *Engineers of the Imagination*, wrote *The Politics of Performance* and has contributed to various journals. He is currently Professor of Theatre and Performance at Lancaster University.

Gwyn Kirk is a writer who has been involved in the peace movement. In 1983, she gathered stories from participants in the women's peace camp at Greenham Common, England and, with Alice Cook, published *Greenham Women Everywhere: Dreams, Ideas and Actions from the Women's Peace Movement*.

Dubravka Kneževic is an ex-Yugoslav dramaturge, playwright, editor, theatre critic and pedagogue. She has a BA in dramaturgy and an MA in theatrology from Belgrade's University of Arts (Faculty of Dramatic Arts) where she taught dramaturgy. The author of nine plays staged all over ex-Yugoslavia and a founding member of many non-government cultural initiatives, she actively opposed the insanity of the Yugoslav fratricidal war.

Leslie Labowitz expressed her commitment to ending violence against women through the creation of public art. She shifted from performance to installations with 'Sprout Time,' extending her concern to violence against the earth. This led to her focus of the past eighteen years – running a health food business and doing occasional installations about food, survival and ecology.

Suzanne Lacy is an internationally known conceptual/performance artist whose work includes large-scale performances on social themes and urban issues. Her best known piece, *The Crystal Quilt* (Minneapolis 1987), was a performance with 430 older women. She has exhibited in the Museum of Contemporary Art in London, the Museum of Modern Art in San Francisco and the New Museum in New York. In 1995 she published *Mapping the Terrain,* on new genre public art.

Jean-Jacques Lebel is a French painter, poet and performance artist. He was instrumental in popularizing the Happenings genre in Europe. The events of May 1968 in Paris catapulted him into the role of political activist as one of the key players in student street actions.

Ngūgī Wa Thiong'o has garnered numerous awards and fellowships as a playwright, novelist and scholar. His work has been translated into more than twenty languages. His books include *Homecoming, Detained: A Writer's Prison Diary 1981, Writers in Politics* and *Moving the Centre: The Struggle for Cultural Freedoms.* He is Professor of Comparative Literature and Performance Studies at New York University.

Adrian Piper is a conceptual artist whose work, in a variety of media, has focused on racism, racial stereotyping and xenophobia. Trained at the School of Visual Arts in New York, she is the recipient of Guggenheim, AVA and numerous NEA fellowships. She has exhibited internationally, and published a two-volume collection, *Out of Order, Out of Sight*. Piper received her PhD from Harvard and is Professor of Philosophy at Wellesley College.

Nelly Richard is best known for her critical work on Chilean unofficial culture post-1977. She was coordinator of art exhibitions and programs for the Museum of Fine Arts, Santiago, and director of Cromo Gallery. She has edited numerous journals, and is the author of *Cuerpo Correccional, Una Mirada sobre el Arte en Chile* and *La Cita Amorosa*.

Cindy Rosenthal is general editor of *The Living Theatre Archive*. Her writing has appeared in *TDR, Women and Performance,* and in the anthology *Jewish American Women Writers*. She has taught, performed and directed at The Bread Loaf School of English as a member of its resident Acting Ensemble since 1986.

Richard Schechner is University Professor at New York University. He is editor of *TDR, a Journal of Performance Studies*. As a theatre director, he created numerous experimental productions with the Performance Group and abroad. His books include *Environmental Theatre, Essays on Performance Theory, Between Theatre and Anthropology* and *The Future of Ritual*.

Edgar Snow was a foreign correspondent in China, Burma, India and Indochina for the *Chicago Tribune,* the *New York Herald* and the *London Daily Herald*. As associate editor of the *Saturday Evening Post,* he reported wartime and post-war events in Asia and Europe. He is the author of ten books including *Red Star Over China, The Battle for Asia* and *Journey to the Beginning*. He died in 1972.

Alisa Solomon is an Associate Professor of English at Baruch College and of English and Theater at the CUNY Graduate Center and a staff writer for the *Village Voice*. She is author of *Redressing the Canon: Essays on Theater and Gender*.

Dan Sullivan reviewed theatre for the *New York Times* for three years before becoming the drama critic at the *Los Angeles Times*.

Mark Sussman lives and works in New York City. A founding member of the East Village collective Great Small Works, he has played bass drum in the Circus Amok band for three summers. He is a PhD candidate in Performance Studies at New York University, and teaches in the Theater Department at Barnard College.

Diana Taylor is Professor and Chair of Performance Studies at New York University. She is author of *Theatre of Crisis: Drama and Politics in Latin America* and *Disappearing Acts: Spectacles of Gender and Nationalism in Argentina's 'Dirty War'*. She co-edited *Negotiating Performance in Latin/o America: Gender Sexuality and Theatricality* and *The Politics of Motherhood: Activists from Left to Right*, and edited three volumes of critical essays on Latin American, Latino and Spanish playwrights.

Vladimir Pavlovitch Tolstoy graduated from Moscow State University Faculty of the History of Art and studied at the Academy of Sciences. He completed a doctorate on Soviet monumental art in 1986. He is departmental manager of decorative and monumental art at the Scientific Research Institute of the Academy of Artists, Moscow.

Marguerite Waller is Professor of English at the University of California, Riverside, where she teaches gender theory, film and Renaissance literature. She is the author of *Petrarch's Poetics and Literary History*, as well as articles on Dante, Petrarch, Wyatt, Shakespeare, Federico Fellini, Lina Wertmuller, Liliana Cavani, Maurizio Nichetti, George Lucas and Hillary Clinton.

David Welch is Professor of Modern History and director of the Centre for the Study of Propaganda at the University of Kent at Canterbury. His most recent books are *The Third Reich: Politics and Propaganda* and *Modern European History 1871–1975*.

General introduction

■   Jan Cohen-Cruz

I

THE FOLLOWING THIRTY-FOUR ESSAYS describing projects in over twenty countries evidence a formidable range of radical street performance in the twentieth century. By *radical* I refer to acts that question or re-envision ingrained social arrangements of power. *Street* signals theatrics that take place in public by-ways with minimal constraints on access. *Performance* here indicates expressive behavior intended for public viewing. It includes but is not limited to theatre, which typically keeps actors and spectators in their respective places through presentational conventions supporting a pre-set script. Radical street performance draws people who comprise a contested reality into what its creators hope will be a changing script.

Typically, theatre transports the audience to a reality apart from the everyday; radical street performance strives to transport everyday reality to something more ideal. Because the desired spectators are not necessarily predisposed to theatre-going, it takes place in public spaces and is usually free of charge. Potentially, street performance creates a bridge between imagined and real actions, often facilitated by taking place at the very sites that the performance makers want transformed. As Diana Taylor states, 'the conscious move out of "cultural spaces" in the strictest sense of the word ... posits that society as a whole is culture – the site in which symbols and identity are forged, negotiated and contested' (12).

Not only space but also time is more contiguous with everyday life in street performance than in conventional theatre. Radical street performances respond directly to events as they occur whereas professional theatre schedules are planned well in advance. The temporal context of radical street performance is the duration not of the show but of the struggle; in her essay here about street performance in the former Yugoslavia, Dubravka Kneževic describes the Women in Black, who staged silent protests in the central square of Belgrade every Wednesday during the years of fratricidal strife. Their only time frame was continuation until the war ended.

The above notwithstanding, radical street performance is a deceptive term about which little can be generalized. 'Radical,' despite its general identification with left-wing projects, can equally refer to right-wing agendas, as Marguerite Waller's excerpt on anti-immigration actions and counter-actions exemplifies. Though usually considered in terms of mass movements, radical street performance may operate on an individual level, inspired by experimenters like Allan Kaprow who merged art, which can raise consciousness about all that it frames, with life, which integrates unexpected stimuli into a general flow. This collection includes radical street acts that range from Adrian Piper's individual strategies to challenge racism as she experienced it in everyday life; to community-wide efforts, as Ngũgĩ wa Thiong'o's work with the Kamĩrĩĩthũ Cultural Center; to that which was global in ambition, as the Nazi Nuremberg Rallies, described herein by David Welch.

The usual rhetoric of street performance configures the street as the gateway to the masses, directly or through the media. But the impulse to perform in the street reflects more the desire for popular access than its sure manifestation. Like community, truly public space may be ever longed for but non-existent materially. (See Anderson 1983.) Space is always controlled by *someone* and exists *somewhere*, so is inevitably marked by a particular class or race and not equally accessible to everyone. Public space has shrunk as private enterprise has taken it over for commercial purposes. What gets called street performance spills beyond the physical street and into parks, cafes and union halls, each with its own clientele. While the mobility of much street performance facilitates the seeking out of diverse audiences, one must question if access to a broader audience really is a difference between performance in the street and in theatre buildings.

Is street performance an indirect conduit to broad and diverse audiences through its ability to attract journalistic attention? In their essay in this collection, Suzanne Lacy and Leslie Labowitz devote as much attention to handling the media as to creating the performance. Of course groups with limited means, less compelling presentation or unpopular messages have a harder time gaining media attention. Even the largest demonstration in American history, the June 12, 1981 Rally for a Nuclear Freeze, received less national coverage than an annual Rose Bowl Parade. Abbie Hoffman constructs the media itself as street theatre, the carrier of expressive action to the broadest cross-section of people.

Who are these masses that street performers hope to reach – the working class, the dispossessed or the disenchanted? Does radical street performance reach only those already convinced, a criticism leveled, for example, at the pro-choice theatrics that I examine?[1] Or in an effort to reach an ideologically broader audience, must practitioners find so entertaining a way of communicating their message – see Baz Kershaw on Welfare State International in a nuclear-submarine producing town – that they risk watering down their ideals? Do street theatre audiences ever include a broad cross-section of people? Or do different street events reach different constituencies while some reach none at all, lost in the hustle and bustle of contemporary public space, or too fleeting to make a difference?

Nor can one generalize about street performers. Some are working actors who explore street theatre as a means of bringing their politics into agreement with their profession. Others are not actors by vocation but rather are driven by a tremendous incentive to change their own reality. Yet others are looking for a form to integrate their political yearnings. My hope is that this book will encourage cross-pollination among such performers whether professional actors or not. All manifest a bravery in taking to the streets, and sometimes also an arrogance, as their shows are often imposed on people who have not chosen to be spectators. Street performing has an altruistic side, too, offering one's body for some common goal, without the safety of an impermeable frame. In my own street theatre days, performing on an open flatbed truck, I was egged by kids from atop a building, gawked at by people watching from their cars, their headlights illuminating the last darkening moments of the show, and propositioned by spectators who associate women in public with prostitution.

The diversity of street performers is manifested in the genres they use. Rallies, puppet shows, marches, vigils, choruses and clown shows are just some of the forms employed to capture both media and popular attention in a plethora of different contexts and circumstances. Sometimes the skills involved are instrumental in drawing a crowd, as with the Danish Odin Teatret in the streets of a small Italian village. Sometimes the utter simplicity, such as that displayed by the Mothers of the Plaza de Mayo in Argentina, merely circling the square displaying photographs of their 'disappeared' children, is equally compelling. Partly because it is so varied, street performance is less easily pigeon-holed, and hence politically devalued, as 'just theatre,' apart from the ebb and flow of life.

The sources for street work are equally eclectic. Whether to support or critique the status quo, performance has a long history in public space. Both

the church and the state have relied on the street for the display and reasser-
tion of power; as far back as the ancient world and prominently again in
medieval and early modern Europe, '. . . the relationship between theatre and
monarchy, processions and power, was intimate' (Davis 1986: 8). The
medieval plays that moved out of the church in the twelfth and thirteenth
century, cosmic in scope, encompassed events from creation to the last judgement and needed more space than the church provided. Going outside also
meant using the vernacular rather than Latin, thus rendering the discourse
understandable to more people. Be it the grisly spectacle of a public execution or the resplendent excess of a royal wedding, powerful groups have long
represented their dominance in the most accessible places.

Examples also abound of performative ways to challenge the status quo.
Mikhail Bakhtin inspired a whole literature around carnival: was it an escape
valve, serving to keep people in their place, or did the taste of a world more
to the masses' liking lead to change? (Historically both have happened. See
Part four, 'Utopia', for references.) Ritual, a conservative force in culture,
providing a structure for people to go through predictable changes, has been
explored as a vehicle for less socially ordained processes of transformation.
Popular forms of entertainment, even if originally produced for commercial
reasons, have frequently been adapted to political ends. Processional forms
used to display power have also been used to amass it; public manifestations
by the disenfranchised have been a way to build resistance to the status quo.
This book documents multiple occasions during which the street regained its
role as an arena for the display and creation of power.

II

Numerous considerations informed the selection and organization of these
essays. One criterion has been an edge of danger; indeed my colleague David
Schechter suggested entitling the book 'Disturbing the Peace', from the
charge most frequently leveled against street performers on the numerous
occasions of arrest. While I did not have a translation budget, I stretched
my reprint fund to commission nine new pieces. I have not included essays
on some of the most renowned companies. Focusing on range of forms first
and nationality second, the US is perhaps over-represented because of the
diversity of work I am familiar with here. I considered arranging the book
according to how theatrically each case study manifests itself on the street,
beginning with invisible theatre and ending with the Nuremberg Party Rallies.
However, after I chose essays that are strong individually and representative
of different currents in street performance, a pattern suggesting five categories emerged. Though a few of the essays might have been at home in

several sections, these categories set up some fascinating juxtapositions, evidencing that a given form may serve quite a range of ideologies. I describe them in more detail at the top of each section, but briefly they are:

1   Agit-prop: Attempts to mobilize people around partisan points of view that have been simplified and theatricalized to capture by-passers' attention directly or by way of the media. Popularly identified with the whole domain of street theatre, this represents but one approach to the form.
2   Witness: Publicly illuminating a social act that one does not know how to change but must at least acknowledge. The site of such performance usually relates directly to the event being scrutinized.
3   Integration: The insertion of a theatrically heightened scenario into people's everyday lives to provide an emotional experience of what might otherwise remain distant.
4   Utopia: The enactment of another vision of social organization, temporarily replacing life as it is, and often performed with public participation.
5   Tradition: The use of a communally shared cultural form bespeaking common values, beliefs and connections, to address a current concern.

Given the wild array of configurations that radical street performance in the twentieth century has taken, individual essays provide examples of particular purposes, forms and historic/geographic moments. The danger is that too much can be looked at through this lens; the danger should be counted on.

III

My first impulse to do street theatre was disappointment at finding the regular theatre world so insular. I had naively thought that a life in the theatre would afford me contact with a great range of people and experiences. Instead I found actors largely spending their time with other actors. When, in 1971, I joined the New York City Street Theatre, I did so to combine making theatre and making contact with people in diverse situations – inner-city neighborhoods, migrant camps, prisons and Indian reservations. I was deeply disturbed by the division of the world into 'haves' and 'have nots.' Certainly the street theatre I'd seen in Paris in 1969 in the aftermath of the celebrated 'events of May' (see Jean-Jacques Lebel's essay) was a major influence.

By the late 1970s, I came to believe that change was brought on more by people making theatre than by watching it. Thus I shifted from performing in traveling street theatre to facilitating community-based workshops. I discovered, researching this book, that such a move was in fact widespread. Sixteen years ago, Welfare State International, for example, gave up its vagabond ways and settled in Cumbria. (See Baz Kershaw's essay.) In both the US and Europe in the late 1970s, on-going drama workshops were established at a range of sites hitherto accessed by street theatre: prisons, senior centers, housing projects, day-care centers, unions, schools, churches; facilities for the physically handicapped, emotionally impaired, retarded, abused, seriously ill. Street theatre is thus one of the sources of the current community-based theatre movement.

The most pervasive pattern to emerge in this collection is the persistence of street performance in periods of social flux – either leading up to, during or just after a shift in the status quo. When one needs most to disturb the peace, street performance creates visions of what society might be, and arguments against what it is. Street performance is porous, inviting participation of all who pass. We make the magic circle round the players; we are the stage. Cultural critic Marshall Berman frames such performances as public dialogue, the creation of which he calls 'the city's most authentic reason for being' (1982: 322). Whether theatre professionals in New York City parks challenging the stereotypical representation of gays and lesbians, or Chinese students dancing their desire for democracy in Tiananmen Square, moments when a new consciousness is trying to come into being are shrieked and celebrated, sung and sashayed, paraded and proclaimed into public awareness by radical street performance.

Note

1   I do not mean to disparage 'preaching to the converted.' See Tim Miller and David Roman's wonderful essay by that name in *Theatre Journal* Vol. 47, No. 2, May 1995.

References

Anderson, Benedict (1983) *Imagined Communities*, London: Verso.

Berman, Marshall (1988) *All That is Solid Melts into Air: The Experience of Modernity*, New York: Penguin.

Davis, Susan (1986) *Parades and Power*, Philadelphia, PA: Temple University Press.

Taylor, Diana (1994) 'Opening Remarks,' in Diana Taylor and Juan Villejas (eds) *Negotiating Performance*, Durham, NC and London: Duke University Press.

Chapter 1

Peter Handke

THEATER-IN-THE-STREET AND THEATER-IN-THEATERS

Translated by Nicholas Hern

WHETHER OR NOT READERS AGREE with Handke's conclusions, his manifesto-like essay vividly sets up two of the major questions of this collection: *Is* theatre in the street intrinsically different from theatre in theatre buildings? And, how does radical street theatre performed by non-actors inform that which is performed by professional actors? Writing in the 1960s, Handke captures the highly polarized spirit of that time in the US and Europe when street theatre burst upon the scene and many of us practitioners, though inspired by Brecht, sought a more direct form of theatrical activism.

Brecht is a writer who has given me cause for thought. The processes by which reality can operate, processes which had hitherto unfolded smoothly before one, were rearranged by Brecht into a system of thinking in terms of contradictions. He thereby made it possible for those processes by which reality operates, which previously one had often seen as operating smoothly, to be conclusively contradicted by means of the Brechtian system of contradictions. And finally the state of the world, which had hitherto been taken as intrinsic and natural, was seen to be manufactured – and precisely therefore manufacturable and alterable. Not natural, not non-historical, but artificial, capable of alteration, possible of alteration, and under certain circumstances *needful* of alteration. Brecht has helped to educate me.

The central contention of the forces of reaction and conservatism about those sections of the population who exist in an untenable situation, namely that these people 'wouldn't want it any other way,' has been shown up by Brecht in his antithetical plays as enormous and vile stupidity. People whose will is dragooned by social conditions into leaving those social conditions as they have always been, and who are therefore actually *unable* to will any change – these people 'naturally' don't want it any other way. It's *natural* that they don't want it any other way! No, it's artificial that they don't want it any other way. The conditions in which these people live are manufactured as a precaution precisely so that they remain unaware of them, and not only are they unable to will any *change*, they are unable to will anything *at all*.

Brecht made plays out of these contradictions – *plays*: in this respect Brecht's only successors are the Berliner Kommune led by Fritz Teufel. They are a Berliner Ensemble whose effectiveness is in marked contrast with that of the legitimate Berliner Ensemble. The legitimate Ensemble sets up its contradictions only so as to show their possible resolution at the end, and it points out contradictions which no longer exist (at least not in that specific social form) and which cannot therefore lead to any conflict. The members of the Kommune, however, have thought afresh; they have shifted their antithetical performances away from accepted antithetical arenas (theatre-buildings) to (still) unaccepted antithetical arenas, and have avoided furnishing (extending) the ends of their performances with manufactured, ready-made recipes for the new order, because the performances themselves, the *form* which the performance takes, has already offered a recipe for the new order. As in football when people 'act out' the possible shots at goal, so Brecht 'acted out' alternatives in his parables, but secure in what was sociologically the wrong arena with what were sociologically the wrong means, infinitely removed from the reality which he wished to change, and using the hierarchical system of the theatre in order hierarchically to destroy other hierarchical systems. Those at peace with the world he left in peace, granting countless thousands a pleasant hour or two.

He did, it's true, change the attitude of actors, but he did not change the attitude of audiences; and it is historically untrue to say that the actors' attitude even indirectly changed the audiences' attitude. Despite his revolutionary intent, Brecht was so very hypnotized by and biased towards the traditional idea of theatre that his revolutionary intent always kept within the bounds of taste, in that he thought it tasteful that the spectators, since they did remain spectators, should (be allowed to) enjoy themselves unlit. To the same end, his last wish for each play was that it should be 'entertaining.' Other people would possibly characterize this attitude as 'intellectual cunning': it would seem to me, however, to be the cunning of a thoroughly selfish intellect.

Add to this that Brecht is not content with the mere arrangement of contradictions: in the end a proposed solution, a proposed resolution comes into play – a future on Marxist lines. I say, comes into *play*: the spectator, who has been made to feel insecure by the play, is now to be reassured because, in the course of the play, a possible solution on Marxist lines is specified or at least suggested to him. What upsets me is not that it is a Marxist solution which is specified, but that it is specified as a solution in a *play*. I myself would support Marxism every time as the only possible solution to our governing problems – 'governing' in every sense – but not its proclamation in a play, in the theatre. That is just as false and untrue as chanting slogans for the freedom of Vietnam when this chanting takes place in the *theatre*; or when, as in Oberhausen recently, 'genuine' coal-miners appeared in the *theatre* and struck up a protest song. The theatre's sphere of relevance is determined by the extent to which everything that is serious, important, unequivocal, conclusive outside the theatre becomes *play*; and therefore unequivocation, commitment and so on become irretrievably played out in the theatre precisely because of the fatal limitations of the scope of the performance and of its relevance. When will people finally realize this? When will people finally recognize that seriousness of purpose in places meant for play is deceitful and nauseously false? This is not a question of aesthetics but a question of truth; therefore it is a question of aesthetics. This, then, is what riles me about Brechtian methods: the unambiguousness and the lack of contradiction into which everything dissolves at the end (even though Brecht pretends that all the contradictions remain open) appears, when it happens in the theatre, purely as a matter of form, a play. Every kind of message, or shall we say more simply: every suggested solution to those contradictions which have just been demonstrated becomes *formalized* on the playing area of the stage. Slogan chanting which aims to be effective in the theatre and not in the streets is modish and kitsch. The theatre, as a social institution, seems to me useless as a way of changing social institutions. The theatre formalizes every movement, every insignificant detail, every word, every silence; it is no good at all when it comes to suggesting solutions, at most it is good for playing with contradictions.

Committed theatre these days doesn't happen in theatres (those falsifying domains of art where every word and movement is emptied of significance) but in lecture-halls, for instance, when a professor's microphone is taken away, and professors blink through burst-open doors, when leaflets flutter down on to the congregation from the galleries, and revolutionaries take their small children with them to the lectern, when the Kommune theatricalize real life by 'terrorising' it and quite rightly make fun of it, not only making fun of it but, in the reaction provoked, making it recognizable in all its inherent dangerousness, in its lack of awareness, its false nature, its false idyllicism, and in its terror. In this way, theatre is becoming directly effective. There is now Street Theatre, Lecture-hall Theatre, Church Theatre (more effective than 1,000 Masses), Department Store Theatre, etc.: the only one that doesn't exist anymore is Theatre Theatre – at least not as a means of immediately changing prevailing conditions: it is itself a prevailing condition. What it could be good for (and has previously been good for) is an area of play for the creation of the spectator's innermost, hitherto undiscovered areas of play, as a means by which the individual's awareness becomes not broader but more precise, as a means of becoming sensitive, of becoming susceptible, of reacting, as a means of coming into the world.

The theatre is not then portraying the world: the world is found to be a copy of the theatre. I know that this is a speculative approach; but I would not accept that the alternative to speculation is action. Admittedly, I do have doubts as to whether the impetus to change conditions in the Marxist sense (which was also mine) can as yet be said to result from a more precise awareness on the part of the spectator or listener, although I hope so; that is, I doubt it the more I hope so. The theatre in the theatre can create only hypotheses, proto-theses of new modes of thought; as a play, it cannot directly and unequivocally demonstrate the thesis itself, the new mode of thought which points to the solution. Brecht of course absorbs the thesis, the solution into the play and deprives it of its force and reality. One might say that the Berliner Kommune, however, who have certainly been influenced by the theatre but certainly not by Brecht (although they may venerate him for all I know) perform their thesis, their argument right in the middle of reality. It is to be hoped they will go on performing until reality too becomes one single performance area. That would be fine.

PART ONE

AGIT-PROP

Introduction

AGIT-PROP IS A MILITANT FORM of art intended to emotionally and ideologically mobilize its audience to take particular action vis-à-vis an urgent social situation. As other commentators have also noted (Stourac and McCreery 1986; Kershaw 1992), the aesthetic elements of agit-prop performance reflect the public streets and squares for which the form was designed: portable sets, visually clear characterizations, emblematic costumes and props, choral speaking, traditional music and character types familiar to the broad range of spectators that may congregate, and ideological resonance with the public spaces/ buildings where they are presented.

The essays in this section provide both historical models and subsequent adaptations of the form. In the early twentieth century, agit-prop was a left-wing project looking to communism for answers and addressing the working class. This is exemplified in the first two essays of the section, set in post-revolutionary Russia and pre-revolutionary China respectively. Although drawing on a range of theatrical genres, the quintessential agit-prop piece was short in length and broad in concept, sharpening class differences and simplifying class warfare into a battle between an idealistic worker protagonist and a top-hatted, cigar-smoking capitalist antagonist.

Conceptualizing agit-prop in Marxist terms became increasingly problematic, even before the fall of the Berlin Wall in 1989 and the subsequent dismantling of the eastern bloc. Baz Kershaw contrasts clearly divided societies like Russia, Germany and Britain of the 1920s and 1930s with Britain in the 1960s and 1970s:

[I]n conditions of cultural pluralism produced by political consensus, relative affluence and the ameliorating force of the mass media, the agit prop form becomes problematic . . . partly because the chief oppositional formations – the counter-cultures – are not at all programmatic in their ideologies, making any kind of didacticism difficult. And it becomes doubly problematic because in a pluralistic society the 'enemy' to be attacked is not easy to identify.

(Kershaw 1992: 80)

Notwithstanding, as other essays in this section illustrate, agit-prop *is* possible in 'culturally pluralistic' societies, but with these caveats: 1. as social contexts become more complex, agit-prop may serve an educational function around a specific issue, not necessarily advocating general revolution; 2. the actors must believe that they know a solution to a compelling social problem *and* be prepared to take the same steps that they are urging upon audiences. Augusto Boal, who has brought an arsenal of activist, dialogic techniques to post-World War II political theatre through his 'theatre of the oppressed,' tells of an experience that supports this second point. Performing for peasants in rural Brazil, Boal's middle-class actors ended an agit-prop play by lifting their prop rifles over their heads and calling for revolution. The peasant leader invited them all to eat together and then take up arms against the local landowner. Boal was ashamed; he and his actors were not prepared to fight but were telling other people to do so. Hence Boal developed theatrical forms through which oppressed people may devise their own solutions to social problems. But he still advocates use of agit-prop when solutions are evident for all concerned (Cohen-Cruz 1992).

References

Cohen-Cruz, Jan (1992) Unpublished interview with Augusto Boal, New York.
Kershaw, Baz (1992) *The Politics of Performance*, London: Routledge.
Stourac, Richard and Kathleen McCreery (1986) *Theatre as a Weapon: Workers' Theatre in the Soviet Union, Germany and Britain, 1917–1934*, London: Routledge & Kegan Paul.

Chapter 2

Introduction by Vladimir Tolstoy Documents edited by Vladimir Tolstoy, Irina Bibikova and Catherine Cooke

from *STREET ART OF THE REVOLUTION*

AGIT-PROP CRYSTALLIZED IN RUSSIA IN the years following the 1917 Revolution, with its clear sense of class differences and straightforward ideology. Add characteristics like the masses as hero, the use of architecture/urban space to reinforce political ideology, and the importance of mass participation beyond spectatorship, and one understands why the events that Tolstoy introduces have served practitioners the world over as a touchstone for agit-prop.

From the Introduction: Art Born of the October Revolution

The October Revolution which took place in Russia in 1917 transformed the face of the contemporary world. Nationally and internationally, it also had a decisive influence on the fate of art.

Within Russia itself, the Revolution changed the ideas and content of art, its forms and methods, and above all changed the audience to which it was addressed. From that time onwards, Soviet art became actively involved in the struggle for national transformation. After the 1917 Revolution, the prophetic words uttered by Lenin at the time of the first Russian revolution in 1905 began to come true. Under socialism, Lenin had insisted, art would

VLADIMIR TOLSTOY

no longer serve the elite of society, that 'upper ten thousand suffering from boredom and obesity; it will rather serve the millions and tens of millions of labouring people, the flower of the country, its strength and its future'.[1]

In the years following the Revolution, the main focus was on various forms of mass agitational art. There was a flowering of innovation in such genres as the political poster, newspaper and magazine graphics, oratorical poetry and heroic theatre, mass dramatizations and popular street processions, murals for agitational trains and decorations for the streets in celebration of Revolutionary anniversaries. In these often new forms of mass agitational art, there was always a live and direct echo of the events of the Revolution itself. In this, as the new Soviet government's famous Commissar of Public Education A. V. Lunacharsky put it, 'there was undoubtedly a happy confluence of the strivings of the youthful branches of art, and the aspirations of the crowd'.[2]

The real architectural arenas for these great Revolutionary events and their later commemoration and celebration were of no small importance in themselves. Of course the people who were creating history did not particularly select special 'architectural backcloths' for their real-life dramas. But the great beauty of many of the sites of Revolutionary events – the Winter Palace, the Smolny Institute, the Field of Mars, the Tauride Palace in Petrograd, or Red Square and the Kremlin in Moscow – will always remain in the popular memory as being a symbolically significant and artistically expressive dimension of the events themselves. Suffice it to look at episodes from the *Storming of the Winter Palace* or from Eisenstein's film *October* to see how the significance of events is emphasized by their magnificent environments.

[. . .]

The fundamental initiative which set this train of state festivals in motion was taken by Lenin himself in April 1918. [. . .] He was concerned with policies for artistic education and for preserving the country's heritage of cultural monuments from any threats of vandalism. In the midst of this he launched his 'Plan of Monumental Propaganda'.

[. . .]

The link between Lenin's monumental propaganda plan and the general enthusiasm of the Revolutionary period for festivals is very significant. It is also important that the roots of Lenin's ideas date back to the humanistic traditions of the Renaissance and the experience of previous revolutions, in particular to the Paris Commune and the French Revolution. The idea coincides with that of Robespierre, delivered to the Convention on 7 May 1794, when he said that the motherland ought to educate its citizens and use popular festivals as an important means of performing such civic education. 'Man is nature's greatest phenomenon', declared Robespierre, 'and the most magnificent of all spectacles is that of a large popular festival'.[3]

However, such historical continuities in no way belittle the novelty and originality of Lenin's proposals. In the entirely new phrase 'monumental propaganda' we can see a reflection of the conception of the artist's social role which was inaugurated with the socialist revolution. We see the aspiration to link fine arts with other forms of mass agitational and propaganda work in the name of larger tasks of ideological education.

On 12 April 1918 the Soviet of People's Commissars passed the decree 'On the Monuments of the Republic' which was published two days later. This historic decree established quite specific tasks for monumental propaganda and revolutionary celebrations. By its nature the plan had a double social function: it was both educational and propagandist. Both these functions were now aspects of art's main task in society, which was to be a participator in the all-embracing business of 'building socialism'. In a conversation with Clara Zetkin Lenin said 'our workers . . . have earned the right to a truly great art'.[4] Lenin shared Tolstoy's view that art must 'have a theme which is significant and important for the working mass and not just for an idle minority'.[5] In relation to all forms of popular education Lenin emphasized that 'it would be the greatest and most terrible mistake which a Marxist could make to think that the millions of craftsmen and peasants could emerge from the darkness along the straight line of pure Marxist education'. These simple people, he said, 'must be approached in such a way that their interest is awakened – they must be roused from all directions and by all manner of means'.[6]

Reminiscences of the architect N. D. Vinogradov, who was charged with realizing the plan of monumental propaganda in Moscow, indicate Lenin's clear understanding of how such re-education could be served by such actions. Vinogradov met Lenin for the first time several days after the suppression of the Socialist Revolutionary rebellion and asked him whether this decree 'On the Monuments of the Republic' really deserved the overriding importance which Lenin was according it. He replied: 'This decree is extremely important. After all you cannot liquidate illiteracy immediately. Just imagine: a statue to a revolutionary has been put up. There is a solemn ceremony . . . An imaginative speech is made . . . and imperceptibly we are achieving our first goal: we have touched the soul of an illiterate person'.[7] The extraordinary way in which a truly mass culture of festivals took off after the Revolution was a testimony to the effectiveness of their appeal to the illiterate Russian population.

[. . .]

The intention was fundamentally to convey something of the historic purpose of the social changes through which they were living to those very people who had in fact created that history: the working masses. As Lunacharsky put it to his audience at the opening of the Free Art Educational Studios in Petrograd in October 1918, 'The need has arisen to change the external appearance of our towns as rapidly as possible, in order to express our new experiences in an artistic form as well as to get rid of all that is offensive to the feelings of the people.'[8] The task was all-embracing: the environment had to be brought to the point where it corresponded to the great social changes whose scale was not yet generally grasped. Each of the city-wide celebrations recorded here generated works which aimed at linking architecture and urban space. They were monumental in scale, in their content, in the epic nature of their language, and in the extent to which they actively invaded the lives of individuals in the city.

[. . .]

The mass became the real hero of events, and how its belief in the future was directly expressed in its re-enactments.

Political clowns

From a report on the 1919 May Day celebrations in Moscow, published in *Pravda*, no. 93, 3 May 1919.

. . . There is a strange procession along Strastnoi Boulevard: Durov the Clown is travelling down the street with his animals on several leads.

The procession is surrounded by large crowds. The carts are entwined with flags with slogans. On the first cart is a shield, on the second a small locomotive puffs and whistles, wrapped in a sash with the inscription: 'Revolution is the Locomotive of History.' [. . .] Next comes a hyena in a cage. The cage is decorated with the coat of arms of the Romanov family and the inscription 'Capitalism'.

The procession comes to a halt and Durov, surrounded by little children, begins a performance with a dog. Durov plays a commanding officer of the tsarist army and the dog plays the lowest rank. The ingenious Durov portrays a picture of previous mockery of soldiers. Both adults and children are amused.

Then a tramcar with circus performers stops on Lubyanka Square. The jokes of the clown are drowned by bursts of laughter, a balalaika is strummed and a performer in the costume of a boyarina dances in the Russian style. The spectators can barely keep from joining in the dance. . . .

Some of the processions were led by allegorical groups, depicting labour, the alliance between the proletarians and the countryside etc. A tram went past with children wearing red caps and shirts and a French tank, a trophy from Odessa, rolled heavily towards the assembly point. Then a vehicle decorated with a horn of plenty rushed past scattering newspapers and brochures. Up in the blue sky soared aeroplanes, occasionally letting go of newspapers and leaflets, like flocks of white birds . . .

A constructive approach

A proposal for the organization of the May Day festivities on the streets of Moscow, drawn up by the Section of Mass Performances and Spectacles of the Theatrical Department of the Commissariat for Education, Narkompros, published in the journal *Theatre Courier* (*Vestnik teatra*), no. 51, 5–8 February 1920.

The task facing the Section of Mass Performances and Spectacles from the first moment of its activity has been to work out the first scenario of mass action, and to work out a magnificent drama in which the whole city would be the stage and the entire proletarian masses of Moscow the performers. What is more, the Section has chosen the correct path. The scenario should be written by the masses themselves in the process of collective work and collective discussion.

The Section is working out only the general principles, a plan for the festivities, which will then be sent for discussion by various proletarian groups: clubs, studios, committees, etc. The detailed work of these groups will serve as material for the final scenario.

Initially, the Section proposed the idea of using an ancient myth as the theme of the festivities, interpreted symbolically in the sense of the struggle of the proletariat against capitalism. The myth of Prometheus was suggested, a myth both rich in content and extensively developed in world literature.

But then the Section came to the conclusion that it would be wrong to restore Greek myths during the celebration of 1 May. They are alien to the proletarian masses and in no way reflect the latter's own ideology or feelings.

The first proletarian festival should protect the purity of its idea from any deposits of alien cults, from Biblical myths or Christian rites, even from the civic festivities of the French Revolution.

The Section acknowledged May Day to be an integral festival of proletarian culture and adopted A. M. Gan's suggestion of basing it on the idea of the International, from which the international festival historically emerges as the first act of mass creativity on a world scale.

The content of the festivities is to be the history of the three Internationals. The proletariat, having travelled in the course of history the path to socialism via three internationals, must travel this path during the May Day celebrations in theatrical forms, giving a vivid portrayal of the great achievements of the October Revolution, the Soviet system and of the transition to forms of socialist life . . .

The overall task of this decorative plan is to imagine the Communist city of the future. All the squares on which the action is to take place will be named after sciences and arts. For example, Geography Square – with a huge globe on which the continents are painted in the red shades of a flaming world revolution – Astronomy Square, Political Economy Square, and so on.

The streets will be decorated with red flags and shop windows with satirical depictions on themes of a topical nature. Somewhere out of town (possibly at Khodynka) a field of the International will be set up with a wireless station and an aerodrome. The main action of the festivities will be played out on this field.

The part of the festival scenario elaborated in most detail by the Section is the prologue, which is outlined in the following form: early in the morning a loud siren will sound from Sparrow [Ed. note: now Lenin] Hills, which will be answered by the horns of all the city's factories.

At this signal, cavalry patrols, motorcycles and vehicles will leave the seventeen outposts of Moscow for the district squares, summoning citizens onto the streets. On the district squares they will be awaited by agitation collectives who will draw the people into active participation in the festival. Here the act of the First International will be performed.

On its completion, the masses will start moving towards the centre, passing along the streets and squares of the sciences and the arts. In the centre the celebration of the Second International will be held.

Finally, the crowds of citizens will move towards the field of the International where the collapse of the Second International will be played out, followed by the emergence of the Third and the transition to a socialist system. Along the way, intervals for rest and food will be organized, which will also take the form of theatre.

This is the basic outline of the plan for the May Day festivities. The Section is aware of the immense difficulties involved in putting this plan into practice. Its vast scope requires the use of totally new methods, and new creative devices.

Rehearsals with performers will have to take the form of manoeuvres with whole groups of people. The vast number of performers will mean that gestures and voices will have to be forgotten. Instead sound and movement will have to be regarded as elements from which to mould the theatrical part of the festivities.

The Section also has to devise methods to involve the masses in the festival action. In this area, V. S. Smyshlyaev has suggested a series of measures that would involuntarily force the masses to move away from passive contemplation to active participation, and would turn them from spectators into performers. The methods include: a series of easily surmountable obstacles along the route of the procession, the arrangement of the crowd into columns which would move in a previously determined direction under the guidance of organized groups, the ascent of steps and slopes, etc.

A number of ideas were also put forward at that first debate on 'mass participation' organized by the section in the Moscow Proletkult.

Mass pantomimes, the dramatization of all aspects of the procession, of rest and food intervals, the use of historical places connected with memories of revolutionary events, should all form part of the festival programme.

It must, however, be acknowledged that the very nucleus of the festivities has not yet been found; there is still only a vague outline of how the movement of individual collectives will be transformed into a harmonious, general 'participation' that is both theatrically fine and fascinating for the performers . . .

To storm the Winter Palace

From an interview with N. N. Yevreinov, Director of the mass dramatization of *Storming the Winter Palace*, to be enacted on Uritsky Square on 6 November 1920, published in the newspaper *Life of Art* (*Zhizn iskusstva*), no. 596–7, 30 September 1920.

N. N. YEVREINOV: The collective of authors comprised ten of Petrograd's best directors and this team worked enthusiastically and extremely smoothly. All the same, an immense project was handed to the director, namely myself, and as a theatrical historian and theoretician I can assure you that the production is of unprecedented complexity. Three stages are to appear simultaneously: two conventional theatrical stages and one real, historical stage. On the first stage, events will be portrayed in the style of comedy; on the second, in the style of a heroic drama, and on the third, in the style of a battle. The director will have to find a common denominator, some purely theatrical style, to unify all three.

. . . Our method of work will be artistic simplification. But it is not enough to co-ordinate mass action on these three platforms, or stages. This co-ordination, incidentally, is ingeniously achieved by plunging each platform by turns into darkness and brightly illuminating the area of the theatrical arena to which the spectator's attention should be drawn. The action will take place not only on the stages, but also on a bridge between them and on the ground, across which the Provisional Government will run attempting to escape from the pursuing proletariat, and in the air where aeroplanes will soar and bells and factory sirens will sound.

Apart from ten thousand performers – actors and persons mobilized from the drama groups of the Red Army and Navy units – inanimate characters will also take part in the production. Even the Winter Palace itself will be involved as a gigantic actor, as a vast character in the play which will manifest its own mimicry and inner emotions. The director must make the stones speak, so that the spectator feels what is going on inside, behind those cold red walls. We have found an original solution to this problem, using a cinematographic technique: each one of the fifty windows of the first floor will in turn show a moment of the development of the battle inside.

Figure 2.1 In 1920 in Petrograd, the mass pageant *The Storming of the Winter Palace* attempted to reproduce the events of October 1917 in the same Palace Square.

In the form of silhouetted groups, pieces of the immense action will light up and vanish in the darkness until everything ends with the finale of shots, hooters and sirens, and lighting effects: fireworks and flags.

Analysing the new genre

From an article by N. P. Izvenkov entitled 'The First of May 1925', published in the book *Mass Festivals. A Collection of Papers from the Committee for the Sociological Study of the Arts* (*Massovoye prazdnestva. Sbornik Komiteta sotsiologicheskogo izucheniya iskusstv*) Leningrad, 1926, pp. 114–16, 120, 124, 126.

. . . The use of actual objects in the May Day celebrations can be broken down into the following four categories.

The first category consists of objects having an independent significance of their own. They provided the centre of attention for the organizations displaying them. All exhibits from factories and workplaces were of this type, when they used stands on vehicles, etc. Thus the Red Putilov factory showed its tractor, and another showed an engine with the inscription 'Give it a Soviet engine!' . . .

The second type consisted of products and objects, but used as a background for some demonstration or action to be staged. . . .

The next, third category consisted of objects used as props in a theatrical action. Such for example was the invariable use of a sledge-hammer or ordinary hammer for beating the head or the back of the bourgeois or the appeaser; such were the ink-well and bast-shoe hung on a string and used as a priest's censer; also the black coffin carried by Red Army soldiers and bearing the inscription 'Here lies the last illiterate Red Army soldier', and so on.

The fourth category consisted of things of a mixed character. On the one hand they were products of the workplace, but at the same time they were used in a special way. Such were the majority of production diagrams: those from the cork factory were made of cork, for instance, or from the Sputskaya Textile factory of ribbon. The Sev cable factory used wire for its decorations and the timber works used shavings, and so on.

Here arises yet another of the principles behind the arrangements for the May Day demonstrations – their close relationship to professional and production traits. As we shall see below, this principle runs like a thread through the entire May Day celebrations and thus serves as one of the major determinants of its character.

The theatre arrived at the morning demonstrations in the most varied of forms, ranging from complete plays to separate fragments of performances. Of course, we are not talking here about traditional theatre and performances, such as we are accustomed to seeing in stone buildings, although these did have some part to play in the demonstrations, albeit a small one. We are in general talking about some kind of theatrical action with which the whole May Day carnival was permeated. There was theatre not only in those groups which dramatized some subject on the platform of a lorry or in the middle of a crowd of demonstrators. Theatre could also be seen occasionally in different installations, from mechanized figures and even exhibits. . . .

One of the factories at the May Day demonstration built, for example, a wooden cottage with a thatched roof on a lorry. A red cock sat on the roof. The scene also demonstrated fire-extinguishers and hosepipes. On the lorry there were about fifteen men and women dressed in a peasant style. All this was constructed on the principle of a 'living picture': one man was standing with a fireman's hook, another with a hose and so on; but two or three comments from the lorry to the crowd were enough for the 'living picture' to turn into a most genuine piece of theatre.

Let us take another example from a different demonstration. Among the columns, not far apart from each other, walked two costumed figures – a Catholic priest and a bourgeois with their arms linked by iron chains. Behind them was a tall, thick set worker, without any make-up and in an ordinary modern three-piece suit with a cap on his head and a heavy mock hammer in his hand with which he occasionally hit the heads of the priest and the bourgeois. All three moved silently, they simply walked in the midst of the marching columns, but the costumes, the make-up, the hammer and its blows all did their bit. This was a complete theatrical act. . . .

Together with this, factories use their products at the demonstration for purely theatrical purposes. Thus one factory took on stage an enormous model of the kind of frying pan it makes. In the huge pan, a Polish bourgeois was being fried. . . .

Political satire, which has worked out a number of contemporary masks, has also, of course, created distinctive costumes to accompany each of them. The bourgeois and the appeaser are unthinkable without their tail-coats and top-hats or bowlers just as the white officer is always in his greenish-blue uniform, epaulettes and sabre. Determining such costumes went along the lines of taking the most characteristic details. These details were particularly strongly marked in the 'Living Newspapers'[9] where a top-hat on the head (even if the person was otherwise in ordinary working clothes) was enough to signify a 'bourgeois,' a 'minister' or an 'appeaser,' in a word the person required from the White Front. In clubs' performances the top-hat played a most significant role and from there it moved also to dramatization at mass festivals. In contrast to the top-hat (worn by the bourgeois and the appeaser) the worker usually wears a cap . . .

It is also necessary to note that make-up was used in the main only for negative and comic characters. All the positive characters in the dramatizations – workers, Red Army soldiers and so on – were merely dressed in an appropriate costume and did not wear make-up.

Notes

1   V. I. Lenin, *Polnoe sobranıe sochinenii (Complete Collected Works)*, vol. 12, p. 104.

2   A. V. Lunacharsky, 'Pervoe Maya 1919 (The First Day of May 1919) in *Vospominaniya i vpechatleniya (Reminiscences and Impressions)*, Moscow 1968, p. 209.

3   Quoted in: Zh. Terso, *Pesni i pravdnestva Franstuskoi revoliutsii (Songs and Festivals of the French Revolution)* Moscow 1933, pp. 139–40.

4   K. Tsetkin (C. Zetkin), 'Vospominaniya o Lenine' ('Memories of Lenin'), in *Vospominaniya o Vladimire Iliche Lenine (Reminiscences of Vladimir Ilich Lenin)*, vol. 5, Moscow 1969, p. 17.

5   V. D. Bonch-Bruevich, *Lenin v Petrograde i Moskve 1917–20 (Lenin in Petrograd and Moscow 1917–20)*, Moscow 1966, p. 35.

6   V. I. Lenin, *Polnoe sobranie sochinenni*, vol. 45, p. 26.

7   Quoted in: A. Yusin, 'Nachalos v 1905-m' ('It Began in 1905'), *Pravda*, 16 December 1975.

8   A. V. Lunacharsky, *Rech proiznesennaya na otkrytii Petrogradskikh GSKhUM (Speech delivered at the opening of the Petrograd State Free Art-study Studios)*, 10 October 1918, Petrograd, 1918, p. 27.

9   Ed. note: Living Newspapers consisted of the reading or enacting of current events, initially in response to widespread illiteracy.

Chapter 3

Edgar Snow

from RED THEATER

I N T H E E A R L Y 1 9 7 0 S , W H E N I happened upon this account of troupes of actors traveling with the Red Army in the years leading to the Chinese revolution, I was astounded that actors were so integrated into the major events of their times. Despite his sometimes condescending tone, Snow, one of the first Westerners to document the Chinese revolution, admiringly depicts the vitality of these theatre contingents in the 1930s and 1940s.

People were already moving down toward the open-air stage, improvised from an old temple, when I set out with the young official who had invited me to the Red Theater. It was Saturday, two or three hours before sunset, and all Pao An seemed to be going.

Cadets, muleteers, women and girl workers from the uniform and shoe factory, clerks from the cooperatives and from the soviet post office, soldiers, carpenters, villagers followed by their infants, all began streaming toward the big grassy plain beside the river, where the players were performing. It would be hard to imagine a more democratic gathering – something like old-time Chautauqua.[1]

No tickets were sold, there was no 'dress circle,' and there were no preferred seats. Goats were grazing on the tennis court not far beyond. I noticed Lo Fu, general secretary of the Politburo of the Central Committee, Lin Piao, Lin Po-Chu (Lin Tsu-han), the commissioner of finance, Chairman Mao Tse-tung, and other officials and their wives scattered through the crowd, seated on the springy turf like the rest. No one paid much attention to them once the performance had begun.

Across the stage was a big pink curtain of silk, with the words 'People's Anti-Japanese Dramatic Society' in Chinese characters as well as Latinized Chinese, which the Reds were promoting to hasten mass education. The program was to last three hours. It proved to be a combination of playlets, dancing, singing, and pantomime – a kind of variety show, or vaudeville, given unity chiefly by two central themes: anti-Nipponism and the revolution. It was full of overt propaganda and the props were primitive. But it had the advantage of being emancipated from cymbal-crashing and falsetto singing, and of dealing with living material rather than with meaningless historical intrigues that are the concern of the decadent Chinese opera.[2]

What it lacked in subtlety and refinement it partly made up by its robust vitality, its sparkling humor, and a sort of participation between actors and audience. Guests at the Red Theater seemed actually to *listen* to what was said: a really astonishing thing in contrast with the bored opera audience, who often spent their time eating fruit and melon seeds, gossiping, tossing hot towels back and forth, visiting from one box to another, and only occasionally looking at the stage.

The first playlet was called *Invasion*. It opened in a Manchurian village in 1931, with the Japanese arriving and driving out the 'non-resisting' Chinese soldiers. In the second scene Japanese officers banqueted in a peasant's home, using Chinese men for chairs and drunkenly making love to their wives. Another scene showed Japanese dope peddlers selling morphine and heroin and forcing every peasant to buy a quantity. A youth who refused to buy was singled out for questioning.

'You don't buy morphine, you don't obey Manchukuo, health rules, you don't love your "divine" Emperor P'u Yi,' charged his tormentors. 'You are no good, you are an anti-Japanese bandit!' And the youth was promptly executed.

A scene in the village market place showed small merchants peacefully selling their wares. Suddenly Japanese soldiers arrived, searching for more 'anti-Japanese bandits.' Instantly they demanded passports, and those who had forgotten them were shot. Then two Japanese officers gorged themselves on a peddler's pork. When he asked for payment they looked at him in astonishment. 'You ask for payment? Why, Chiang Kai-shek gave us Manchuria, Jehol, Chahar, the Tangku Truce, the Ho-Umetsu Agreement, and the Hopei-Chahar Council without asking a single copper! And *you* want us to pay for a little pork!' Whereupon they impaled him as a 'bandit.'

In the end, of course, all that proved too much for the villagers. Merchants turned over their stands and umbrellas, farmers rushed forth with their spears, women and children came with their knives, and all swore to 'fight to the death' against the *Jih-pen-kuei* – the 'Japanese devils.'

The little play was sprinkled with humor and local idiom. Bursts of laughter alternated with oaths of disgust and hatred for the Japanese. The audience got quite agitated. It was not just political propaganda to them, nor slapstick melodrama, but the poignant truth itself. The fact that the players were mostly youths in their teens and natives of Shensi and Shansi seemed entirely forgotten in the onlookers' absorption with the ideas presented.

The substratum of bitter reality behind this portrayal, done as a sort of farce, was not obscured by its wit and humor for at least one young soldier there. He stood up at the end, and in a voice shaking with emotion cried out: 'Death to the Japanese bandits! Down with the murderers of our Chinese people! Fight back to our homes!' The whole assembly echoed his slogans mightily. I learned that this lad was a Manchurian whose parents had been killed by the Japanese.

Comic relief was provided at this moment by the meandering goats. They were discovered nonchalantly eating the tennis net, which someone had forgotten to take down. A wave of laughter swept the audience while some cadets gave chase to the culprits and salvaged this important property of the recreation department.

Second number on the program was a harvest dance, daintily performed by a dozen girls of the Dramatic Society. Barefoot, clad in peasant trousers and coats and fancy vests, with silk bandannas on their heads, they danced with good unison and grace. Two of these girls, I learned, had walked clear from Kiangsi, where they had learned to dance in the Reds' dramatic school at Juichin. They had genuine talent.

Another unique and amusing number was called the 'United Front Dance,' which interpreted the mobilization of China to resist Japan. By what legerdemain they produced their costumes I do not know, but suddenly there were groups of youths wearing sailors' white jumpers and caps and shorts – first appearing as cavalry formations, next as aviation corps, then as foot soldiers, and finally as the navy. Their pantomime and gesture, at which Chinese are born artists, very realistically conveyed the spirit of the dance. Then there was something called the 'Dance of the Red Machines.' By sound and gesture, by an interplay and interlocking of arms, legs, and heads, the little dancers ingeniously imitated the thrust and drive of pistons, the turn of cogs and wheels, the hum of dynamos – and visions of a machine-age China of the future.

Between acts, shouts arose for extemporaneous singing by people in the audience. Half a dozen native Shensi girls – workers in the factories – were by popular demand required to sing an old folk song of the province, accompaniment being furnished by a Shensi farmer with his homemade guitar. Another 'command' performance was given by a cadet who played the harmonica, and one was called upon to sing a favorite song of the Southland. Then, to my utter consternation, a demand began that the *wai-kuo hsin-wen chi-che* – the foreign newspaperman – strain his lungs in a solo of his own!

[. . .]

With infinite relief I saw the curtain go up on the next act, which turned out to be a social play with a revolutionary theme – an accountant falling in love with his landlord's wife. Then there was more dancing, a 'Living Newspaper'[3] dealing with some late news from the Southwest, and a chorus of children singing 'The International.' Here the flags of several nations were hung on streamers from a central illuminated column, round which reclined the young dancers. They rose slowly, as the words were sung, to stand erect, clenched fists upraised, as the song ended.

The theater was over, but my curiosity remained. Next day I went to interview Miss Wei Kung-chih, director of the People's Anti-Japanese Dramatic Society. [. . .] She told me something of the history of the Red Theater. Dramatic groups were first organized in Kiangsi in 1931. There, at the famous Gorky School (under the technical direction of Yeh Chien-ying) in Juichin, with over 1,000 students recruited from the soviet districts, the Reds trained about sixty theatrical troupes, according to Miss Wei. They traveled through the villages and at the front. Every troupe had long waiting lists of requests from village soviets. The peasants, always grateful for any diversion in their culture-starved lives, voluntarily arranged all transport, food, and housing for these visits. [. . .] 'Every army has its own dramatic group,' Miss Wei continued, 'as well as nearly every district. The actors are nearly all locally recruited. Most of our experienced players from the South have now become instructors.'

[. . .]

What surprised me about these dramatic 'clubs' was that, equipped with so little, they were able to meet a genuine social need. They had the scantest properties and costumes, yet with these primitive materials they managed to produce the authentic illusion of drama. The players received only their food and clothing and small living allowances, but they studied every day, like all Communists, and they believed themselves to be working for China and the Chinese people. They slept anywhere, cheerfully ate what was provided for them, walked long distances from village to village. From the standpoint of material comforts they were unquestionably the most miserably rewarded thespians on earth, yet I hadn't seen any who looked happier.

The Reds wrote nearly all their own plays and songs. Some were contributed by versatile officials, but most of them were prepared by story writers and artists in the propaganda department. Several Red dramatic skits were written by Ch'eng Fang-wu, a well known Hunanese author whose adherence to Soviet Kiangsi in 1933 had excited Shanghai. More recently Ting Ling, China's foremost woman author, had added her talent to the Red Theater.

There was no more powerful weapon of propaganda in the Communist movement than the Reds' dramatic troupes, and none more subtly manipulated. By constant shifts of program, by almost daily changes of the 'Living

Newspaper' scenes, new military, political, economic, and social problems became the material of drama, and doubts and questionings were answered in a humorous, understandable way for the skeptical peasantry. When the Reds occupied new areas, it was the Red Theater that calmed the fears of the people, gave them rudimentary ideas of the Red program, and dispensed great quantities of revolutionary thoughts, to win the people's confidence. During the Reds' 1935 Shansi expedition, for example, hundreds of peasants heard about the Red players with the army, and flocked to see them.

The whole thing was 'propaganda in art' carried to the ultimate degree, and plenty of people would say, 'Why drag art into it?' Yet in its broadest meaning it was art, for it conveyed for its spectators the illusions of life, and if it was a naïve art it was because the living material with which it was made and the living men to whom it appealed were in their approach to life's problems also naïve. For the masses of China there was no fine partition between art and propaganda. There was only a distinction between what was understandable in human experience and what was not.

One could think of the whole history of the Communist movement in China as a grand propaganda tour, and the defense, not so much of the absolute rightness of certain ideas, perhaps, as of their right to exist. I was not sure that they might not prove to be the most permanent service of the Reds, even if they were in the end defeated and broken. For millions of young peasants who had heard the Marxist gospel preached by those beardless youths, thousands of whom were now dead, the old exorcisms of Chinese culture would never again be quite as effective. Wherever in their incredible migrations destiny had moved these Reds, they had vigorously demanded deep social changes – for which the peasants could have learned to hope in no other way – and they had brought new faith in action to the poor and the oppressed.

Notes

1   Ed. note: The Chautauqua movement began in New York State in 1874. A traveling lecture series and summer school, it was the prototype of institutions to further popular education in the US.

2   The 'decadent' and 'meaningless' Chinese opera died hard. Thirty years later the GPCR drafted opera stars wholesale to produce modern plays in forms which would 'serve the people' by dramatizing revolution and the Thought of Mao Tse-tung, and which were not susceptible to undesirable historical analogies. *The Red Lantern*, a play of the 1960s popularized during the GPCR [Great Proletarian Cultural Revolution], was in content basically the same play as *Invasion*, of 1936 – lacking only the comic relief of the marauding goats.

3   Ed.: See note 9, p. 25.

Chapter 4

Safdar Hashmi

from *THE RIGHT TO PERFORM*

U NLIKE HANDKE, HASHMI FAVORS conjoining street and institutional theatre, hoping to provide a performative alternative to what he decries as the mediocre films dominating Indian popular culture. Hashmi situates Indian street theatre in the tradition of agit-prop, with its working-class protagonist, commitment to socialism as *the* political solution, and adaptation of popular cultural traditions. The militant aspect of agit-prop, too, was tragically present in Indian street theatre; Hashmi was murdered by his adversaries while performing in the street.

I. From 'Jana Natya Manch: The First Ten Years Of Street Theatre, October 1978–October 1988'

Contemporary Indian street theatre has been drawing in equal measure from our folk and classical drama as well as from western theatre. The political pamphlet, the wall poster, the agitational speech, the political demonstration – these have all gone into creating the diverse forms adopted by our street theatre.

Street theatre had become inevitable when the workers began organising themselves into unions in the late nineteenth and early twentieth century. As such, it is a twentieth century phenomenon, born of the specific needs of the working people living under capitalist and feudal exploitation.

31

It is basically a militant political theatre of protest. Its function is to agitate the people and to mobilise them behind fighting organisations.

In India, however, street theatre has developed in a different and more ambitious manner, especially during the last dozen years or so. The street theatre workers of the present generation, unlike the pioneers of the forties and the fifties, have become more conscious of its distinctly formal aspects. While unabashedly accepting the ideological nature of their theatre and its unconcealed alignment with political forces, they are no longer producing only poster plays.

In our view there are two reasons for this new development. Firstly, in our cities, with one or two exceptions, there is no tradition of theatre-going. The masses of our urban population have never been to a theatre. Our theatre, even the best of it, has remained mostly confined to a very select group of theatre-goers. The theatre, on its part, has also not been addressing itself to the common, working people. If our urban theatre had been a major cultural force – a living and popular art form reflecting the hopes, aspirations and struggles of the people – then perhaps our street theatre too would have remained only a functional propaganda device, surfacing every now and then to focus attention on burning issues. But since our mainstream theatre is by and large out of tune and touch with the majority of our people, the need remains for a fully developed people's theatre, a theatre which is available to the masses. The street theatre workers now have first hand experience of the artistic inadequacy of poster plays. Such plays serve a purpose, but they satisfy neither the people's need for a fuller theatre, nor the actors' and directors' craving for more challenging and stimulating material. Since conditions have continued to be unfavourable for a mass expansion of proscenium theatre, they have been seriously seeking to develop street theatre itself. Secondly, their long association with street theatre has gradually opened before them the unforeseen possibilities of the development and flowering of street theatre into a full fledged art form. The circular acting area, the conditions of performance, the proximity of the actor and the spectator have all demanded a new acting style, new dramatic structures, new writing skills, a new kind of training, a new use of music, verse and chorus and a new method of theatre management. Even the audience–performer relationship in street theatre is something unique and new and demands have already led to some amount of serious work on the language, structure, grammar and aesthetics of street theatre.

This new street theatre, though still in its infancy and struggling to discover itself, needs to be seen against the backdrop of its phenomenal expansion. During the last dozen years or so it has spread to almost all corners of India. Today there are hundreds of amateur troupes writing their own plays or freely adapting and translating scripts from other regions and languages and giving an enormous number of performances. Jana Natya Manch alone has given 4,300 performances of 22 different plays, in 90 cities, during the last 10 years, seen by over two-and-a-half million people. This body of theatre, though still by and large disregarded by the mainstream theatre, has today become an inseparable part of the theatrical landscape of India. Especially in North India, after the sharp decline of the already weak proscenium theatre in the past few years, street theatre appears to have become at least in terms of the number of performances and the size of its audience, the major theatrical activity. In our opinion, today it is not possible to form a complete picture of contemporary Indian theatre without including street theatre.

This brings us to the unfortunate tendency to project street theatre as a rebellion against the proscenium theatre, or as standing in opposition to it. This absolutely erroneous notion has been created by adherents of both kinds of theatre. On the one hand, some exponents of street theatre have tried to counterpoise it against proscenium theatre, dubbing the latter as a bourgeois, decadent and constricting genre, condemning it as a theatre of irrelevance, of airy-fairy philosophy, of frivolity, and concluding thereafter, that a genuine people's theatre is impossible on the proscenium stage; on the other hand a large number of proscenium wallahs[1] have consistently refused even to accept street theatre as a valid form of dramatic art.

In our view it is absurd to speak of a contradiction between proscenium and street theatres. Both belong equally to the people. Yes, there is certainly a contradiction between the proscenium theatre which has been appropriated by the escapists, the anarchists and the revivalists and the street theatre which stands with the people. Just as there is a contradiction between reactionary proscenium theatre and progressive proscenium theatre, or between democratic street theatre and reformist and sarkari [Ed. note: government-sponsored] street theatre.

Equally absurd is the tendency to dismiss street theatre as political advertisement or a mobile poster. One reason for such comments is of course the voluntary insulation of the proscenium wallahs from street theatre. It is a fact that most of them have not been able to keep themselves abreast of the latest developments in street theatre. The other equally important reason is the extraordinary amount of shoddy fare that has been produced in the name of street theatre. However, there may be another, deeper reason for such comments.

Historically, proscenium theatre has become a place where one concentrates on the finer and subtler aspects of life, a place for meditation, reflection and introspection. All this is fortified by the serious and formal atmosphere in the hall, the silence and the darkness.

Since this kind of intensity and concentration is not obtainable in a street situation it is asserted that it is impossible to achieve any depths of analysis or beauty or any force of presentation in street theatre.

We believe, and we are certain you will all agree with us, that the implements and devices of artistic expression are created by the dramatist's creative perception of life, and not the other way round. True one artist may find it possible to work only within his inherited or acquired discipline. Nobody need quarrel with that. But to reject as incomplete, indeed unrecognisable, one or all disciplines other than his, is wholly unacceptable and unscientific.

Let us be very clear on this. Theatre cannot be dependent on the frills and trappings which surround it. Drama is born with force and beauty in any empty space whether square, rectangular or circular. The play comes alive whether the spectators are on one or all sides, in darkness or in light. One of the greatest bodies of theatrical work that mankind has ever known, the Greek classical drama, used to be performed in sunlight, in front of some 15,000 people on all three sides of the acting area. Shakespeare performed his plays in the courtyards of inns, market places and gardens. His Globe theatre had the reputation of being one of the noisiest places in London where ale was sold in the pit even as a scene was in progress. Brecht described his ideal audience as one which could smoke and drink while watching the play, and vocally express its expert opinion of the agent on the stage like soccer or boxing fans at a match. Closer home, many of the most vibrant theatres of India are traditionally performed in the fields or in open stages. Theatre did not begin with proscenium, nor has its evolution reached the final stage, with it.

Polemics apart, we believe that street theatre is doing something which is of singular significance. At a time when all forms of community entertainment are fast disappearing, when the video and TV have started marketing encapsulated entertainment to be consumed at the level of the nuclear family or the individual, street theatre is once again reviving art which can be enjoyed at the community level, in large gatherings. In this sense it is already playing the role that a fully developed and popular theatre should.

We think it is high time that a living relationship was formed between all those who are committed to healthy theatre whether they are in the proscenium theatre or in street theatre. When new approaches to street theatre are being adopted, the theatre fraternity has a role to play in development of new techniques, new skills and new training methods. The established and the gifted playwrights of the mainstream theatre too have a role to play in enriching the repertoire of scripts for the street theatre. The critics have a role to play in devising new criteria for evaluating this theatre in its own terms. The talented directors and teachers have a role to play in helping street theatre realise its potential.

On the occasion of the tenth anniversary of our street theatre, we extend an invitation to our colleagues in the mainstream theatre to cooperate with us in developing and enriching our street theatre.

(October 29, 1988)

II. From 'Concept of People's Theatre:
A Jana Natya Manch Experience'

[. . .] Any gathering of organised or unorganised workers, students or any group of general public can be an occasion for Janam to stage their playlets. A circle of 15–20 feet radius and people around it is sufficient for it to stage a play. A students' convention against communalism, authoritarianism and unemployment; a demonstration against computerisation; a preparatory meeting for some working class rally; strikes and lockouts; literary seminars or even the victory celebrations of trade unions can be the right opportunity for a performance by Janam. The themes of its plays always keep a close touch with popular mass movements. Its plays on communal riots, the defective education system, the Industrial Relations Bill, women's emancipation, or the political economy of the bus-fare hike achieved phenomenal success only because of the emotional nearness of the themes to the everyday life of the people. For that matter all street plays have to be bold, succinct and direct; and so they are. These aspects of street theatre are necessitated by its limitations of time, space and money.

In order to keep itself alive and involved in the day-to-day people's movement, it can't afford to wait for relevant scripts to be written by professional and celebrated dramatists. Involvement of culture with people's movements requires immediate analysis of the current political and socio-economic developments and preparing a new play on that within a day or two, if not in a couple of hours. This leaves no scope for professionals and celebrities to come into the picture. In this matter Janam is not dependent

Figure 4.1 Hashmi's company, Jana Natya Manch, performing in Sahibabad.

on any professional's services. It is competent enough to write, design, visualise, direct and present plays on its own. All the script writing, designing, direction, music composing, etc. are done collectively in Janam.

In 1973, when the Delhi branch of IPTA [Ed. note: Indian People's Theatre Association] almost became inactive and defunct, a few members came out of it and formed Jana Natya Manch. Its first play was a Bengali play *Mrityur Atit (After Death)* by Utpal Dutt. Thereafter *Bharat Bhagya Vidhata*, a satirical play in Hindi by Ramesh Upadhyay on the misuse of election machinery, was taken up and shown in the far-flung working class colonies and factory gates in addition to colleges, public parks and middle class areas. It was also staged in a few towns of UP [Ed. note: Uttar Pradesh (Northern Province)] during the 1974 mid-term assembly elections.

[. . .]

Due to the high cost and resources involved in these full length plays and paucity of usual sponsors, mainly the trade unions, totally shattered and impoverished during the nightmare of the emergency, not many shows could be done. But Janam felt the huge cultural gap before the demoralised working class and decided to fill it up with an alternative healthy culture. At this specific juncture the need for low cost and need based topical theatre was seriously felt. Hence the necessary drift to street theatre.

Its first post-emergency street play *Machine*,[2] depicting the machinations of the establishment in collusion with the police and security forces against industrial dissent, just coincided with the first ever all-India all trade union rally against the Industrial Relations Bill at the Boat Club on November 20, 1978. This play helped to rejuvenate the morale of a working class audience of about one lakh [Ed. note: a lakh = 100,000] at the joint rally. Since then over 70 shows of this play have been done, mainly in working classs audiences.

[. . .]

In December '78 the news of communal riots in Aligarh shook the country and within a week Jana Natya Manch was out in the streets with its play *Hatyarey*, analysing the political and economic factors which antagonise the traditionally harmonious co-existence of two communities. Performance of this play, ironically, coincided with the second phase of communal violence let loose on the common people of Aligarh. Contrary to Janam's apprehension, they have in fact strengthened the communal harmony by performing this play in troubled, sensitive and minority localities.

In February '79, the state owned Delhi Transport Corporation burdened the common commuter by suddenly raising its fares sky high. Within 24 hours, Jana Natya Manch took the 12-minute play *DTC Ki Dhandhli* to the bus stops exploring the political economy of the fare hike including mismanagement, corruption and rackets of the top bureaucracy. Instant success of the play was evident from the mass appeal and participation it received along with the conversion of each show into a street corner meeting in protest against the fare-hike. This play was shown to about 30 thousand people in 35 performances in different bus-stops of Delhi within a week. Ultimately, the corporation had to partially withdraw the raised fares and even rationalise the fare structures being followed prior to the hike.

JANAM's next play, *Aurat*, depicting the plight of working women, is a universally successful play. Primarily written for and first staged to meet the specific requirements of the first Northern Indian Working Women's Conference (CITU), this play has been performed over 70 times till now. In several glimpses it shows the various stages of woman's life as a daughter, as a wife, as a student, as a mother, as an unemployed young woman, as a worker and finally as a revolutionary; all within 27 minutes. The argument of the play is that women's struggle for equality is only a part of the broader united struggle of the working classes.

In July '79 many All India students and youth organisations of divergent opinions converged in Delhi for a seminar on authoritarianism and communalism. The seminar focussed attention on unemployment, educational reforms and lowering of the voting age to 18 years. This congregation of students from all over India was presented with the 15-minute play *Teen Crore* [Ed. Note: teen means three; crore is a large numerical unit], specially in incorporating the three problems facing our student and youth. Thereafter it was performed in various colleges also.

[. . .]

Due to the topicality and mass involvement of all these plays the audience participation has become a regular feature with Jana Natya Manch. It gets regular suggestions from its audience about improvements and themes of new plays. [. . .] To meet the increasing demand for an alternative and healthy cultural form they have to often go out of Delhi . . . This way Jana Natya Manch is almost leading an All India People's theatre movement emanating from the Hindi heartland.

Notes

1   Ed. note: Difficult to translate precisely, a wallah is a professional, an advocate, a practitioner.
2   Ed. note: The 'emergency' was a maneuver by Prime Minister Indira Gandhi to run the country along dictatorial lines in the name of internal security.

Chapter 5

Suzanne Lacy and Leslie Labowitz

from FEMINIST MEDIA STRATEGIES FOR POLITICAL PERFORMANCE

FOR OVER TWO DECADES, LACY has experimented with forms that combine her personal artistic imagery with political issues. In the context of the women's movement during the 1970s in California, Lacy and Labowitz developed 'feminist media art.' Resonant of agit-prop, they positioned women rather than the working class as protagonist, and the media as their audience and often target.

It was violence – in the media and in society – that gave birth to feminist media art. By 1977 feminists had brought the subject of sexual violence into cultural dialogue; at the same time, an increased social permissiveness allowed more obviously violent and pornographic imagery to 'leak' into the dominant culture through media. Across the country women formed groups to protest snuff films, one of the most shocking manifestations of glamorized violence. These groups did not focus on direct services to victims, as did rape centers formed earlier, but on the social effects of popular imagery. A natural liaison developed between activists who criticized violent images and artists who worked to expand their audience base with critical issues.

In 1978 we formed Ariadne: A Social Art Network, an exchange between women in the arts, governmental politics, women's politics, and media. The focus was sex-violent images in popular culture. Through Ariadne we developed a media strategy for performance artists, one applicable to a wide range of experiences, expertise and needs. For the three years of Ariadne's existence, we produced seven major public performance events dealing with advertising, news media, and pornography. From its inception, our work together combined performance and conceptual art ideas with feminist theory, community organizing techniques, media analysis, and activist strategies. The first of these was *Three Weeks in May* (1977), a performance that laid the groundwork for a form we called the public informational campaign.

[. . .]

Three Weeks in May, with assistance from the Women's Building and its artists, Los Angeles, May 1977

Each day the red stain spread further over the bright yellow map of Los Angeles. One red-stamped 'rape' marked occurrences reported to the police department; around each of these, nine fainter markings represented unreported sexual assaults. Installed in the City Hall Mall, the twenty-five-foot map sat next to an identical one that listed where victims and their families could go for help.

This performance focused attention on the pervasiveness of sexual assault through a city-wide series of thirty events. Performances, speak-outs, art exhibits and demonstrations were amplified by media coverage. In one particularly striking series of street performance, Leslie Labowitz focused on myths of rape, men's role conditioning, and self-defense. Lacy's performance *She Who Would Fly* provided a ritual exorcism. Other artists included Barbara Smith, Cheri Gaulke, Anne Gaulden, Melissa Hofman and Laurel Klick. *Three Weeks* brought together normally disparate groups – including artists, self-defense instructors, activists and city officials – in a temporary community that suggested future collaborative possibilities.

[. . .]

Record Companies Drag Their Feet, Leslie Labowitz in collaboration with Women Against Violence Against Women and the National Organization for Women, Los Angeles, August 1977

How do you bring attention to a national boycott? Working with Women Against Violence Against Women (WAVAW), Leslie Labowitz designed a performance specifically for television news coverage. A parody of the recording industry's greed, which enables it to ignore the effects of its violent advertising on women's lives, this performance was held on Sunset Boulevard, the symbolic heart of the industry. A mock executive's office was set up under a huge billboard for the latest album by the rock group KISS, along

Figure 5.1 In *Mourning and in Rage*, 1977. Seven-foot-tall veiled women in front of Los Angeles City Hall.

with a counter-billboard announcing rape statistics. Three record company moguls – portrayed by women dressed as roosters – arrived in a gold Cadillac, strutted into their 'office' and began to count their 'blood money.' Women pleaded against, they protested their exploitation to no avail. The performance ended when twenty women draped the set with a banner that read, 'Don't Support Violence – Boycott!'

Covered by all major television stations in the city and by *Variety*, a trade journal for the entertainment industry, the event launched a successful campaign against the record companies Warner, Atlantic and Electra for their use of violated images of women in their advertising. This performance was not only powerful as a one-time media event, but it also provides one example of how artists can collaborate effectively with an activist organization.

In Mourning and in Rage, Suzanne Lacy and Leslie Labowitz with assistance from Biba Lowe, Los Angeles, December 1977

Ten seven-foot-tall, heavily veiled women stepped silently from a hearse. As reporters announced to cameras, 'We are at City Hall to witness a dramatic commemoration for the ten victims of the Hillside Strangler,' the women in black delivered an unexpected message. They did not simply grieve but attacked the sensationalized media coverage that contributes to the climate of violence against women. One at a time, the actresses broke their ominous silence to link these murders with *all* forms of sexual violence (an analysis missing from the media) and to demand concrete solutions.

City council members promised support to activists, Holly Near sang 'Fight Back' (written especially for the performance), and news programs across the state carried reports of the performance and its activist message. *In Mourning and in Rage* was perhaps our most compelling example of a one-time media performance, staged as a guerrilla intervention to the conventions of sex crime reportage. Follow-up talk show appearances and activities by local rape hot line advocates created a much broader discussion of the issues than could be covered at the performance itself. [. . .]

Chapter 6

Alisa Solomon

AIDS CRUSADERS ACT UP A STORM

SOLOMON DESCRIBES THE CONSCIOUS theatricaliza-tion of AIDS issues in order to capture media attention and catalyze political action. This article was written in 1989 during the heady early days of ACT UP, the group most responsible for mobilization around AIDS in the US.

A dozen young men sit in a circle with their arms linked tightly. Rocking a bit, they chant, 'Act up, fight back, fight AIDS!' Their melodic mantra takes on urgency as the 'up,' sung a minor third above the 'act' and tunefully prolonged, gives way to the staccato calls to fight. On and on they croon, their voices becoming tarnished with hoarseness. Soon, another dozen men approach, ordering the chanters to disperse. They do not move. One by one, each man is torn from the group and dragged away. His body goes limp, but his voice keeps going strong.

Once the circle has been demolished, the two groups of men change places. The ones who dragged the chanters off now sit down, lock arms and start sounding the battle cry. After they are hauled asunder, they change roles and begin again. ACT UP – the AIDS Coalition to Unleash Power – is rehearsing for its next major action.

Since it began in New York only two-and-a-half years ago, ACT UP, the fastest-growing AIDS activist group in the country, has been hitting the streets to educate Americans about acquired immune deficiency syndrome and to shake some movement out of bureaucratic government agencies that tie up experimental drugs in astonishing tangles of red tape – while the number of AIDS cases rises past 100,000 (more than twice the number of American soldiers who died in Vietnam).

From the beginning, the AIDS epidemic has taken hold of the theatre. Some of the earliest calls to awareness and action came from the stage – in William Hoffman's *As Is* and Larry Kramer's *The Normal Heart*, both first produced in early 1985. And it took the death of an actor, Rock Hudson, later that same year for mainstream media and the public to take note of the devastation that had already been claiming lives for five years. Meanwhile, the theatre community itself suffered one loss after another after another.

Recently, AIDS has fallen off as a central subject for new drama. It's no wonder. When, for instance, spectacle and public ritual are so movingly combined in the image and action of the Names Project Quilt,[1] conventional theatre seems redundant – at best a pale imitation of the formal, mass expressions that help give shape to real grief and anger. Time and again the spirited protesters of ACT UP have demonstrated that the theatre of AIDS is in the streets.

'The whole idea,' says playwright Kramer, who founded the group, 'was to get drugs into bodies.' It's been working.

The group's very first demonstration, in March 1987, was a protest against drug-company profiteering from the exorbitantly priced AZT (the only drug approved for AIDS treatment by the Food and Drug Administration). Some 300 outraged New Yorkers sat down in traffic on Wall Street and hanged FDA commissioner Frank Young in effigy. (The puppet lookalike was built by Kramer's friends in the prop shop of the New York Shakespeare Festival.) The FDA then promised to shorten the drug approval process by two years. On the evening news, Kramer recounts in his book *Reports from the Holocaust*, 'Dan Rather gave credit to ACT UP. It was a wonderful beginning.' Just a few months ago, ACT UP scored its biggest victory yet: Under pressure from activists, the pharmaceutical giant Bristol Myers agreed to distribute the experimental drug, ddI – which is far less toxic than AZT – outside the sluggish formal clinical trials.

Among its triumphs along the way, ACT UP managed to persuade organizers of last June's AIDS conference in Montréal to open up the proceedings to people with AIDS; in one of many successful bouts with publishers, it convinced Malcolm Forbes to run a retraction of an article in his business weekly that dismissed the seriousness of the epidemic; it forced New York City health commissioner Stephen Joseph to back off from his plan to institute contract tracing for carriers of the HIV virus when he had barely finished announcing it; and, though far more difficult to measure, ACT UP has without a doubt brought news of the government's lethargy on AIDS into living rooms across the country.

In the meantime, ACT UP has also won a Bessie award, the Oscar of performance art, and wide-ranging respect from researchers and people with

AIDS alike. For all their impressive knowledge of AIDS etiology and experimental drugs, it's their rowdy, flamboyant tactics that have garnered the activists' attention and adulation – as well as opposition. Theirs is the theatre Artaud envisioned: It generates the electricity of a mob rushing into the streets by doing just that.

Good political protest has always been consciously theatrical. Jailed 19th-century Suffragists paraded in a pageant alongside a giant statue with broken chains in her hand under the banner, 'From Prison to Citizenship'; today's No More Nice Girls march for the right to choose abortion, wearing pregnant bellies (pillows under black tunics) bound in chains. The 1980 Women's Pentagon Action wove a peaceful web around the Washington weapons wigwam; 15-foot-high puppets of Ronald Reagan, George Bush, Jeanne Kirkpatrick and Caspar Weinberger stood trial for the crimes of American foreign policy in a 1984 Manhattan rally. Activists have always counted on dramatic devices to get their causes noticed. But more than that, they have tapped into theatre's special union of representation and community to symbolically demonstrate our personal stakes in political issues.

ACT UP has rambunctiously run forward in these radical footsteps. They stole the show, for instance, at the 1987 New York Gay and Lesbian Pride Parade, upstaging glorious drag queens, marching bands and the brilliant banners of the Lesbian Herstory Archives with their compelling float: A rubber-faced Ronald Reagan grinned maniacally from behind the wheel of a flatbed, while on the platform behind him, men in prison uniforms crouched, cordoned off by concentration-camp barbed wire and escorted by guards in surgical masks and gloves.

ACT UP's young members pay little homage to the models their forebears have provided for such tried-and-true histrionic techniques. Despite elder statesmen like veteran activists Vito Russo and Marty Robinson and feminist stalwarts like Maxine Wolf, ACT UP is comprised mostly by a new generation who were not out of diapers when the SDS's Mark Rudd threw a lemon meringue pie in the face of an army recruiter at Columbia University, and not even born when school children marched valiantly against the violent spray of firehoses in Birmingham, Ala. Indeed, for many of the more than 400 men and women who crowd into a dank, dim hall in Manhattan's Lesbian and Gay Community Services Center for ACT UP meetings every Monday night, even the Stonewall riot that kicked off the gay rights movement in 1969 is ancient history.

Many of ACT UP's young professionals – there are lawyers, stockbrokers, teachers, artists, advertisers, publishers, writers, doctors in the group – readily admit that, until joining, they considered protesting the thing you did when your steak came to the table too rare. Now, in these cynical 'postmodern,' 'post-feminist,' 'post-'60's' late '80s, ACT UP is making activism hip again. Some 3,000 New Yorkers have signed on to ACT UP, and there are upwards of 60 chapters across the country and in Canada. Some observers go so far as to claim that ACT UP is ushering a new era of radicalism into the '90s. Indeed, when ACT UPpers tell their friends they're planning a demo, they no longer have to explain that they aren't talking about a music session. Suddenly 'CD' no longer evokes compact discs and certificates of deposit – civil disobedience has become fashionable again.

Among its many styles of spectacle, civil disobedience is perhaps ACT UP's most choreographed mode of work. Ever since the sit-ins of the Civil Rights Movement caught local officials unawares, legal restrictions have made massive arrests an elaborate, pre-arranged *pas de deux* between demonstrators and police. Along with the national coalition of AIDS activist groups, ACT NOW, ACT UP staged one of its most intricate and lively duets at the Food and Drug Administration in Rockville, Md. On Oct. 11, 1988. While the group followed what have become the common procedures of CD – taking over an unauthorized area and staying put until arrested by police prepared and waiting in advance – they stretched the form with unbridled theatrical flair. 'Each action is like an enormous show,' says Kramer. 'We're divided into committees doing banners, logistics, media, just like a producer would hire people for scenery, costumes, publicity.'

Experienced activists (mostly women) lead workshops in nonviolent CD for small squads called affinity groups for weeks before busloads of these newly trained shock troops arrive at the bleak 18-story FDA office – to find a hostile audience of 50 riot police and a dozen cop cars. Blocking entrances, posting their signature 'silence = death' banner on the building's roof, ACT UP closes the building within half an hour. For six hours more, the performance continues. Every 32 minutes – the rate at which an American dies of AIDS – one group of demonstrators cuts through the incessant chanting with shrill air-raid whistles and falls 'dead' to the pavement. Another affinity group made up of people with AIDS collapses to the ground beneath cardboard tombstones reading, 'I needed aerosol pentamadine' (a drug that treats pneumocystis pneumonia, an opportunistic disease common to people with AIDS). 'AZT wasn't enough,' another tombstone explains. 'Buried by the System,' adds yet one more. Of more than 1,000 protesters, nearly 180 are arrested. They go limp and are dragged off, just as they rehearsed it.

Meanwhile, a group that wants to break the tired conventions of CD comes up with a new twist on environmental theatre. Richard Elovich, a Manhattan-based performance artist, is with the faction that, in his words, is 'looking for something that is not just reactive, but will set up an alternative model, one that is visionary.' The group takes over the FDA's nearby ethics building. Decked out in labcoats, they proclaim themselves a new center for drugs and biologics and issue edicts announcing all kinds of fantastic plans for government initiatives against AIDS. They use letterhead stationery created for the occasion.

These are some of ACT UP's most obvious forays into acting – but in its subtler forms, there's a paradox in acting up. Because so many of its

45

Figure 6.1 ACT UP member being arrested for civil disobedience at the San Francisco Conference on AIDS, June 1990 (photo by Ann Meredith).

members are new to activism, many admit to feeling that marching in the streets involves a kind of role-playing. 'I know how I'm supposed to look, what I'm supposed to wear – jeans and an ACT UP T-shirt – and how to do the chants and shake my fists,' one young newcomer told me, 'but it took me a long time until I felt like it was really *me* doing those things.' In one sense, this acting is Brechtian: the activist plays the part with a detached self-awareness, often commenting on the role.

On the other hand, it is akin to the kind of avant-garde acting that seeks to erase the boundary between performer and role. After all, for the large percentage of ACT UP members who are gay, simply saying so aloud in this homophobic culture is a political act. Marching in the streets is just saying it louder. Moreover, working with ACT UP provides a direct outlet for all-too-real emotions. After helping to care for a friend who died of AIDS, Elovich saw ACT UP march at a Gay Pride Parade and 'felt I belonged there because of the anger. The fact that there was no hospice for my friend to go to, that he couldn't get experimental drugs, upset me.' Echoing many ACT UP members, he notes, 'ACT UP was a place to deal with my anger over that situation, and to do something about it.' When hundreds holler, 'Fight back, fight AIDS,' their fists clenched with rage, their jaws tight with fear, this is not acting.

Sometimes these boundaries get so blurred that things turn anarchic. Fired by fury and armed with facts, demonstrators have on occasion crossed non-violent activism's invisible fourth wall between peaceful outrage and potentially explosive provocation. Last summer, during festivities celebrating the 20th anniversary of Stonewall, a playful, camped-up reenactment of the rebellion (which was itself full of campy performance as rioters formed kick-lines or teased the cops with come-ons) turned violent as some ACT UP members, not acting under the authority of the organization, decided spontaneously to 'take Seventh Avenue.' Some activists were hit by vehicles; one car was completely smashed, its sides kicked in and its windshield shattered.

The threat of such eruptions always seethes beneath the surface of even the most measured ACT UP strike, creating a heightened dramatic tension that has been missing from much routine protest for years. Among the committed, charged bastions of ACT UP, anything can happen – and it often does.

The day before Gay Pride Day this year, ACT UP sponsored its own march up Sixth Avenue 'to put some politics back into the weekend,' as one participant said with a sneer toward the carnival-like spirit of the annual Sunday parade. 'We have to do more than celebrate when so many of us are dying.' Whereas the traditional event resembles the political pageantry of the Bread and Puppet Theatre or of Britain's Welfare State International, ACT UP marches are sharp, urgent, purposeful.

Several thousand stream up the street, propelled by the rambunctious pleasure of stopping traffic without a permit – a rare occurrence in New York and a testament to the police department's respect for the group's unprecedented ability to do what it wants, permission or no. Small bands of ACT UPpers part the sea of traffic by linking hands across the intersections. Once the march passes by, they run on ahead to stretch across another block. In the meantime, they dance the can-can.

As usual, ACT UP makes a splash on the evening news. Using theatricality to attract the media is, of course, nothing new. In the '60s, the Yippies played for the cameras too. (Both these generations of activists, it's interesting to note, were galvanized by personal threats: the draft, and now the specter of a horrifying disease.) 'Our thing's for TV,' Abbie Hoffman once said, 'Long hair is just another prop.'

But this TV generation has learned how to use television rather than be used by it. In a 1971 article, 'Rethinking Guerilla Theatre,' San Francisco Mime Troupe founder R. G. Davis criticizes the Yippies for 'fail[ing] to recognize the medium of their message.' Television, he explains, is not owned by the people – 'advertisers own it. They rent the space. If you can't rent space, you must do somersaults to obtain coverage. Somersaults create news and created news adds spice to the commercials. The object of privately manipulated mass media is not to distribute news but to create demand for consumer products.'

No ACT UP activist could disagree with Davis's point, but while people are dying, ACT UP doesn't worry about the long-term revolution. To get drugs released, treatment programs funded and consciousness awakened, ACT UP gleefully beats the media at its own game. You could almost say, following Davis's analysis, that they present their *cause* as a consumer item and make it at least as appealing as a cold Coors or a cruising Camaro. TV news reports of their events are commercials for ACT UP.

The anti-war student movement of the '60s lost credibility in mainstream America when news cameras insisted on following the most flamboyant hippies while ignoring massive grassroots activity and its actual leadership. (In much the same way, reports on Gay Pride parades often focus on drag queens and leather men.) ACT UP prevents such skewed reporting by first being painfully democratic in its structure and decision-making, then by blitzing networks and newspapers with glossy, highly professional media kits. Formal press releases go out well in advance of actions, and afterwards activists have often been booked on the talk-show circuit.

One ACT UP member who once worked as a network anchorwoman coaches fellow activists in how to give sound bites. The group's visual imagery is hard-hitting, quickly digested and memorable – just like advertising.

When ACT UP was first getting off the ground in the spring of 1987, Larry Kramer recalls, posters with the slogan 'silence=death' under a pink triangle (the symbol Nazis forced homosexuals to wear) began appearing mysteriously all over New York. An art director named Avram Finklestein (who has since left his corporate job to concentrate on activism) showed up at an early ACT UP meeting and offered the logo. Stickers bearing the haunting image have been plastered on subways, payphones, billboards, even the backs of unsuspecting policemen's jackets; it has become as familiar and desirable a part of Manhattan's bombarding visual landscape as the similarly shaped Mercedes Benz emblem.

More recently, a group called Gran Fury has been supplying ACT UP with such startling symbols as a dripping red handprint with the text, 'You've got blood on your hands, Ed Koch.' Elovich, who works with Gran Fury, says the group consciously relies on advertising strategies. 'It's the opposite of developing performance art, where I start intuitively and hone down. Here we begin with clarity – what exactly we want to say – and then determine how best to say it.' In recent months Gran Fury produced city bus posters (already displayed in San Francisco but not yet accepted in New York) that look, at first glance, like Benetton ads. Three separate, attractive mixed-race couples – two men, two women, a man and a woman – kiss in a closeup punched-out photo. 'Kissing doesn't kill,' reads the legend. 'Greed and indifference do.'

Some traditional radicals scoff at this 'MTV activism.' ACT UPpers Ray Navarro and Catherine Saalfield counter the criticisms (in an article called 'Shocking Pink Politics' in the Manhattan weekly *Downtown*) by pointing out, 'We have reclaimed style as a weapon . . . Well-designed propaganda products provide revenue for the group's actions. And through our media work, we have seduced other communities into recognizing why we fight.' A couple of decades ago in *Performance* magazine, critic Todd Gitlin questioned whether theatricality really served political movements in the end: 'Dramaturgy is not the revolution, it is a phase, and it cannot itself create the conditions for mass change in consciousness or materiality . . . Theatre has its place, but unless its revolutionary politics is embedded in the ordinary lives of the people, it becomes Broadway.'

Television, perhaps; Broadway never. For ACT UP's work *is* embedded in the ordinary lives of the people involved – ordinary people who might be face-to-face with death.

In addition to playing to the camera, ACT UP often performs for a specifically targeted live audience. The second anniversary City Hall demonstration last March 28 [1989] – which made the covers of New York dailies and was the lead story on the network news – singled out city government for its message. One affinity group – out of several devoted to demonstrating links between America's health crisis and other issues such as housing and reproductive freedom – sat down in the street penned in by little individual cardboard houses. Poking out like jacks-in-the-box, they called attention to the thousands of New York homeless with AIDS.

But even more directly than in its mass demonstrations, ACT UP targets special audiences with its ubiquitous 'zaps' – guerilla theatre strikes that respond, most often within 24 hours, to a specific, dangerous act. Outside *Forbes*'s Fifth Avenue office in June, some 35 demonstrators marched around the sidewalk chanting, 'They print lies, we die.' Their placards, decorated with plastic toy shovels, asserted, 'Your capitalist tools are digging our graves.'

At *Cosmopolitan* magazine headquarters a year earlier, at a zap called by ACT UP's vocal, exemplary women's caucus, infuriated activists distributed condoms and safer-sex information to passers-by – the magazine had published an article saying women are not at risk for AIDS. There have been phone zaps – when Northwest Airlines denied passage to a person with AIDS, ACT UPpers jammed their circuits with thousands of calls for bogus plane reservations. And even postal zaps – when New York's post office issued a cancellation commemorating the 20th anniversary of the Stonewall rebellion, ACT UP sent countless postcards to ultraconservative Senator Jesse Helms – who had vehemently objected to the special stamp.

ACT UP has been bringing its campy shock tactics to demonstrations called by other groups with related agendas. At an outdoor 'Brunch at the Plaza Hotel' for the homeless, ACT UP passed condoms and clean drug-work kits; in Washington last April, the AIDS activists joined hundreds of thousands of pro-choice marchers with chants, banners and outrageous costumes. A couple of stiltwalkers loped down Constitution Avenue with giant red coathangers for hats; a woman fringed head-to-toe with condoms held up a sign, 'Dress for Safe Sex.' And ACT UP has staged countless kiss-ins (same-sex, of course) – including at the 1988 Democratic Convention – as a wet reminder that saliva does not transmit AIDS.

This tongue-in-cheek edge keeps ACT UP's theatrics from getting stale. 'A great part of what keeps us together, besides our common goals,' says Kramer, 'is that it's a lot of fun.'

ACT UP has even gone to baseball games together. Hoping to reach out to a more general audience – an issue ACT UP's Women's Caucus and Majority Actions Committee (so named because the majority of people with AIDS are black and Hispanic) have been particularly pushing – the group bought several hundred seats for a Mets game and brought their message to Shea Stadium's bleachers. 'We wanted to find a way to make the idea of using condoms visible to a heterosexual male population,' says Women's Caucus member Debbie Levine. Since 40 tickets entitles a group to a message on the scoreboard, 'Strike Out AIDS' flashed over the outfield. Meanwhile, ACT UP members unfurled a series of banners that, stretching across several 80-seat blocks, counseled, 'Don't balk at safe sex.'

Dramaturgy might not have been so crucial an element of the revolution in the '60s, but nowadays, when it is a basic component of government, it is also a logical means of resistance. In the 20 years since the anti-war movement, the ground has shifted seismically. On the one hand, the Reagan–Bush era has so theatricalized us, so saturated the culture with superficial imagery, that simply attaching symbols to an emotional and political reality becomes radical. Think of the difference between a Reagan-endorsed sham like Hands Across America, whose empty rhetoric served to *allay* concern about world hunger by giving people the illusion that they were doing something about it, and ACT UP's second anniversary sit-in at City Hall, whose hard-core information combined with powerful images to *provoke* concern.

At the same time, since the '60s, feminism – followed by the gay rights movement – has taught us how the personal and political intimately connect. Protest actions, as a result, have blurred the boundaries between performance and engagement. The Argentinian mothers of the Plaza de Mayo, for instance, assemble weekly in Buenos Aires wearing scarves embroidered with the names of their disappeared children, not just for TV (in Abbie Hoffman's version of protest) but for themselves. Women living in tents at Greenham Common's peace camp in England have not only demonstrated against nuclear weapons, but totally changed the conditions of their lives.

ACT UP, too, draws upon this ancient theatrical impulse of empowering a community through ritual. Andrew Velez, chair of ACT UP's actions committee, which orchestrates many of its demonstrations, talks about the group's poster-painting parties with the fervor of someone who has just discovered what it's like to work in the theatre: 'It's thrilling just to watch people make posters – drawing, spray-painting, laughing and really getting juicy with their imaginations. Everyone has an opportunity to make a difference.'

For Debbie Levine, who holds a masters from Columbia University in directing, this recognition runs deeper. 'I actually went into ACT UP because I didn't feel comfortable doing theatre any more,' she says. 'I admired a lot of experimental work, but was frustrated by its coldness and limited audience.' Hoping to create a play about AIDS, Levine went to an ACT UP meeting for advice. She dropped the theatre project and stayed with the activists. 'For a long time,' she says, 'I felt guilty that I wasn't doing theatre any more, but I felt satisfied that I was reaching a large, diverse audience with an intrinsic message of universalism – and my guilt resolved itself. I realized theatre *was* what I was doing.'

Note

1   Ed. note: The AIDS Quilt is composed of over 40,000 panels, each commemorating a person who died of AIDS. Each panel typically includes birth and death dates, photographs and momentos.

Chapter 7

Dubravka Kneževic

MARKED WITH RED INK

KNEŽEVIC'S PIECE RESPONDS TO THE fratricidal war during the early 1990s in the former Yugoslavia. She depicts a society in which as recently as the late 1970s, political street theatre was 'the first and only opposition movement in the one-party system of ex-Yugoslavia.' Agit-prop no longer points to any one ideology, least of all Marxism; the mere act of questioning is the political act exemplar. Theatre is as much a tool of the state as of the opposition, for whom sometimes the only action is standing in public, neither agitating nor propandizing, but bearing witness to events to which there is no obvious or immediate remedy. Here Kneževic's essay bleeds into the next section of this book, 'Witness.'

In *Danton's Death* — arguably the best historical play ever written, at least from a European, and especially from an Eastern European point of view — Georg Büchner contrasts scenes of revolutionary passion and suffering with grotesque sketches of crowds in the street — with the savage, farcical, and naturalistic side of the same phenomenon. What is first presented as a refined human, philosophical, life-and-death dilemma instantly repeats as a blood-thirsty farce, a vicious Grand Guignol with no return. The former belongs to the theatre, the latter to a reality that is by definition always theatrical-ized in oppressive totalitarian and inhuman regimes.

Abraham-Joseph Bénard Fleury, one of the most outstanding French actors before and during the Revolution, vividly depicts the societal mode in which the theatre, and the people, had to survive:

Nothing was fixed, nothing was settled, nothing was permanent; everything was, as they say in financial circles, to come due this month, or to come due next month. It was a time when kings lasted three months, books an hour, plays half an evening, and constitutions fifteen days. The scene shifted constantly, the nation lived in tents, and as we were part of the nation, we followed the trend.

(Fleury 1966: 244)

Fleury, leading actor of the Comédie Française, was one of those theatre practitioners jailed because they were considered to be counterrevolutionary, performing in luxurious costumes that might provoke memories of the ancien régime. By the time a long and exhaustive court procedure finally began after he had been imprisoned for eleven months, the mark in red ink already had been written beside his name – 'G,' for 'guillotine.' Some others had more luck – they got only 'D,' for 'deport.'

Dealing with theatre in Eastern Europe, particularly with theatre addressing broader, even accidental groups of spectators on the street, always has been a kind of hazardous, unsafe, breakneck activity. But what we cannot learn without personal engagement and experience is the response from both sides – the regime and the spectators. Any prediction is absolutely impossible in some drastic situations, such as war, destruction, lack of any system of values – especially in a climate of socio-psychosis caused by the devastations of fratricidal war and by living under long-term oppression permeated with hatred and inflamed by jingoistic propaganda.

Street theatricality and the nationalistic regime(s)

Based on experiences in ex-Yugoslavia following the hippie movement, and under the impact of 'documentary' theatre, a strong wave of provocative, polemical theatre arose during the late 1970s and the early 1980s in ex-Yugoslavia, a wave called 'political theatre.' When nothing else could be done, theatre took responsibility for interrogating reality, unmasking prejudice, negating dogma, and slapping awake society's atrophied moral sense. It could be said that political theatre, by taking the crucial step in introducing alternative political views, has been for many years the first and only opposition movement in the one-party system of ex-Yugoslavia.

If the theatre was so important and active in creating public opinion, it is unavoidably necessary to ask whether theatre practitioners were able to stop the war in ex-Yugoslavia, or at least to reduce its atrocities. Unfortunately, the nationalistic elites were faster and more perfidious. Their recipe for obtaining power by the destruction of everything existing, including culture and theatre, counted on theatrical means and the exceptional popularity of the theatre among so-called 'ordinary people.' The use of theatre effects for the purpose of unscrupulous political propaganda and manipulation always has been a habit of all oppressive regimes. The Serbian nationalistic regime, which for a long while preceded all other regimes in the region, became quite experienced in all three of the main genres of street performance that theatre sociology has identified at work in eighteenth-century France. (Cf. Kernodle 1944, Duvignaud 1973.)

The first genre consists of spontaneous manifestations or manifestations organized under the auspices of agitators; these were at once the most 'popular' and the most numerous. They were extremely important in generating the climate for the rise of today's Serbian president. The most 'spontaneous' part of these gatherings were the busses by which 'unintentional' demonstrators were taken to a predetermined place.

Also quite popular was an old, pagan ritual of 'second entombment': reinternment of the bones of a dead and until recently forgotten 'father' of the nation – a spectacle that included regular media updates of the bones' progress as they were carried over sometimes transatlantic distances. Finally, the third 'classical' genre consisted of celebrations with purely ideological content, usually disguised behind cultural or religious purposes. The best-known example in ex-Yugoslavia is the celebration of the 500th anniversary of the battle of Kosovo Field (1389), aimed at raising the 'spirit of the nation' while emphasizing territorial claims.

Our politicians of the late 1980s added to the French model an aggressive, violent, inflammatory vocabulary full of pornographically abused terms like 'statehood,' 'sovereignty,' 'national self-determination,' 'irreconcilable territorial claims' – all wrapped up in garish, colorful flags, emblems, seals, slogans, icons, and banners of hate-mongering. In other words, by making use of all possible means of street theatre, and of spectacle in general, our politics have become a self-sufficient para-theatrical spectacle that counts on an emotional, cathartic response.

The opposition strikes back

Theatre practitioners in Belgrade, in Serbia, and in what is nowadays called the FRY (Federal Republic of Yugoslavia) were spared direct exposure to the war disaster and the savage bloodshed. But they have been faced with the victimization of both the whole society and each individual, with hundreds of thousands of refugees and unknown numbers of casualties, with a rigid and vicious war policy, and with the meteoric escalation of chauvinistic euphoria. They have witnessed the organized exhumation of deeply patriarchal heroic clichés and myths; the contamination by pseudo-religion, history, and tradition; and the disastrously hazardous reshuffling of values and priorities. And they have been forced to live in a twilight zone of total economic and ethical collapse. They did not actually support that insanity of mass proportions, they did not take part in stirring up the collective national trance. But neither did they do anything against all this.

A different sort of theatre took place in their stead. On 9 March 1991, three months before the beginning of civil war, Yugoslav army tanks were sent against demonstrators in Belgrade for the first time in the history of ex-Yugoslavia.[1] From that moment on, the role of radical street theatre was taken over by opposition parties, movements, and associations, primarily those of civil orientation. In contrast to the regime, these theatre non-practitioners have never claimed that their street activities were occurring 'spontaneously'; their events were carefully planned, with all their theatricality, very often quite conceptual, and always graced with more-than-symbolic titles.

Many street actions, especially those addressed to the Serbian president and his clique, took place in front of the Federal or Serbian Assembly, depending upon where the president was scheduled to appear that day. For example, early in the war the Center for Anti-War Action and Civil League organized 'The Last Bell' – a literal expression of the widely shared belief that the last bell for the Serbian president had rung and that he must resign. The participants were asked to bring and use anything that could make a clinking sound, and they stood for an hour in front of the Assembly concertizing with their chimes, carillons, sheep and cow's bells, cymbals, sets of keys, and noisy mechanical alarm clocks. Another action in the same period was 'The Last Prayer,' organized by the Belgrade Musicians' Guild. The image of a thousand people kneeling for one hour in front of the Assembly, each whispering her or his own pleas, proved highly impressive – to everyone but those to whom the performance was addressed.

At the very beginning of the war in Bosnia, Youth Radio B-92, the most prominent opposition medium, organized an action entitled 'All the President's Babies' – a reference both to the war's atrocities and to the fact of Serbia's negative birth rate. A thousand parents and their babies, each carrying flowers or candles for all the victims of the war, formed a large circle around the Assembly; but nobody inside the building was moved.

Student protest '92

In the summer of 1992, during two-and-a-half months of protest, students at Belgrade University organized numerous street theatrical actions aimed at capturing the attention of Belgrade's citizens and media and simultaneously at consolidating the spirit of the movement itself.[2] Apart from taking over university buildings, halting the work of all the faculties in the city, and protesting in their halls, students expressed their dissent through another popular form of organized street protest – thematic processions. The first one, 'Prisoners of Shortsightedness,' was organized in support of an opposition meeting and also to answer the charge that student protest 'must have been organized by someone else,' not by the students themselves. The students pinned prisoners' numbers onto their shirts and walked with one hand holding their student identification cards high in the air, the other covering their eyes.

Another action provoked a brutal response by a radical right-wing leader. The action took place at the beginning of a severe economic crisis in the first few weeks of the UN sanctions, a first sign of which was a lack of elementary hygienic supplies. The action, called 'Washing Up,' was addressed to all members of the Serbian parliament – concerning their dirty hands, faces, and minds. Every student in the long line brought their last hygienic supplies from home – soap, a handful of detergent, a half-used tube of toothpaste – and left them in front of the Assembly. While they were leaving the 'symbols' on the front steps of the Assembly, the right-wing leader came out of the building and began to swear and threaten the protesters, continuously pulling out his revolver. The students responded by shelling the mad chauvinist with a rain of soap-bars. Luckily, the police intervention this time was not directed against the students.

The most important procession of the Student Protest was 'Coffee with the President.' One afternoon, students joined by many other Belgrade citizens took a long walk from the University Rectorate, headquarters of the protest in the city center, to the president's residency in the fancy part of Belgrade, ten kilometers away. The students decided to visit him at his home, greet his wife with flowers, have a coffee with him (a traditional sign of Balkan hospitality), and hand-deliver a list of their demands – the first point in which was a call for his immediate resignation. The procession was stopped a few hundred meters in front of the residency by numerous special police squads. A few days later they performed a theatrical replica of the same procession, called 'Five O'Clock Coffee.' For this event, students of fine arts made two-meter-tall rug puppets of the president and his wife, students of architecture designed a stage representing their house, and the whole procession, with flowers and the list of demands in the fore, was repeated. What could not happen in reality happened in this Grand Guignol.

Some student actions went on even after the protest had been definitely defeated. One of these took place in the fall of 1993, about half-way into the worst period of inflation, poverty and hunger, when the appearance of even a trivial article in the local grocery immediately resulted in a kilometer-long queue of frustrated customers. The students put an iron cage in the center of the city where a few, experienced in pantomime, started selling the 'invisible thing.' The action, lasting several hours, was intended to provoke conscientious objection and civil protest in the place of patient obedience and submission.

Women in Black against the war

A group of women, none of whom had any kind of theatrical training or previous experience, has been playing a distinctive role in Belgrade anti-war street theatre. Before the beginning of war they gathered around a nucleus of the non-existent women's movement which dealt primarily with basic theoretical feminist issues in this patriarchal Balkan country – a country that always has been led, ruled, seduced, and destroyed by omnipotent and omnipresent macho males. Their initial appearance on Belgrade streets was allied to the preliminary, completely spontaneous response of Belgrade citizens to the madness of war. The evening after the news broke about the first deaths in the ex-Yugoslav carnage, all members and supporters of civil-oriented associations assembled in front of the Serbian Parliament to light candles in memory of all the victims of the war, no matter of which nationality. A group of women of various ethnic origins and with quite different social and educational backgrounds wanted to enhance the 'Candles' event by adding even more dignity, engagement, and significance in order to obtain broader attention for it. They dressed in black and went to the main Belgrade square carrying black banners, candles, and flowers; there they stood in silent vigil for one hour. Since then, they have kept on standing there every Wednesday afternoon, regardless of the permanent changes in the official Serbian policy, right-wing provocation, or meteorological circumstances.

It is amazing what a simple way they found to express what they think, feel, want, and how easily they can communicate on any level. They call themselves simply Women in Black, the sessions and workshops they hold in their modest premises are simply 'meetings,' and their protest in the streets is just 'standing.'[3] But their 'standing' constantly includes theatrical elements that vary from one Wednesday to another. The only constants are the color of the clothing and the banners. There is always a certain choreography that depends on how many women have joined the particular 'standing.' Sometimes the women simply stand in line or in a circle, sometimes the circle is a moving one, sometimes it sways from a line to circle, then to a line again, or to a semi-circle. The shape is usually derived from an energy field that originates with the participants themselves, then transfers to the surrounding spectators, and gets broader if the energy feedback is generally positive. Sometimes spectators/passers-by may respond quite roughly or aggressively; if so, the women move closer together, generating strength and energy within the group and staying quiet and in full concentration.

Women in Black also initiated some street actions themselves and shaped some according to the patterns just described. The one that gathered the greatest number of people together took place in April 1993. Called 'Black Ribbon,' it was a procession paying tribute to all victims of war and marking the first anniversary of the war in Bosnia. A long line of participants covered with a long construction of black fabric – a ribbon of mourning – occupied

Figure 7.1 Women in Black at a central square in Belgrade (photo by Vesna Pavlović).

the whole length of Belgrade's main street. The event took place in absolute silence and with the dignity that is characteristic of Women in Black.

Breath(e) to stay alive

While opposition on the streets was taking over the role of theatre, Belgrade's institutional theatres – safe behind their shields during almost three years of war – were not able to get out of a vicious circle of lethargy. What they did not want to do, could not do, or were afraid to do, was done by a small, alternative, experimental theatre group. A group of young theatre professionals, led by two female theatre directors, decided to start working when everything else in ex-Yugoslavia was stopped by the war; the company, Dah Teatar, is determined to oppose the destruction and political insanity through theatrical creation.[4] In the summer of 1992, the group went into the main Belgrade street with its production of *This Babylonian Confusion*, a piece that combined Brecht's most daring anti-war poetry and songs with performance techniques drawn from several avant-garde models.

Everything worked against them. There was no trace of a professional street-theatre tradition in ex-Yugoslavia, especially in Serbia, and women directors are not in favor with the rather patriarchal Serbian audiences.[5] Besides, to say something in public against Serbian war policy – to say it from the 'stage,' whatever that stage might be – was at that time almost a crime, a form of disobedience typical of tiny civil and peace groups. When Dah Teatar went into the street, one third of their 'audience' of ordinary passers-by was wearing various kinds of uniforms, and many were armed to the teeth. Twenty meters down the street from the place they performed was a stand where the extreme right wing sold posters, badges, flags, and emblems while rowdy war songs blared out from 'ghetto blasters.' But, when the performance started and four persons dressed in black appeared with golden angel wings, everything came to a halt. Many people who were just passing by were caught unaware. The words they heard were not their cup of tea; in some other situation they would have pulled the trigger and killed such a traitor, but they could not resist the pure emotion and positive energy that stood behind this 'traitorous' verbal disturbance.

This Babylonian Confusion was performed for fifteen days in a row – absolutely unusual in Yugoslav theatre custom. Although some kind of unpleasant incident seemed quite possible, not one occurred.

Interestingly, at the beginning, Dah Teatar members did not think about doing a street piece. But all their productions grow out of questions they ask themselves in the particular moment of the working process, and taking to the streets was the logical answer at that moment. The question was: in times of blood and crime, what are we, as artists and human beings, supposed to do? Even without any previous street-theatre experience, Dah Teatar

59

intuitively found a way to communicate directly with its spectators, to make them at the same time witnesses of reality and of the performance that cross-examined it.

After this production, Dah Teatar continued its theatrical mission by founding the International Network of Young Research Theatres and by organizing a project named 'Art Saves Lives.' In June 1994, during the second year of the project's existence, Dah Teatar led the participants of a Belgrade meeting to the same street where they had performed *Babylonian Confusion*; here, they all took part in an improvised performance. Performers from Sweden, Denmark, Italy, Spain, Hungary, Norway, Greece, and Dah Teater itself jammed together, each in her or his own language, on the theme of freedom and oppression, handing lighted candles to the spectators.

Post-Dayton conclusion

Despite a definite cultural hibernation, it was again theatre, or at least theatrical elements, that on certain rare, extreme occasions embodied the last bit of common sense, showed us light at the end of this endless tunnel of horrors, and directed us toward honest human and moral behavior. These examples have had a real, healing effect on politically unconscious, illiterate, and hysteric entities in certain groups of people.

On the other hand, lack of information about what was happening on Belgrade streets, lack of support even from colleagues abroad, and disregard not only by the Serbian government but also by the international community keep telling us that there is less and less sense in what we are doing. Halting the spirit of freedom, freezing it, driving it into hibernation, even erasing it —everything that could not be accomplished by the Serbian regime despite all its efforts during these five war years was accomplished by the international authorities, by the measures they keep taking to stop or thwart the regime itself. Three years of UN sanctions did not destroy the Serbian ruling party, but they did diminish an already fragile opposition. The sanctions have not in any way endangered the popularity of the Serbian president; on the contrary, they have strengthened and even expanded his power.

In other words, what was happening on the highest international levels during the last five years and what finally happened following the signing of the Dayton Accord in fact aided and abetted the Serbian regime. At the moment, any public show of dissatisfaction, disobedience, or protest against the Serbian government is countered by the absolute legitimacy the government has been granted by the international community; to resist the regime is to resist the international authorities themselves. Being internationally recognized as a peacekeeper and as a legitimate representative of 'the people's will,' the president of Serbia is now free to do whatever he wants. Not many of us who were openly against this war and openly showed our dissatisfaction with the regime – with actions as well as words – will live long enough to see where this will lead.

One thing is sure – the first step taken by every internationally recognized dictator is to sweep his rivals – even the weakest ones – under the carpet and to destroy everything documenting their existence. Neither oppressive regimes nor world politics need the witnesses. And there is no doubt that somewhere, on some list written in some dark chamber – whether of the ex-Yugoslav mayhem or the international political circus – our names have been marked with red ink for quite a long while. Writing this essay, bearing witness to the street events I have described above for every possible reader, is nothing more than an attempt to save some evidence of our existence. As long as it is possible to share the information, some last dinosaurs in Serbia will have the proof that they are still humans and alive – before the guillotine's blade falls.

Notes

1   Although not well known abroad, the events of 9 March 1991 mark the key point in the development of the Serbian opposition. A meeting of the leading opposition party turned into a serious mass demonstration. Battalions of police violently attacked unarmed people; the tanks appeared later in the evening.

2   Student Protest '92 became the most powerful, largest, and longest-lasting in this part of the world; however, like the events of 9 March 1991, it was arrogantly ignored – not only by the Serbian regime, but also by international authorities and by the media. During this summer, students unexpectedly united across widely differing social and professional backgrounds. The protest's failure combined with the effects of war, mobilization, poverty, economic crisis, and a sense of not having any kind of future to impel 350,000 graduates and undergraduates to leave the country during the period from the beginning of the war through the end of 1993.

3   'Women in Black' is a non-government, not-for-profit, Belgrade women's peace association whose activities have largely taken over other forms of peace protesting. They are extremely active in facilitating the resocialization of refugees, taking care of several refugee camps in Serbia completely forgotten by both domestic and international administrations.

4   'Dah' means 'breath' in Serbo-Croatian; the word has synonyms similar to those for the English – including breeze, air, and life.

5   The Department of Theatre Directing at Belgrade University of Arts, from which all Belgrade theatre professionals come, is attended by an equal number of female and male students. But it is always the men who get the first chance in the theatres. The list of extraordinary women directors, some with international reputations, who have left Serbia or given up directing in the last ten years is painfully large.

References

Duvignaud, Jean (1973) *Les Ombres collectives: sociologie du théâtre*, 2nd edn. Paris: Presses Universitaires de France.

Fleury, Abraham-Joseph Bénard (1966) *Memoirs*, 2:398, quoted and trans. In Marvin Carlson, *The Theatre of the French Revolution*, Ithaca, NY: Cornell University Press.

Kernodle, George R. (1944) *From Art to Theatre: Form and Convention in the Renaissance*, Chicago: University of Chicago Press.

PART TWO

WITNESS

Introduction

Hope is an orientation of the spirit, an orientation of the heart. It is not the conviction that something will turn out well, but the certainty that something makes sense, regardless of how it turns out.

Vaclav Havel

BEARING WITNESS AS RADICAL STREET performance uses heightened means to direct attention onto actions of social magnitude, often at sites where they actually occur, and from a perspective that would otherwise be missing. Witnessing supposes a connection between knowledge and responsibility. As Steven Durland states in the first essay of this section, 'A person who bears witness to an injustice takes responsibility for that awareness. That person may then choose to do something or stand by, but he may not turn away in ignorance.'

The acts under scrutiny tend to be of such great force that the efficacy of bearing witness is often questionable. But at least they are brought to public view, thus fulfilling theatre's role as embedded in its etymological root *theatron*, seeing place. Playwright Karen Malpede uses the term 'theatre of witness' for plays that respond to acts of genocide, 'seek[ing] to reverse trauma's debilitating effects on self and society by giving shape to the complex and cyclical stages of remembrance and recovery' (1996: 233).

As the following essays attest, street theatre as witness manifests both personal and collective, therapeutic and political dimensions. I hope these essays contribute to a fuller conception of street performance as not a two-dimensional, soapbox affair but a multi-faceted, multi-purpose form of expression.

Reference

Malpede, Karen (1996) 'Thoughts on a Theater of Witness and Excerpts from Two Plays of Witness,' in Charles Strozier and Michael Flynn (eds) *Genocide, War, and Human Survival*, Lanham, MD: Rowen & Littlefield.

Chapter 8

Steven Durland

WITNESS: THE GUERRILLA THEATER
OF GREENPEACE

DURLAND CITES THE QUAKER PRACTICE of bearing witness as the source of the environmental activism of Greenpeace. Quaker meetings feature silent meditation followed by telling the congregation what one has heard inside, understood as a manifestation of the presence of God. Quakers believe that this inner voice guides their actions, including speaking out against social wrongs.

In 1968 a dozen members of the Yippie movement, led by Abbie Hoffman and Jerry Rubin, went to the visitors gallery of the New York Stock Exchange and threw money on the brokers below. 'We didn't call the press,' wrote Hoffman, 'at that time we really had no notion of anything called a media event.' But the press was quick to respond and by evening the event was being reported around the world. Within the month the stock exchange had spent $20,000 to enclose the gallery with bullet-proof glass.

Hoffman continues, 'A spark had been ignited. The system cracked a little. Not a drop of blood had been spilled, not a bone broken, but on that day, with that gesture, an image war had begun. In the minds of millions of teenagers the stock market had just crashed. . . . Showering money on the Wall Street brokers was the TV-age version of driving the money changers from the temple.'[1]

In 1971 an ad hoc group of activists in Vancouver who for two years had been protesting American nuclear tests on Amchitka Island in the

Aleutians without success, decided they too needed to ignite a spark. Their plan was to sail a broken-down boat named the *Phyllis Cormack* to Amchitka to 'witness' the next bomb test. Hampered by storms and the US Coastguard, they were forced to turn back, with expectations that their venture had been a failure. But thousands of supporters who had been following their efforts in the newspapers greeted their return and a second boat was immediately sent out. The second boat was still 700 miles from the island when the bomb went off and it appeared that all had been for naught. But as a result of the worldwide media attention the US announced an end to tests on Amchitka and the island was restored to its prior status as a bird sanctuary. It was the first victory of Greenpeace.

For Hoffman and the Yippies their actions and the ones that followed were part of the long history of guerrilla theater, 'probably the oldest form of political commentary,' says Hoffman. 'We would hurl ourselves across the canvas of society like streaks of splattered paint. Highly visual images would become news, and rumor-mongers would rush to spread the excited word.'

For the Canadians their Alaskan Sea adventure grew out of a Quaker belief called 'bearing witness.' A person who bears witness to an injustice takes responsibility for that awareness. That person may then choose to do something or stand by, but he may not turn away in ignorance. From this belief and a modest first adventure has grown the organization that claims over 1.5 million contributors and offices in seventeen countries. The organization's name was coined in preparation for that first adventure, *green* to signify the activists' conservation interests, and *peace* to signify their second goal.

The 'actions' of Greenpeace have always been discussed in terms of the organization's ecology concerns, but it seems appropriate to include it in the history of protest theater, and in fact, Greenpeace might well lay claim to being the largest and most successful guerrilla theater of all. During the past seventeen years they have conducted innumerable actions around the world and can take or share credit for such accomplishments as the reduction of international whaling by 84 percent, a ban on disposing of nuclear garbage in the Atlantic Ocean, the near elimination of mass slaughter of nursing harp seals, and significant reductions in acid rain production, nuclear weapons testing and toxic waste disposal.

Of course Greenpeace is much more than a theater company, but its strength, and the element that differentiates it from other environmental organizations, is the impact of its visual and theatrical actions. According to Steve Loper, Action Director for Greenpeace USA, 'Greenpeace believes that an image is an all important thing. The direct actions call attention to the issues we're involved in. We put a different point of view out that usually ends up on the front page of the paper. *Then* we have people who've done research and people who are lobbying so that once the attention is there it gets more done. We've embarrassed people for not doing their job, or we've called attention to facts that the general public wasn't aware of so they question their local politicians. If we just did research and lobbying and came out with a report it would probably be on the 50th page of the paper.'[2]

Greenpeace focuses its efforts in three major campaign areas: toxic waste, nuclear issues and ocean ecology. It has been the organization's efforts to save the whales that has brought Greenpeace much of its attention. Since the initial exploit of the *Phyllis Cormack*, the organization has built an 'econavy' ranging from converted fishing trawlers to inflatable rubber dinghies called Zodiacs. They have used their fleet to document and interfere with illegal whaling as well as toxic dumping and nuclear testing and transport on the seas. Their most famous vessel, the flagship *Rainbow Warrior*, was sunk in 1985 off the coast of New Zealand by French military intelligence. The *Rainbow Warrior* was in the Pacific to protest French underground nuclear weapons testing near the Mururoa Atoll. The incident created an international scandal for the French government, and in October 1987 an international arbitration tribunal headed by UN Secretary General Javier Pérez de Cuéllar awarded Greenpeace $8.1 million in damages from France for the sinking. Two French agents were sentenced to ten years in jail by the New Zealand court after pleading guilty to sabotage and manslaughter.

One of Greenpeace's more potent images was created in England in 1985 where internationally known photographer David Bailey directed a sixty-second film showing a glamorous fashion show in which one of the models comes out in a fur coat which suddenly begins spurting blood until the whole audience is splattered. In the final shot the model exits the ramp, dragging her fur coat and leaving a wide swath of blood behind her. The last image has also been produced as a billboard with the caption, 'It takes forty dumb animals to make a fur coat. But only one to wear it.'

Greenpeace's actions frequently consist of plugging pipes that discharge toxic waste or climbing structures and hanging banners from such places as nuclear cooling towers, smoke stacks, buildings and such famous symbols as the Statue of Liberty and Mt. Rushmore. The Mt. Rushmore action in October 1987 was an acid rain protest; the plan was to stretch a banner shaped like a gasmask over the mouth of George Washington. The banner said, 'We the People Say No to Acid Rain.'

Local authorities interrupted the Mt. Rushmore action before it was completed but the image still appeared in numerous papers across the country and had its impact. 'A symbolic image like Mt. Rushmore is a very powerful image,' said Loper. 'It lends a great deal of weight. It's almost like those Presidents against the Reagan administration. These people gave us this clean, beautiful country and we're not caring about it.'

In 1984 Loper was involved in hanging a banner on the Statue of Liberty that read 'Give Me Liberty From Nuclear Weapons, Stop Testing.' 'That picture went around the world,' Loper said. 'Every August 6th [the anniversary of the Hiroshima atomic bomb] the media is looking for an image that

Figure 8.1 Greenpeace action at Belgium's largest municipal incinerator to stop waste from being burnt (photo by Buyse).

denotes protests against nuclear weapons. What we did in '84 was give them the perfect image. It was one of the most enjoyable I've done.'

Greenpeace's actions often are directed at specific problems and specific companies. Loper helped plug an underwater pipe at a CIBA-Geigy chemical plant in Lavallette, New Jersey, that was dumping over 200,000 gallons of chemicals a week into the ocean. 'A lot of toxic chemicals are odorless and colorless so it's hard to convince people they're dangerous,' he said. 'But the effluent from CIBA-Geigy looked like spent motor oil. We brought big water jugs of it ashore where people were sitting or swimming or sunning. Their mouths just fell open. They knew just by looking that this stuff didn't belong in the water. A guy from the Chamber of Commerce tried to steal a bottle of the effluent. After the action an organization started in the community called the Ocean County Citizens for Clean Water.

'Sometimes it seems like the government, the Environmental Protection Agency, is more like a defensive organization for the industry than it is a protection agency for the people. For example, Dow Chemical in Midland, Michigan, has a risk assessment for the plant. Someone decides that it's okay, for instance, for five people or ten people in every million to die because the plant is there. That's not realistic in our opinion.'

New York governor (and then presidential candidate) Mario Cuomo was the focus of a Greenpeace action last spring when it was learned that New York was going to permit Occidental Chemical to open an incinerator in the Niagara region, an area already suffering from an overdose of toxic waste. 'We're fighting to have people reduce the production of toxic waste at the source if it can't be dealt with,' said Loper. 'Currently there is no technology that does anything but put it somewhere else.'

Loper and fellow activists climbed the state house in Albany at night and attached a banner that read 'Niagara: Still Toxic After All These Years. Why, Governor Cuomo?'

'He was having a press conference,' Loper said, 'and people were asking him "What's going on with Niagara? How come you're permitting this?" These are the kinds of questions we hoped to have asked. At the time he may have been a political candidate so he was in a position to have pressure affect him. He really got angry. He swore we were lunatics and equated us with Oliver North, but two months later we were invited by the governor's office to a signing of a toxic waste agreement at Niagara Falls. There's a grudging respect he's paying us.'

Like the best guerrilla theater, the daring escapades and visual images take a backseat to results in the Greenpeace resume. 'In some cases we do a protest and there's too much publicity on the protest itself – how high up we were, how we got there, how cold it was – so we defeat ourselves,' said Loper. 'We try to downplay the thing we've done. We tell the media that our people are professional climbers, etc. What I always say after I come down is that it wasn't much of a chance I was taking because I'm trained, and the people who are taking a real chance without any choice are the people who are having all this toxic waste foisted on them. We try to get the light off the climb, or whatever we've done, and get it on the issue.'

But Greenpeace often does get the attention on the issue and, according to Loper, they are suffering the results of their success. 'In recent years some of the things Greenpeace has done have caused retribution against us and I think that's a signal that we're being more effective. That includes prison terms and the sinking of the *Rainbow Warrior*. The more effective you are the more you piss people off. For instance the Mt. Rushmore climb wasn't successful in that we didn't get the whole banner up, but the event evidently went into 300–400 papers in the United States including the *Washington Times*, the paper Reagan reads. Who's to say that he didn't say, 'Who are these little assholes?'

'Before we climbed Mt. Rushmore our lawyer's assessment was that we'd be fined $500 and that would be it. Then after we actually did it word came that there was high pressure from Washington to curtail our personal activities. The plea bargain the prosecution is offering right now is $250 fine and three weeks in jail.

'What's surprising is that most people in the system that is prosecuting us support us. The policemen will tell you, "I think you guys are doing great. We respect what you did." The policeman in Albany who arrested us for the climb apologized the entire time for having to do it. Our banner was soaking wet because it rained that night. He took it out and told us, "We had it dried." We couldn't believe that.

'There was a prosecutor on the East Coast who told the judge that he refused to prosecute the case because what we were saying was true. Then he walked over to the guy from Greenpeace who was on trial, handed him $15 for a membership and walked out of the courtroom.'

Certainly, in Greenpeace's case, its protest theater is aimed at issues that are of concern to everyone, even the perpetrators. 'I'm a philosophical person,' said Loper, 'and I don't feel that these are bad people. These are good people who are ignoring something that they know. The scientists and the government are telling them that what they're doing isn't hurting anybody and I believe they want to believe that. Anybody who's making money doesn't want to believe that they're hurting people. But somewhere inside themselves I think they know what they're doing is wrong. I think that's why when we do a protest so much energy is released because when we're down there plugging the pipes we're a part of them they've denied.'

Loper finds Greenpeace's work helps empower the rest of the audience as well. 'We always give people the feeling that something can be done. The power of individual action. When you go on the property of the company that's doing the damage and actually drape your feelings from their property it's a very distinctive defeat for them. It makes what you're saying true. The company is psychologically towering over those who would oppose it and this is like a slap in the face. It's motivating people to act. When we come along, a little three or four of us, take on the big company, it's giving the giant a whack on the nose. And it's a good thing.'

In contemporary American culture the actions of Greenpeace, like the guerrilla theater of the Yippies and all effective creativity with a mission, are rarely considered art by those given to determining such matters. Interestingly, the more successful political theater is, the less important it becomes to those affected that it *is* called art. It certainly isn't a problem Greenpeace is worrying about. But as the function of art in our culture drifts steadily toward becoming investment commodity and entertainment, it might well be worth the art world's time to expand its narrow definitions to include activities that have a function more in keeping with traditional art values – creating images that have an impact on people's lives.

Notes

1   Abbie Hoffman, 'Museum of the Streets,' in Douglas Kahn and Diane Neumaier, eds, *Cultures in Contention* (The Real Comet Press, 1985), pp. 134–140.
2   Steve Loper, all quotes from an interview with the author, December 1987.

Chapter 9

Diana Taylor

MAKING A SPECTACLE
The Mothers of the Plaza de Mayo

TAYLOR DESCRIBES WOMEN WHO BORE public witness to the 'disappearance' of their children by a brutal military dictatorship, using their role as mothers for protection. The women made their audience witnesses, too, with the responsibility that comes with knowledge.

Arm in arm, wearing their white head scarves, the Mothers of the Plaza de Mayo slowly walk around the Plaza de Mayo, Argentina's central square. Some carry huge placards with the smiling faces of their missing children. Others hang small photographs around their necks. Turning their bodies into walking billboards, they carry banners demanding 'Aparición con vida' – that their children be brought 'back alive.' On any given Thursday afternoon at 3:30, hundreds of women meet in the square to demand justice for the human rights violations committed by the brutal military dictatorship that abducted, tortured and permanently 'disappeared' 30,000 Argentineans between 1976 and 1983, a period that came to be known as the 'Dirty War.' The Plaza, facing the Presidential palace, lies in the heart of Buenos Aires' financial and economic district. Businessmen and politicians hurry to and fro, sometimes crossing the street to distance themselves from the Mothers. The women continue to talk and comfort each other as they walk, stopping every so often to gather around the microphone from which they and their leader, Hebe de Bonafini, broadcast their accusations to the country's president. *Where are our children? We want them back alive! Why did their torturers and murders get away with murder? When will*

Figure 9.1 Las Madres de la Plaza de Mayo (photo by Cristina Fraire).

justice be done? Until these issues are resolved, the women claim, the Dirty War will not be over. Nor will their demonstrations.

The spectacle of elderly women in white scarves carrying placards with the huge faces of their missing children has become an icon of women's resistance movements, especially in Latin America where their group has become the model for dozens of similar grass-roots, human rights organizations. This essay focuses on how the Mothers of the Plaza de Mayo staged their opposition to the military juntas that controlled Argentina between 1976 and 1983. While much has been written on the Mothers' movement, few people have looked at how their spectacle fit into or contested the military junta's spectacle of national identity and cohesion. As the political Fathers of the nation persecuted and killed its opposition in the name of Christian, Western and family values, the Mothers made visible the violence and hypocrisy that underwrote the junta's 'process of national reorganization.'

In its first pronouncement immediately following the coup (literally *blow*), published on the front page of a major centrist daily paper, *La Nación*, March 24, 1976, the junta declared itself the 'supreme organ of the Nation' ready to 'fill the void of power' embodied by Perón's widow, María Estela Martínez de Perón ('Isabelita'), Argentina's constitutional president. With a show of muscle, the junta undertook its exercise in national body-building, determined to transform the 'infirm,' inert, Argentine masses into an authentic, implicitly masculine, 'national being.' The military heralded its accession to power as the 'dawning of a fecund epoch,' although the generative process was not, as it recognized, strictly speaking 'natural.' 'Isabelita's' government was sick; its 'productive apparatus' was exhausted; 'natural' solutions were no longer sufficient to insure a full 'recuperation.'

The military represented itself as a disciplined masculine body, aggressively visible, all surface, identifiable by its uniforms, ubiquitous, on parade for all the world to see. The display of the military leaders in church or with the Catholic archbishops aligned military and sacred power. Staging order was perceived as a way of making order happen. The junta's display both re-enacted and constituted the new social order: all male, Catholic and strictly hierarchical. The unholy trinity – Army, Navy and Air Force – were depicted as one entity, set-apart as in religious iconography, the embodiment of national aspirations of grandeur. They spoke as one central, unified subject; their 'we' supposedly included everyone. Visually, the spectacle affirmed the centrality of the junta and emphasized the importance of hierarchy and rank by distancing the great leaders from their undifferentiated followers.

From its opening address, the junta made explicit that the maternal image of the Patria or Motherland justified the civil violence. The military claimed it had to save 'her,' for 'she' was being 'raped,' 'penetrated' and 'infiltrated' by her enemies.[1] But 'she' was also the site of the conflict, as the Dirty War was carried out in the interstices of the Patria, in her very entrails. General Jorge Videla, President of the junta, declared that the *Patria* was 'bleeding to death' (Troncoso 1989: 59). But it is interesting to note that *Patria*, which comes from Padre or father, does not mean *fatherland* in Spanish. Rather, the word Patria signals the image of motherland as envisioned by patriarchy. Thus, the word itself alerts us to the dangerously slippery positioning of the 'feminine' in this discourse. There is no woman behind the maternal image invoked by the military. The term Patria merely projects the masculinist version of maternity – patriarchy in drag. In the name of the Patria, this nonexistent, yet 'pure' feminine image, the military justified its attack on its own population. However, depicting the physical site of violence as feminine had devastating repercussions on the lives of real-life women. The very notion of the feminine was split in two, the 'good' woman and the 'bad.' On the one hand, the junta honored the symbolic image of pure motherhood associated with the Patria, the 'good' woman, and made clear to women that their role was also to be 'pure,' that is non-political, mothers confined to the private sphere. On the other hand, active women were 'bad,' associated with deviance and subversion. Women who were not content to stay home were often targeted as enemies of the State.

During the Dirty War – so called because it was a terrorist civil conflict rather than a conventional war with two armed sides that abides by the international rules of war – some mothers were willing to go along with the junta's version of 'good' women. They supported the military's mission and encouraged it to exercise even more control over the public good. In 1977, the League of Mothers of Families, sounding much like the Christian Right in the US today, urged their rulers to ensure that 'education strengthened traditional and Christian values' and asked that 'the media be truly instruments of culture, diffusing good examples and healthy entertainment' (Avellanada 1986: 148). The media, under military direction, not surprisingly carried interviews and reports on 'good' women, those who were happiest in the home, looking after their children. Mothers were warned that their sons and daughters were in grave danger because the *guerrillas* were just waiting to lure them into subversion. The radio, television, and magazines bombarded women with the question, 'Señora, do you know where your children are?' The junta demanded that women put State interests over familial bonds.

In the midst of this brutal and repressive political climate, when most members of the opposition were either in exile, in hiding, in concentration camps or jails, the Mothers went to the Plaza de Mayo, the most public space in Argentina, to protest that it was the military that posed the gravest threat to their children. To protest the Armed Forces' 'disappearance' of their children, the Mothers had to manipulate the maternal image that was already rigorously controlled by the State. They claimed that it was precisely their maternal responsibilities as 'good' mothers that took them to the Plaza in search of their children.

In 1977, fourteen women first took to the Plaza to collectively demand information concerning the whereabouts of their missing children. They had met in government offices, prisons and courts looking for any sign of their sons and daughters. Little by little, the women came to identify as a group, calling themselves the 'Mothers of the Plaza de Mayo.' They started wearing white head kerchiefs to recognize each other and to be recognized by onlookers. The Mothers realized that only by being visible could they be politically effective. Only by being visible could they stay alive in a society in which all opposition was annihilated by the military. The role of 'mother' offered the women a certain security in the initial phase of their movement. The junta, which legitimated its mission with the rhetoric of Christian and family values, could hardly gun down defenseless mothers in public. So it tried dismissing the Mothers as 'crazy old women' and threatened them individually in their homes and on their way to and from the Plaza. But still the Mothers returned to the Plaza every Thursday afternoon.

Gradually, the number of women grew. They belonged to different social classes, though the majority were working class. They represented different religious groups and came from different parts of Argentina. In July there were 150 Madres. Most Argentines tried to ignore them, crossing the street to distance themselves as much as possible. Some passersby insulted them. Others whispered support and solidarity. On October 5, 1977 the Mothers placed an ad in *La Prensa* demanding the 'truth' about 237 disappeared persons, accompanied by pictures of the victims and the signatures and identity card numbers of the women in the movement. They got no reply. Ten days later, hundreds of women delivered a petition with 24,000 signatures demanding an investigation into the disappearances. The police tried to disperse them – spraying tear gas at the women, shooting bullets into the air and detaining over 300 of them for questioning. Foreign correspondents, the only ones to cover the event, were also arrested.

News of the Mothers and their anti-junta activities soon spread internationally. The battle for visibility commanded more and more spectators. Largely due to public recognition and financial support from human rights groups from the Netherlands, Sweden, France and Italy, the Mothers were able to survive politically and financially. Amnesty International sent a mission to Argentina in 1976 to report on the disappeared. In 1977, President Carter sent Patrica Derian, US Assistant Secretary of State, to investigate the accusations of human rights abuses. She estimated that three thousand people had been executed and five thousand disappeared (Simpson and Bennett 1985: 279). The United States cut military aid to Argentina and canceled $270 million in loans. The junta realized that they could not dismiss the Mothers as 'madwomen'; they had to get rid of them. So in December of 1977, the junta infiltrated the Mothers' organization and kidnapped and disappeared twelve women. But in spite of the danger, the Mothers returned to the Plaza.

During 1978, the military intensified its harassment and detentions. In 1979, the Plaza was cordoned off by heavily armed police. The women would dash across the square before the Police could stop them, only to remind the world and themselves that this was still their space. That same year, the Organization of American States (OAS) sent the Inter-American Human Rights Commission to Argentina. The Mothers brought women from all over the country to testify before them, as many as 3,000 people lining up at a time (Navarro-Aranguren 1989: 253). The junta, unable to block the investigation, launched its own counter-attack, mimicking the Mothers' visual strategies. They made up posters and used people's bodies as walking billboards marked with a pun on human rights: 'Somos derechos y humanos.' ('We are right and human.') The Mothers formed the Association of the Madres de la Plaza de Mayo and in January, 1980, returned to the Plaza, ready to face death before relinquishing it again.

The Mothers' performance of motherhood tried to bridge the schism between the 'good' and the 'bad' woman belabored by the military. The women consciously modeled themselves on the Virgin Mary, the ultimate mother who transcends the public/private bind by carrying her privacy with her even in public. Thus, Christian and Jewish women alike exploited a system of representations and stereotypes that had so effectively limited most forms of female visibility and expression: 'At first they marched as if in ritual procession: faces serious, eyes turned upward in supplication, heads covered . . . peaceful, rapt, pleading' (Diago 1988: 29). The virginal role allowed the women to perform traditionally acceptable 'feminine' qualities – self-sacrifice, suffering, irrationality. Even as they took one of the most daring steps imaginable in their particular political arena, they affirmed their passivity and powerlessness. Yet even that role did not protect the women for long. Their public exposure resulted in ostracization from the Church. They had gone beyond the representational constraints of the role: pain was permissible, perhaps, but not anger. Silence, maybe, but not protest. As one of the Church leaders commented: 'I can't imagine the Virgin Mary yelling, protesting and planting the seeds of hate when her son, our Lord, was torn from her hands' (Rossi 1989: 149).

Over the years, the Mothers' notion of motherhood had gradually became political rather than biological. They came to consider themselves the mothers of all the disappeared, not just their own offspring. Their spectacles became larger and increasingly dramatic. They organized massive manifestations and marches, some of them involving up to 200,000 people. In 1983, at the end of the last military junta, they plastered Buenos Aires with the names and silhouettes of the disappeared. However, even with the return of a democratic government, their demands for information about the fate of the children and justice for their tormentors had not been addressed. In spite of the Trial of the Generals, only a handful of the military leaders had been sentenced to prison terms. All those who had served as torturers and on the para-military 'task forces' that abducted, tortured and killed thousands of people were still free. In 1986, when it became clear that Raúl Alfonsín's elected government would do nothing meaningful to punish those responsible for the atrocities, the Mothers staged the March for Human Rights as a procession of masks.

The Mothers spoiled the junta's parade by responding to the military spectacle with a spectacle that inverted the focus. While the military attempted to make their victims invisible and anonymous by burying them in unmarked graves, dumping their bodies into the sea or cutting them up and burning them in ovens, the Mothers insisted that the disappeared had names and faces. They were people; people did not simply disappear; their bodies, dead or alive, were somewhere; someone had done something to them. Instead of the military's a-historical forgetting, the Mothers inscribed the time and dates of the disappearances. Instead of dismembering, remembering. The Mothers challenged the generals' claim to history by writing themselves and the 'disappeared' into the narrative, literally as well as figuratively. Opposed to the image projected by the junta of a lone, heroic male leaving family and community behind, the Mothers emphasized community and family ties. Instead of the military's performance of hierarchy, represented by rigid, straight rows, the Mothers' circular movements around the Plaza, characterized by their informal talk and pace, bespoke values based on egalitarianism and communication. While the soldiers' uniforms, paraphernalia and body language emphasized the performative aspects of gender, the Mothers too were highly conscious of the importance of their gender, specifically maternal role, and played it accordingly. The Mothers also had their 'uniforms,' presenting themselves as elderly, physically weak and sexually non-active women. Yet they resisted even the most brutal treatment. When the military tried to force the women from the Plaza, they marked their presence indelibly by painting white kerchiefs around the circle where they usually walked. Instead of the empty streets and public spaces mandated by the military curfew, the Mothers orchestrated the return of the repressed. Buenos Aires was once again filled with people; spectacular bodies, ghostly, looming figures who refused to stay invisible. The public spaces overflowed with demonstrators as the terrorized population gradually followed the Mothers' example and took to the streets.

However, re-defining motherhood was a painful process for the Mothers. Individually, many of the women admitted that they had lost hope of finding their children alive: 'We know we're not going to find our children by going to the square, but it's an obligation we have to all the *desaparecidos*' (Fisher 1989: 153). The tension between the biological death of their children and the living political issue of disappearance and criminal politics placed them in a conflicted situation. Were they now simply the mothers of dead children? If so, should they claim the dead bodies offered up by forensic specialists, accept compensation for their loss, and get on with their lives? Or did they need to hold on to the image of the 'disappeared' in order to bring the military to justice and continue their political movement? Could the Mothers, now a political organization, survive the death of their children? By 1986, the dilemma had split them in two. The group that now calls itself the Madres de la Plaza de Mayo, headed by Hebe Bonafini (as opposed to the 'Linea Fundadora,' 'Founding Group,' of the fourteen original members), continues to demand 'Aparición con vida' ('Back Alive') for all the disappeared. They refuse to give up the struggle until justice has been served. The Linea

Fundadora, though accepting that their children are dead, work to bring the perpetrators to justice. However, the women felt that many of the working-class members of the organization needed the economic compensation offered by the government in order to keep up their struggle. Members of both groups travel, lecture abroad and document their history. Both groups, made up mainly of women in their sixties and seventies, continue to march around the Plaza de Mayo.

Commentators find it hard to agree on the short- and long-term effects of the Mothers' activism. During the Dirty War, the Mothers provided the families of the disappeared with a model of resistance to atrocity as well as a network of communication and support. The Mothers would find out information about a detained or disappeared person and transmit it nationally. The women raised money to allow families around the country to travel to ask about their missing children or to visit a political prisoner. The Mothers' organization contributed money to raise the children of the disappeared who had been left behind with relatives or friends. Long term, however, some commentators stress that the Mothers changed little in Argentina. Fewer women were voted into positions of power after the Dirty War than before. Some say that the Mothers' grass-roots movement lacked any lasting organizational structure. The women undoubtedly called international attention to civil rights violations taking place in Argentina. But that, in itself, did not topple the dictatorship.[2] Moreover, though the Mothers' spectacle was a powerful manifestation of personal courage and moral resistance to oppression, it did little to stop international aid to the Armed Forces. Though Carter cut aid, Reagan increased US support of the Armed Forces' 'war' on subversion.

So how to assess and understand the Mothers' movement given its many contradictions? It attacked the legitimacy of the military but left a restrictive patriarchal system basically unchallenged. The Mothers won significant political power, but they claim not to want that power, or to want it only for their children. The women's shared struggle for missing children bridged class and religious barriers, but the Mothers have not politicized those issues. They recognize that 'women are doubly oppressed, especially in Catholic-Hispanic countries' (Fisher 1989: 155), and have formed alliances with women's coalitions in various Latin American countries. But they are not feminists, if by feminism one refers to the politicization of women's subordinate status. Hebe de Bonafini states:

> I don't think the Mothers are feminists, but we point a way forward for the liberation of women. We support the struggle of women against this *machista* world and sometimes this means that we have to fight against men. But we also have to work together with men to change this society. We aren't feminists because I think feminism, when it's taken too far, is the same as *machismo*.
>
> (Fisher 1989: 158)

The Mothers left the confines of their homes, physically and politically, but they have not altered the politics of the home – for example, the gendered division of labor. After demonstrations most of them still cooked and did housework for their remaining family, even when husbands were at home full time. The Mothers took to the streets in order to protect their children and families; nonetheless, their political activity estranged many of them from the surviving members of their families who were not prepared to accept the women's new roles: 'They say if you stop going to the square, you're one of us again. My family now are the Mothers of the Plaza de Mayo,' says one Mother (Fisher 1989: 156). Having left home, they have established a new *casa* (or *home*) for their new family. There, they continue their unpaid labor, their political activity. There, too, they nurture the young people who come to talk to them: 'We cook for them, we worry about their problems, we look out for them much as we did for our children' (Diago 1988: 187).

How to explain these contradictions? Some of them can be understood, I believe, by distinguishing between the Mothers' performance of mother-hood and essentialist notions of motherhood which, in all fairness, the Mothers themselves often accentuate. Although much has been written about the Mothers' strategy of politicizing motherhood, little has been said about the fact that motherhood, as a role, had already been socialized and politicized in their patriarchal society. What we see, then, are conflicting performances of motherhood, one supporting the military's version of social order, one defying it.[3] Once the Mothers decided to march, their self-representation was as theatrical as the military's. The Mothers' movement did not begin when the individual mothers became acquainted in their search for their chil-dren. It originated when the women consciously decided to protest and agitate *as* mothers. That *as* marks the conceptual distance between the essentialist notion of motherhood attributed to the Mothers and the self-conscious manip-ulation of the maternal role that makes the movement the powerful and intensely dramatic spectacle that it has been. The women, most of whom had no political background or experience, realized that they were part of a national spectacle and decided to actively play the role that had traditionally been assigned to them – the 'good' women who look after their children. Yet, they shifted the site of their enactment from the private sphere, where it could be construed as essentialist, to the public, where it became a bid for political recognition and a direct challenge to the junta. The Mothers' decision to make their presence visible in the Plaza, stage center so to speak, was a brilliant and courageous move. While the Plaza had often been used as a political stage throughout Argentina's history, no one had used it as the Mothers did, much less during a state of siege in which public space was heavily policed. They perceived and literally acted out the difference between motherhood as an individual identity (which for many of them it was) and motherhood as a collective, political performance that would allow women to protest in the face of a criminal dictatorship. The role of mother was attractive, not because it was 'natural,' but because it was viable and practical. It offered the women a certain legitimacy and authority in a society that values mothers almost to the exclusion of all other women. It offered them visibility in a representational system that rendered most women invisible. For once, they manipulated the images which had previously controlled them.

Looking beyond the maternal role, however, and looking at the individual women who walked away from the Plaza, I see a group of women who redefined the meaning of 'mothers,' 'family' and 'home' in a patriarchal society. Mothers, flesh and blood women, are now more free to act and take to the streets. They can be bold, independent, political and outraged even as they take on the role of the submissive, domestic creature. Their new 'home' is a negotiated space; their new 'family' founded on political rather than biological ties. What has been accepted as the Mothers' traditionalism in fact has more to do with the negotiated alliances advocated by feminists. The women may choose to adhere to their old ways, re-create a 'family,' and cook for the younger members of the group, but that is now a choice they exercise. Their political activism, explicitly designed to empower the new 'Man,' in fact made new people out of the Mothers, people with options. As Hebe says:

> For me cooking for twenty is the same as cooking for one, and we like to eat together because this is also a part of our struggle and our militancy. I want to continue being the person I've always been. Sometimes I'm criticized for wearing a housecoat and slippers in public but I'm not going to change. Of course my life is different.
>
> (Fisher 1989: 158)

The performance of motherhood has created a distance between 'I' and the 'person I've always been.' It is as if the women's conscious performance of motherhood, limited though it was, freed them from the socially restrictive role of motherhood that had previously kept them in their place. The performance offered that disruptive space, that moment of transition between the 'I' who was a mother and the 'I' who chooses to perform motherhood.

The performative aspect of their movement, though seldom commented upon, was a politically vital and personally liberating aspect of the Mothers' activism. The demonstrations offered the women a way of coping with their grief and channeling it to life-affirming action. Rather than trivialize or eclipse their loss, the performative nature of their demonstrations gave the women a way of dealing with it. Much as in the case of mourning rites, aesthetic distancing is an enabling response to pain, not its negation. Then too, the ritualistic and 'restored' nature of their demonstrations succeeded in drawing much-needed public attention to their cause. This put them in contact with human rights organizations worldwide and provided them with financial and moral support as well as the much-needed legitimacy to offset the junta's claims that the women were only raving 'madwomen.' Moreover, the 'restored' nature of their public action in itself was a way of restoring the disappeared into the public sphere, of making visible their absence. And, by bringing motherhood out of the domestic closet, the Mothers showed up the predicament facing women in Argentina and the world over. Traditionally, mothers have been idealized as existing somehow beyond or above the political arena. Confined to the home, they have been made responsible for their children. But what happens to the mothers who, by virtue of that same responsibility to their children, must go looking for them outside the home and confront the powers-that-be? Do they cease to be mothers? Or must onlookers renounce notions of mothers as a-political? Their transgression of traditional roles made evident how restrictive and oppressive those roles had been. Thus their performance of mothers as activists challenged traditional maternal roles and called attention to the fact that motherhood was a social, not just biological, construct.

The Mothers' performance challenged the onlooker. Would the national and international spectators applaud their actions, or look away? Join their movement or cross the street to avoid them? One letter to the editor of La Nación asked the authorities to put an end 'to the sad spectacle that we must endure week after week' (June 1, 1981, p. 6). But there were spectators who were able to respond as reliable audiences/witnesses. They helped introduce different perspectives and disrupt the show the military was staging about itself. The fact that the Madres could not do *everything* – i.e., seriously challenge patriarchal authority – does not mean that they did *nothing* to ruin their parade. The Mothers' efficacy and survival relied on capturing the attention of spectators – Argentines who might dare to re-interpret the junta's version of events as well as the foreign spectators who might feel compelled to bring pressure to bear on their governments.

The Mothers had the courage to show the world what was happening in Argentina. They still continue their walk around the Plaza at 3:30 on Thursday afternoons. They vow to do so until the government officially explains what happened to their missing children and brings their murderers to justice. There has been no closure. The drama of disappearance is not over.

Notes

1   President Videla of the junta, in his first address to the nation on March 25, 1976 (La Nación, p. 14). Other military spokespeople warned against 'Marxist penetration' and 'ideological infiltration' (La Nación, August 5, 1976, p. 1).

2   The downfall of the military came with its invasion of the Islas Malvinas, the British-owned Falkland Islands that lie off the coast of Argentina. Plagued by a crashing economy and an increasingly irate population, the

military decided to bolster their popular support by taking back the islands. The Armed Forces miscalculated Britain's resolve to keep the islands, given their substantial oil deposits and Margaret Thatcher's own need of a boost in popular opinion. The humiliating defeat of the Argentine military, which was also held responsible for the death of a thousand very young conscripts who had not been prepared for war, brought down the last of the juntas.

3   A pro-military league of mothers, 'La Liga de Madres de Familia,' organized to ask the junta for a more forceful implementation of 'family values' (Avellanada 1986: 148).

References

Avellanada, Andres (1986) *Censura, autoritarismo y cultura: Argentina 1960–1983*, Vol. 2, Buenos Aires: Biblioteca Política Argentina.

Diago, Alejandro (1988) *Hebe Bonafini: Memoria y esperanza*, Buenos Aires: Ediciones Dialéctica.

Fisher, Jo (1989) *Mother of the Disappeared*, Boston, Mass.: South End Press.

Navarro-Aranguren, Marysa (1989) 'The Personal is Political: Las Madres de la Plaza de Mayo', in *Power and Popular Protest: Latin American Social Movements*, ed. Susan Echstein, Berkeley: University of California Press.

Rossi, Laura (1989) '¿Cómo pensar a las Madres de la Plaza de Mayo?' in *Nuevo texto crítico* 4 (Año II), eds Mary Louise Pratt and Marta Morello Frosch, Stanford, Calif.: Stanford University Press, 145–53.

Simpson, John and Jana Bennett (1985) *The Disappeared: Voices from a Secret War*, London: Robson Books.

Troncosco, Oscar (1989) *El proceso de reorganización nacional: Cronología y documentación*, Buenos Aires: Centro Editor de America Latina, Vol. 1.

Chapter 10

Marguerite Waller

from *BORDER* BODA OR DIVORCE *FRONTERIZO?*

LAS COMADRES, A MULTICULTURAL WOMEN'S group in a US/Mexican border region, collaborate on visual and performance art. In this excerpt from a longer essay, Waller describes one of Las Comadres' activist projects that pivoted on a dual act of witnessing.

The second event was a right wing, populist campaign, called 'Light Up the Border,' begun in the fall of 1989 and continuing through the summer of 1990. To protest the crossing by 'illegal aliens' (mostly Native American *indios*) of a border that blocks a centuries-old migration route, a border that was nonexistent until 150 years ago and entirely open through the 1970s, Muriel Watson, a town councilwoman from the suburban/agricultural community of Encinitas, and Roger Hedgcock, a local radio talk show host and former mayor, urged the 'Americans' living in San Diego to converge at a prearranged point on the border on the third Thursday of every month. There they would line up their cars at dusk and send a wash of light into the no-man's land marking the boundary between the two countries. The demonstrations were intended to discourage the 2,000-plus undocumented workers who negotiate the border every day and to signal the US federal government that the border needed more lights, more INS officers (or better, an armed military presence, according to some of the demonstrators), more detention centers, and a better fence. From numerous conversations in which members of Las Comadres engaged demonstrators, and from Hedgcock's own broadcast conversations with listeners who called in, it became evident that neither the demonstrators nor their organizations knew the Indio, Spanish, and Mexican history of the region, let alone the current Mexican political and economic situation, and least of all the complex, self-serving, and immensely profitable games US business, manufacturing, agriculture, and government have been playing with Mexican labor for generations. Instead, Watson and Hedgcock promulgated, uncynically it seemed, a racist (and implicitly sexist) fantasy of a beleaguered United States threatened with inundation by a 'flood' of polluting 'aliens' pouring through its leaky border.

A coalition of community activists, teachers, artists, and students from both sides of the border devised a performance art piece in response to this scapegoating of Mexican workers for the economic and emotional deficits of the local Anglo community. Members of the Border Arts Workshop/Taller de Arte Fronterizo, the Union del Barrio, members of our reading group, and several hundred other activists, artists, and students positioned themselves opposite the headlights of over a thousand cars, and by holding up mirrors and mylar- or aluminum-covered cardboard reflectors, returned the wash of light back on the vehicles' owners. Doubling the gaze, undoing the Watson-Hedgcock faction's implied monopoly of the power to 'illuminate' the border, the counter-demonstrators made looking, at least symbolically, reciprocal and interactive.

For the April demonstration, Las Comadres (naming ourselves for the occasion) hired a plane to fly before the evening's light show, towing a banner that read, '1000 points of Fear – Another Berlin Wall?' This provocative reference to current events in Eastern Europe brought a perceptible gasp from demonstrators, some of whom drove away after they read it, apparently moved by the analogy to reconsider what they were doing. This left a larger proportion of White Supremacist groups, like the 'WarBoys' and 'The Holy Church of the White Fighting Machine of the Cross,' to be faced by the counterdemonstrators, and a hostile, potentially dangerous confrontation ensued. Though cause and effect are impossible to determine in such situations, it seems likely in retrospect that the counterdemonstrators' upping of the ante on this occasion thus contributed to the subsequent decline of the 'Light Up the Border' movement over the summer. Neither its leaders (two politicians, after all) nor their more moderate followers wanted to be associated with physical violence, a feeling shared by the counterdemonstrators who on subsequent occasions merely stood in silent witness or quietly recorded the event on film and videotape.

The tense April 'Light Up the Border' demonstration also catalyzed significant internal changes in our group. Some apprehension of the spiritual and political power that could be tapped by working together despite and through the 'interference' of the historical and political divisions that unite and separate us was born that night. Comadre Aida Mancillas subsequently wrote about the new depth of communication that occurred when she confronted some of her own childhood demons in the company of another Comadre, Cindy Zimmerman. As she and Cindy drove to the designated border location together, they discovered that each was contending with her own point of fear, that they shared a dread of reactivating trouble from the past in the scene that lay ahead of them:

> In an hour we would meet our individual nightmares across a police barricade. Mine was about the Ku Klux Klan and how they would ride into the Mexican neighborhoods in Santa Ana, California where my mother's family lived during the 1920s. My anger was part of a collective anger, huge because at the base of it was the shame of knowing the obscenity had gone unchallenged. I could smell the hate of the nightrider's descendants as we got closer to the gathering of cars, and I was grateful for the television crews whose presence somehow protected me from harm. Her nightmare was confronting the racism of her own kind; of seeing her people, the neighbors so like those she had grown up with in Oklahoma, lining their cars up along the road, headlights pointed at Mexico to shine light on the problem of foreigners. . . . She was ashamed of their ignorance and bigotry; ashamed of them and for them. And as we gazed into our respective mirrors, we both hated and loved what we saw there because it was part of us, part of our inheritance, our burden and responsibility.

Surprisingly, the evening created a space where something wonderful occurred. Cindy found the courage to cross the road and converse calmly with the demonstrators about what they were doing. Aida found the tenor of her family story subtly changing:

> I learned her people had come West from Oklahoma during the years of the Dust Bowl and the Great Depression. I had heard of these people coming to work in the fields and factories of California from my mother and aunts. In many places they replaced the Mexican field hands in a struggle between the disinherited. But in my idealized memory I like to think her people worked alongside mine in the groves of walnuts and apricots of Southern California. Perhaps they worked a swingshift at the local defense plant. Perhaps they showed up at the same dancehall. Perhaps the wall between them was only a window.

[. . .]

Works cited

Mancillas, Aida. '1,000 Points of Fear – The New Berlin Wall: Impressions of a Weekend on the Border San Diego, California/Tijuana, B.C., April 1990.' Unpublished manuscript.

Chapter 11

Jan Cohen-Cruz

AT CROSS-PURPOSES
The Church Ladies for Choice

IN ANOTHER ACT OF WITNESSING witnessers, the Church Ladies for Choice undermine US anti-abortion groups like Operation Rescue that blockade women's health clinics under the banner of 'rescuing unborn babies.' This essay was written in 1993, when anti-abortion activity was especially aggressive.

It is 7:30 on a Saturday morning, and the Church Ladies for Choice are getting dressed for a morning of street performances outside of abortion clinics. Though usually the epitome of modesty – 'sensible shoes, floral print polyester frocks, and earrings that pinch – that's what keeps us so angry!' – today they are in a daring mood. Phyllis Stein, 'the Jewish Church Lady,' shows off some pearls that were once his mother's. 'Are these too much?' he asks. 'No,' answers Sister Mary, aka Yasha Buncik. Stein is disappointed: 'I'd hoped they were too much. I'll wear them anyway.'

The Church Ladies are a pro-Choice counterpart to right-to-lifers who 'blockade women's health facilities that offer abortions, forcing the clients to run a gauntlet of harrassment' (Buncik 1993). The first Ladies were established in Pittsburgh; a second group was founded in Washington, D.C. Impressed by their ability to entertain the crowd and diffuse tension, two members of WHAM! (Women's Health and Mobilization) joined with two male ACT UPpers to inaugurate a New York contingent.

Membership in the New York Church Ladies is loose; currently they number about eighteen, mostly gay men and a few straight women, all of whom dress as either ultra-feminine, church-going ladies or members of the cloth. Their character names are word plays about sex, like Bessie Mae Mucho; religion, as Cardinal Sin; and pro-choice politics, as Harmonie Moore who pleads, 'How many More women must die of botched illegal abortions due to the fascist injustices of the American right and their psycho-Christian lapdogs?' They describe themselves as 'gals' who lift spirits and provide comic relief at clinic defense and abortion-related demonstrations. The USO[1] of clinic defenders; the cheerleaders for choice' (Church Ladies 1993: 1).

The singing of '*Hers* – the word *Hymns* is just so sexist!' (Church Ladies 1993: 7) – is at the heart of Church Ladies' performances. Sharon Flewitts explains the genesis of this choice:

> It was in New York, at the 1992 Democratic Convention. Randall Terry [founder of Operation Rescue] was surrounded by the media. We arrived, in our Church Lady garb, and redirected the media our way, a good thing in itself. But we didn't know what to do once we had their attention. That's why we developed the song.
>
> (Flewitts 1993)

The songs are familiar melodies with rewritten pro-choice lyrics. For example, *This Womb is My Womb*, sung to the tune of *This Land is Your Land*, attests, 'This womb is my womb, it is not your womb, and there is no womb, for Wandell Tewwy.' As the Ladies dress and make up this particular May morning, some of them run through a new song that Bessie Mae Mucho has written to the tune of Mary Poppins' *Super-cali-fragilistic-expealidocious*: 'Christian-fasco-Nazi-nutso-psycho-right-wing-buuull-shit.'

The songs are one of the Church Ladies' strategies for putting the normal into question. The rewritten Poppins song, for example, undermines the heightened feminine demeanor of the Church Ladies and the properness of the Poppins association through its unladylike combination of 'Christian fasco,' colloquial 'nutso,' and unchurchlike 'bull shit.' *God is a Lesbian*, sung to *God Save the Queen*, brings into question the very idea of being created in His image. At the same time, the song plays *on* the double meaning of queen and plays *with* the solemn, religious-like tone affected for royalty.

The use of drag underscores the social construction of morality as embodied by church-going, conservatively dressed, sensibly shoed, always smiling females. This might appear to be a self-defeating choice, given the group's feminist politics and drag's erstwhile hostile overtones. According to Carole-Anne Tyler, 'Not so long ago camp languished, theorized as the shameful sign of an unreconstructed, self-hating, and even woman-hating, homosexual by gay, feminist, and lesbian feminist critics alike' (1991: 33). But in contrast to the glamour of most drag, the Ladies' careful exposure of a stubble of beard and fully hairy legs makes this a kind of Brechtian drag, whose seams are intended to show. Their obvious masquerade puts the 'for realness' of their adversaries into question by suggesting that any appearances can be put on or taken off. Still, aware that drag can be read as misogyny, the Ladies always include at least one biological woman dressed as a 'Lady' or a nun (Buncik 1993). Women and men in drag together suggest that everyone is disguised to conform to societal norms.

The Ladies also expose the ideological construction of words in the abortion controversy. Conscious of the power of language to shape public perception and aware, along with other pro-choice advocates, that the religious right's term 'pro-life' is emotionally stronger than 'pro-choice' (Faludi 1991; Phelan 1993), the Ladies have renamed their adversaries 'antis,' 'lifers,' and 'the religiously-challenged.' The religious right also expresses its views through renaming, referring to the clients at clinics as 'whores and dykes' (Phelan 1993: 131), an amazing conflation of women who choose abortion as either just into sex for the money or not attracted to men. Buncik refers to their local adversaries as 'HOGPI(E)s,' the acronym for the New York City clinic attack group, Helpers of God's Precious Infants. Members of HOGPI hold prayer meetings in front of clinics, hand out anti-abortion literature, and try to convince clients not to 'murder their babies.'[2] Consequently, most clinics have clearly designated volunteer escorts waiting to whisk the women in.

The Church Ladies describe themselves as 'publicity whores.' Each member is well-informed and articulate about the abortion issue, all part of their effort to 'speak through, not to' the media (cited by Buncik 1993). The goal is to get the pro-choice message out at the sites where the so-called pro-life message is most harmful. The strategy is to make themselves a news-attracting event. This thinking reflects their roots in ACT UP, whose modus operandi was 'to go to the furthest extreme in order to get the center to take notice' (Signorile 1993: 72).

At ACT UP, the founding mothers also experienced the power of theatrical street actions through an affinity group called Action Tours.[3] 'Do you remember the Santa Claus who lost his job at Macy's in 1991 when they found out he was HIV positive, and then it got a lot of publicity and he got his job back?' Buncik asks. 'That's because twenty-eight of us, dressed like Santas, converged on Macy's, chained ourselves to the cosmetics department and demanded that he be reinstated.'

Today the Church Ladies plan to perform at four clinics, and I am to be their driver. I begin the day dubious, while interested. The Church Ladies know that they will not convince the 'antis' to change their opinions. Supporting the escorts is considerate, but why entertain a small group of people who are already pro-choice? The Church Ladies will not draw crowds for unpublicized actions on this Memorial Day weekend. I wonder about the clients. Having an abortion is no pleasure; nobody talks about 'pro-abortion,' only 'pro-choice.' It is an intensely private, often painful decision, the result

Figure 11.1 Church Ladies for Choice (photo by Lisa Kahane).

of real soul-searching as regards readiness to take on the enormous task of parenting. How do they feel about these ostentatious people drawing more attention to the clinic? And why do gay men, who make up the Ladies' majority and are the adult population least directly affected by abortion rulings, get up early on Saturday mornings to do free street shows?

We arrive at the first clinic and, as carefully staged as conventional theatrics, the Ladies begin about a half block away so they can make an entrance. They unfurl a long banner, waist high, that reads in bold large letters, CHURCH LADIES FOR CHOICE. One Church Lady plays the bag-pipes as they move ceremoniously toward the clinic, holding the banner at their waists like a portable lower frame. The police direct them to one side of the clinic door, well apart from the antis. Once in place, the Ladies sing through their repertoire, with a little playful banter between songs, as the escorts cheer and the antis grimace. The Ladies are high-spirited and tuneful, sashaying along to the music and playing right to the audience, flirtatious toward the escorts and passers-by and with an undercurrent of one-upmanship toward the antis.

The songs are sung collectively, with occasional solos; some have chore-ography. *High Court Boogie*, a song about the Supreme Court sung to the tune of *The Bugle Boy of Company C*, features three of the Ladies while the rest do back-up:

> Well George and Ronny put them on the bench to say
> Women in the kitchen they would have to stay
> When Casey came to town
> We-e-ell that's when they said
> Oh boy the shit will go down!
> They're on the High Court now
> They're after you and me
> They are Clarence, Tony, Billy, Dave and Sandra D.

Generally the escorts flock around the Ladies, delighted for the energetic support. As they sing, the Ladies gather an additional audience of passers-by, some delighted, some confused. They also give out pro-choice literature.

The right often frames its clinic appearances as religious revivals; according to Peggy Phelan, they 'generate a feeling of terror, and thereby produce the feeling that one needs to be saved' (1993: 131). They do this through intense prayer and concentration, and through passionate efforts to convince women entering the clinics not to 'murder their unborn children.' Sometimes the antis display two different posters of fetuses in what Faye Ginsburg has described as a pattern of dual representations: the one, an 'inno-cent' fetus, photographed 'in warm, amber tones, suffused with soft light . . . [and the other,] gruesome, harshly lit, clinical shots of mutilated and bloody fetal remains' (1989: 105). The Church Ladies neutralize this with a totally contrasting display of irreverence and good humor, thus undermining the atmosphere that the religious right tries to create.

At one of the clinics we visit, an anti falls to her knees in prayer near the clinic door. She is holding a three-inch tall-plastic model of a fetus that resembles a baby Jesus icon, sending clients a message that they are killing God. I ask her how she got involved with the Helpers. She tells me she had two wonderful children, and then she had a miscarriage. Responding to her resulting depression, Bishop Daly at her local Queens parish put her in touch with this group to participate in their prayer meetings outside clinics and 'do the work of God.'

She rushes up to a client entering the clinic, but the escorts get the woman in before she can say more than a few words. A police officer directs her to the side with the prayer group. A man waiting for his girl friend who is inside getting an abortion says the right-to-lifers make them furious; an abortion is traumatic enough but the lifers only make them feel worse, not change their mind. They were both glad that people expressing the other side were at the clinic so that it did not appear 'all bad' to get an abortion.

In front of another clinic, a male 'anti' approaches me with a right-to-life magazine and shows me an article about a tortuous new method of abortion in which 'they suck out a baby's brain.' He speaks softly and with great concern. Were I not so ardently pro-choice, I can imagine wanting to dissociate myself from anyone who would do such a thing to a baby. But we are talking about fetuses, not babies. Again I am reminded, words are a weapon of this war. He refers to the Church Ladies as a 'bunch of lesbians trying to mock what we're doing here.' He not only misses the fact that most of the performers are men, complete with hairy arms, deep voices, tall statures, and in some cases beards, but that they are a group of men and women. He also assumes that they are lesbians, as if that were the only reason one would be pro-choice.

The Church Ladies mimic the religious right as through a funhouse mirror, reflecting back their own version of the antis' gestures, songs and clothing. When the lifers hold crosses up toward the Ladies, the Ladies hold up costume jewelry and make the sign of the cross back at them. When the HOGs begin singing *Amazing Grace*, the Ladies join in, with their rewritten words:

> Amazing grace, how sweet the sound
> That saved a wretch like me
> I once was lost, now I'm Pro-choice
> was blind, but now I see

Carole-Anne Tyler links mimicry and camp, stating that in both realms 'one "does" ideology in order to undo it, producing knowledge about it' (1991: 53). The Ladies pushed this tactic all the way in their creation of an alter-ego street performance group, Transvestites for Life:

If we can have Christian rock n'roll and Christian rap, then why not
Christian drag queens for life? If it really is a sin for a man to wear a
dress then our own Pope would have to parade around nude!

(Church Ladies 1993: 10)

Having created a camp version of the lifers, the Church Ladies expose their
'logic' (sic):

They've rewritten the words to the song, 'If You're Happy and You
Know It, Clap Your Hands' into, 'If you think you own your womb,
show me the deed,' or, 'If you want to get a life, be a wife.' Worse
yet are their own versions of the anti's ubiquitous ABORTION KILLS
CHILDREN signs [such as] 'Destroy third world nations, not fetuses.'

(10)

Oddly enough, when the Church Ladies march up to the antis at this
site, the police do not try to separate them. The two groups, side by side,
are quickly surrounded by some thirty people. Audience sympathy is clearly
with the Ladies, causing the antis to pack up and leave. They would have
only looked foolish if they stayed; a straight man automatically becomes part
of the joke when partnered with a comic.

The Church Ladies entertain the crowd for about forty minutes. Most spectators are delighted; someone gives the group a bouquet of flowers, someone else
calls out happily, 'Only in New York.' The Church Ladies sell a number of their
18-minute tapes (free with a $15 contribution to WHAM!). On this up note, the
group marches out of the ad-hoc performing space, to vigorous applause.

Returning to my earlier question: why do gay men, who make up the
Ladies' majority and are the least likely to be directly affected by abortion
rulings, get up early Saturday mornings to do clinic defense shows? I believe
that they are engaged in a 'cross-dressing' of queer concerns with those of
feminists. The term 'queer,' according to Michael Warner, 'rejects a minori-
tizing logic of tolerance or simple political interest-representation in favor
of a more thorough resistance to regimes of the normal' (1993: xxvi). The
Church Ladies go beyond identity politics by resisting anti-choice and anti-
gay actions simultaneously, recognizing that 'Psycho-Christians usually also
oppose safer-sex education and condom distribution in schools, lesbian and
gay male rights, and wearing mixed fibers' (1). They thus support the larger
idea of sexual freedom, manifested as a woman's right to choose an abortion
or anyone's right to choose his/her sexual partners.

A number of the songs articulate this connection. *Stand By Your Clinic*
attests that 'when they're done with the women, they're coming after us
queers.' *We're Off to Fight the Bigots* has one verse for women's healthcare
and another in support of the Rainbow Curriculum. The second verse of
Psycho-Christians, to the tune of *Little Boxes*, warns:

Psycho-Catholics, taunting homos
That's the way they buy indulgences
Psycho-Catholics, taunting homos
And they all look just the same
There's a closet-case
and a closet-case
and a closet-case
and a closet-case
Psycho-Catholics, taunting homos
And they all hide just the same.

(Church Ladies 1993: 367).

The Church Ladies thus counter Operation Rescue's conflation of 'the "unnaturalness" of women who would abort [as] much the same as those who engage in nonreproductive sexuality' (Phelan 1993: 136), with a queer consciousness resisting any imposed sexual norms.

Equally significant, the Church Ladies carry the torch of one of the earliest feminist insights – the personal is the political. Performing has given them the opportunity to publicly play out deeply felt personas, be it ladies for the men or the ethically upright nuns for the two core biological women in the company. The male Ladies get a palpable pleasure from making-up, exchanging necklaces and earrings, and zipping each other's dresses. The biological women dressing in the moral authority of the nuns enjoy the unique pleasures of that persona. For even as identity politics focuses on under- and mis-represented *groups*, the Church Ladies concentrate on under- and mis-represented *selves*. Bessie Mae came to the performance in jeans and pearls. He changed into his dress, keeping on the same pearls. Yasha Buncik speaks with a compelling sense of moral outrage. She works as a copy editor, correcting other people's mistakes for a living; but mistakes of form, not substance. As Sister Mary, she addresses people's ethical errors, and shows them the way. This crossover between personal pleasure and political passion suggests that individual aspects of ourselves need expression just as do collective racial, cultural and sexual identities. Perhaps playing out internal personas also functions as an anti-burnout strategy, nourishing the participants and furthering their growth. Personal expression is, nevertheless, subsumed by their overarching political agenda, as evidenced in their desire to be duplicated via Church Ladies contingents elsewhere, like a radical chain of McDonalds.

The group's critique of the church may be seen as itself at cross-purposes to its pro-choice, pro-gay rights message. Some religious people, while pro-choice, are offended by songs like 'God is a Lesbian' and snipes at religious leaders. On the other hand, the connection between anti-choice, anti-gay attitudes and certain church politics is precisely what attracts other religious people to the group. The question arises as to how focused a group need

97

keep its agenda and whether it seeks the broadest possible base of support for a short-term goal or more far-reaching social change.

Surely a critique of the church motivates these ladies to get up early on Saturday mornings to do free street shows. Further, they fulfill their desire to take on the religious right by appearing with them on the only stage where such a duet would be possible, namely at the site of the controversy. And whereas in the late 1970s and 1980s, *differences* among people had to be stressed – for example, the shift in the women's movement from a hegemony of the white heterosexual middle class to acknowledgment of difference as regards race, class, ethnicity and sexual orientation – in the 1990s, connections need to be forged among internally strengthened but separate groups with compatible goals. This the Church Ladies achieve by interpreting choice vis-à-vis the whole realm of sexuality. They thus please themselves, fight the good fight and build coalitions, breaking the political hold that identity politics has had on leftist organizing over the past twenty years.

My day with the Church Ladies comes to a close. They thank me for being their driver, tell me to send my travel receipts to the Vatican and disappear into the city.

Notes

1   The USO, United Service Organizations, are performers who travel to combat zones in order to entertain American troops.

2   Most of the materials that the religious right hands out at New York City clinics is undated and unascribed to any one individual. For example, one leaflet urging women not to 'kill a preborn child' read at the bottom, 'Distributed and paid for by you [sic] neighbor.' The Helpers of God's Precious Infants is directed by Msgr. Philip J. Reilly, in residence at The Monastery of the Precious Blood, 5300 Fort Hamilton Parkway, Brooklyn, New York, 11219.

3   ACT UP is composed of a number of ongoing committees – such as fundraising, media, needle exchange, People With AIDS (PWA) Housing – created by vote from the membership (Elbaz 1993: 79). Members can also take the initiative and form constantly changing Affinity Groups, an important component of the self-empowering dynamic and a direct action conduit of the organization (Elbaz 1993: 80).

References

Buncik, Yasha (1993) Interview with the author, June 10.
Church Ladies for Choice (1993) *Starter Kit*, New York.

—— (1993a) *In Your Face with Amazing Grace*, Video, New York: Land of Fire Productions.

Elbaz, Gilbert (1993) *The Sociology of AIDS Activism: The Case of ACT UP, 1987–1992*, unpublished dissertation, New York: ACT UP archive.

Faludi, Susan (1991) *BACKLASH*, New York: Crown Publishers.

Flewitts, Sharon (1993) Interview with the author, May 29.

Ginsburg, Faye (1989) *Contested Lives: The Abortion Debate in an American Community*, Berkeley: University of California Press.

Moore, Harmonie (1993) Interview with the author, May 29.

Phelan, Peggy (1993) *Unmarked*, London and New York: Routledge.

Signorile, Michelangelo (1993) *Queer in America*, New York: Random House.

Tyler, Carole-Anne (1991) 'Boys Will Be Girls: The Politics of Gay Drag,' in *Inside/Out*, ed. Diana Fuss, London: Routledge.

Warner, Michael (1993) *Fear of a Queer Planet*, Minneapolis: University of Minnesota Press.

Chapter 12

Dan Sullivan

THEATER IN EAST HARLEM
The Outdoor Audience Gets Into the Act

SULLIVAN, WRITING AS A THEATRE critic for the *New York Times*, describes what might be considered a play of witness, created by inner-city youth, shedding light on urban conditions that have loomed out of control. A good example of the close relationship that often exists between street and community-based performance, the play is described by Sullivan as 'speak[ing] not just to an audience but for it, and with it.' Soon after this production, playwright Maryat Lee returned to her rural southern home and helped develop eco-theatre there.

The young people of East Harlem's Soul and Latin Theater (SALT) say that after their first summer performing in the streets, they are going to find indoor audiences 'sort of pale.' After spending an evening with them, you know what they mean.

SALT's show the other night on 117th Street off First Avenue was illuminating in a couple of ways. First: the plays themselves, homemade ones full of the rage and gaiety and despair of the ghetto. Second: the way the audience took them.

The audience would have reduced even the cast of *Dionysus in '69* to tears. They milled around the stage, jumped up on it, yelled at the actors, never stopped moving or talking. Some of the people on the fire escapes even dropped water-filled balloons that crashed through the plastic roof of the stage.

But none of it damped SALT, not even the balloons (which the cast immediately worked into the show – 'Hey, rain!'). Since the young actors know the neighborhood so well (they are students at Benjamin Franklin High a couple of blocks away), they could tell that the audience, except the balloon throwers, was not rejecting the show but reveling in it.

Once you opened your ears and shed your downtown prejudices about how a proper audience should behave, you knew they were right. The three plays on the program – *After the Fashion Show*, *Day by Day*, and *The Classroom* – were in essence dramatized arguments, and the crowd was reacting as spontaneously as if they were real.

They knew, of course, that it was just a show. But they pitched in joyously anyway, taking sides, shouting encouragement to the good guys, pitilessly booing the bad. 'I had a teacher like that once!' yelled a young man during a tense scene in *The Classroom*. 'Lay it on her, baby!'

You felt yourself very much in the presence of the fabled ritual power of drama, its ability to speak not just to an audience but for it, and with it. It is a power our finest downtown playwrights and directors try for and miss. Here, it was in the hands of an untrained group of slum teenagers, black and Puerto Rican.

They got together last spring at Benjamin Franklin with the idea of doing a play about dope addiction for some of the other students. The high school has one of the highest addict counts in the state. A VISTA volunteer, Sandy Hoffman, suggested that they contact Maryat Lee, who teaches a course in street theater at the New School and who had written such a play, *Dope*, in the 1950s.

Miss Lee, who is white, said she didn't want to revive *Dope*, but would help them write and stage some other plays about social problems. Thus, *After the Fashion Show* (homosexuality); *Day by Day* (drugs); *The Classroom* (bad schools).

The scripts, worked out in rehearsal from scenarios by Miss Lee, are as true to the vocabulary and rhythms of street talk as a tape recorder. They are also true to life; the problems do not go away at the end of the play.

As good as the words are on paper, they attain full life only when whanging around SALT's tiny stage-on-wheels. 'Can't you follow rules?' yells the white principal in *The Classroom*. 'It's not the rules; it's that you look down on us, right?' yells the student, and the audience all but roars olé! They are so glad to have somebody say it straight out like that.

When the people don't pay attention, the SALT kids know how to get them back (ignore it, or, in extremis, grab the mike and tell them – but never beg them – to listen. When somebody tries to heckle, the kids know how to put him down ('Are you a student?' said the boy playing the principal to a heckler. 'You look like a dropout!')

It is all very noisy and tiring, and the young actors will probably be glad to get back to school next month, after their first fling at the theater, which was subsidized by funds from the Government and the Vincent Astor Foundation. But they have achieved their objective: 'to get across what's happening in the schools and the neighborhood by acting out how people treat one another.'

Some of their names – Norma Acevedo, Maria Gonzalez, Janet Bond, Gwen Braddock, José Mojica, Lucy Figueroa, Esteban Seaton, José Colon. Mr. Colon had the last defiant word for the water throwers the other night: 'We'll be back on this block next year with a better show! And a stronger roof!'

Chapter 13

Sudipto Chatterjee

STAGING STREET, STREETING STAGE
Suman Chatterjee and the new Bengali Song

THE AUTHOR TRACES THE MUTUALLY nourishing relationship between stage and street in Suman Chatterjee's music. He highlights Chatterjee's street singing to support, not speak for, workers.

This essay has been extracted from a longer article on the sociology of the music of Suman Chatterjee.

> I will make you think, I will
> Whatever it is that you may say
> I'll get you out on the streets, I will
> However much at home you stay.[1]

Suman Chatterjee

In 1989, when Suman Chatterjee (Bengali Caṭṭopādhyāy[2]) returned to Calcutta from almost a decade and a half of life in exile to resume his career as a Bengali music-maker, he did not think he was destined for super-stardom. He had ended his second contract as a broadcast journalist with the German International Radio and returned to Calcutta to make a final, somewhat desperate attempt to present the Bengali songs he had been composing in exile before the Calcutta listeners. Having realized the personal nature of his songs and equipped now with the newly mastered classical guitar, he had decided on going solo. *Tomāke Cāi* (*Want You*), his first solo album, released in 1992, was an instant hit. *Business Standard*, an English daily from Calcutta, cried in an elated headline as early as 1991, 'The City Finds Its Chansonnier.' Loud speakers in neighborhood social gatherings played his songs in loops. T-shirts, carrying lines from his songs, were up for sale. Song excerpts were cited like proverbs. Suman's second and third albums did not belie the expectations of the first and he continued to top popularity charts.

Suman had wrought distinctive changes on the physiognomy of modern Bengali music. The freshness of his lyrics, their poetic beauty, economy of expression and, in cases, biting satire, coupled with the syncretic quality of his music, assembling traits from music all over the world, have made for a new kind of song. Much in the mold of the Latin American *nueva canción*, it offers a platform for lay people to express their innermost thoughts and feelings. Suman's songs encapsulate and are nurtured by the cultural nuances of life in Calcutta, its pedestrian tragedies and catastrophic trivialities. In an urban musical tradition that has emphasized melody over lyrics, where the normative expectation of traditional aesthetics keeps the so-called 'prettiness' of song lyrics immunized from the dissonances of daily life, Suman's arrival was a major rupture in the status quo.

But Suman was doing more than making and inspiring new music. He interlaced his songs on stage with provocative polemical utterances, including sharp criticisms of both the powerful Left Front government of West Bengal, led by the Communist Party of India (Marxist), a.k.a. CPI(M), which he had supported not too long before, and the right-wing religious fundamentalist parties. His aggressive stage sermons augmented the protest inherent in his songs with direct calls for action and condemnation of social wrongs. Suman has written and sung numerous songs on the ills in Bengali society, speaking out against government policies and wrong-doings quite openly in concerts and interviews. But perhaps the biggest blow to Suman's steadily souring relationship with the party and government was his active participation in the directly anti-government Kanoria Jute Mill agitation in 1993–94.

In December 1993, Kanoria Jute Mill, on the banks of the river Hooghly, a little north of Calcutta, had been closed by its owners. The official explanation was the mill could not afford to run its own expenses and make a profit large enough to pay the employees. A majority of the employees thought otherwise, although many of the party-based unions agreed with the owners. A non-partisan union was established, which most of the workers joined. The new union disobeyed the court's stay order and forced the mill gate open to resume work. The mill was closed down again. Negotiations continued, but there was no resolution in sight. No one got paid, yet the workers continued to resist. They built community kitchens to feed their families with support from local farmers and the middle class. The support grew with newspaper coverage and direct encouragement from leading intellectuals extending their hands from Calcutta. Kanoria became a subject of great discussion among the urban intelligentsia.

The situation took a critical turn when a group of mill workers went on a hunger strike. Suman Chatterjee came forward to urge people to continue to support and participate in the Kanoria agitation. He sang for days near the mill premises to motivate the workers, and at street fairs and public gatherings to raise money. The Bengali daily *Pratibedan* (*Dispatch*) reported on December 19, 1993:

> Music, too, is a weapon for struggle. [. . .] The way Suman usually extends his anger towards decaying values and a worm-ridden establishment was the modus operandi today when he expressed resentment at the corrupt political parties. [. . .] Cautioning [workers] against the so-called progressive parties, he said, 'Stay away from them. And keep yourselves united. Or else, they'll create differences among you on lines of caste and religion and lead the agitation astray.' [. . .] Thanking the local farmers who have helped the workers with food, Suman said, 'You can find me in any of your struggles. When you need it, my voice will always deny the lures of slavery.'
>
> (Kanoria Jute Workers' Revolutionary Union 1994: 51)

On December 26, the *Saṅgbād Pratidin* (*News Daily*) reported: 'Suman Chatterjee said that "the way the Kanoria Workers are conducting their agitation is nothing short of a revolution. So, I will write a song about it. That's all I am thinking about these days amidst all my other chores" ' (Kanoria Jute Workers' Revolutionary Union: 52). In a few days Suman had, indeed, come up with a new ballad:

In the mills	the workers work	and perspire
Profits made	from their work	owners acquire.
Boats sail on	sweat (not water)	dash'n'lash.
[. . .]		
Tell us River	tell their stories	back'n'flash –
Splish'n'splash	splish'n'splash	splish'n'splash.

(Chatterjee, 1994: 67)

On January 3, Suman raised funds for the Kanoria workers at a concert in Calcutta. The *Saṅgbād Pratidin* reported it in the following words:

> For the first time Suman Chatterjee has, transgressing preventative governmental sanctions, raised funds for the Kanoria Jute Mill. All proceeds, after production costs, will go to the Kanoria funds. On Wednesday Suman announced from the Biśwarūpā stage, 'If there are any people from the party or the government among the audience, do not try to stop the concert. I won't stop singing.' [. . .] When representatives of the Kanoria workers showed up in the auditorium, he said to them, 'You are re-writing history. . . .'
>
> (Kanoria Jute Workers' Revolutionary Union 1994: 55–56)

On another occasion, Suman performed at one of the busiest intersections in downtown Calcutta. The sound system was no more than a microphone better suited to neighborhood political rallies. It was during the evening rush hour and armed police sergeants intervened, trying to prevent the workers from collecting money from the audience that gathered spontaneously. Suman interjected, 'What do you have against the workers? You, too, can starve to death tomorrow. Why are you doing this? Why don't you help instead? You'll see the workers will help you.' And the workers did help. In just a few moments the situation was reversed. The sergeants began encouraging spectators to donate money while workers got busy managing rush hour traffic! 'And there I sang. It was a good three to four hours' concert, with at least a thousand people around, who were constantly singing along.'[3]

The Kanoria situation propelled political activism on a different footing: a non-partisan group of workers claiming what rightfully should have been the job of the left-wing party-backed unions, who the workers thought had sold out. The workers needed a better alternative, leading to the formation of a new union which, despite its non-partisan orientation, was ultra-left, its position defined not merely by its ideological orientation but because the existing leftist parties had moved closer to the center. It reflected the quizzical, if not hypocritical, turn leftist politics had taken in West Bengal since Perestroika and the fall of the Soviet Bloc. In the specific labor situation of Kanoria at least, the leftist parties had decidedly chosen to stand by the seat of capitalist power rather than champion the rights of the workers. While the workers expressed their disgruntlement at this reversal of ideological position, the party administration applauded their own restraint in not letting this turn violent as, according to them, may have happened in a number of other states. Kanoria offered an alternative to traditional party-based workers' union politics where workers' rights was the issue for a change, not party lines. It mirrored the larger political theatre of West Bengal where the Left Front was in power largely by default, because none of its oppositions were viable alternatives.

The situation had drawn Suman Chatterjee's studio and stage-bound music – playable comfortably on Walkmen and stereo systems – to the streets, working as an active agent to create progressive public opinion. Studio music and stage performance finally interfaced with the street. The stage and the studio had, in a manner of speaking, been 'streeted.' Suman confessed in an interview with a representative of the Kanoria Revolutionary Workers' Union:

> I am not really a worker. I sell songs to live. But, when I see a group of workers uniting to make their demands, I want to be a part of it. . . . People coming together, without shouting any religious fundamentalist war-cries, without raising political flags of any particular color, to make legitimate demands. I don't have a stake in their demands since I don't live their lives, I don't live in their homes. But I'm putting

myself in that space because theirs are human demands. I cannot deny
the demands of the times. That's all.

(Rāy 1994: 21)

It wasn't just Suman who inspired the Kanoria workers; their grit and determination inspired him. Suman said in the same interview with the Kanoria
representative:

> I participated in the revolution in Nicaragua. . . . That's where I learnt
> about the structure of a revolutionary organization. . . . I even had to
> learn combat. . . . I know how it feels to walk through a mined area,
> how a man could shit in his pants. . . . I have seen mechanized warfare.
> . . . And I am somewhat bull-headed, which is why I can even think
> of making a living out of singing/making Bengali songs at 40 some-
> thing. But here [in Kanoria] I saw people whose bull-headedness was
> of a better kind, without any restlessness, devoid of histrionics. Here
> I learnt something new, the strength of *satyāgraha* . . . the strength of
> non-violence. . . . I went there to see, to be a supporter-spectator, but
> I ended up being their student.

(Rāy: 23–24)

Suman served the Kanoria agitators with music, not only his own but
also that of older writers and composers; even songs that were once the
rallying slogans, now sanctimonious passwords, of the same Communist Party
of India that opposed the Kanoria workers' struggle. Suman also sang traditional love songs, outside the factory gates (since only employees could enter
the premises), with a broken harmonium played into a street-vendor's bull-
horn as the workers re-ignited the furnace. 'At times,' he said later, 'love
songs can inspire more than protest songs!'
    But Suman's relationship with Kanoria became tenuous when the middle-
class leadership of the workers was eventually co-opted by the CPI(M):

> Blessings [were] being sought from the same person in whose regime
> factory workers can't find work. When I heard that the middle-class
> leader – he is not a worker, he had nothing to do with the movement,
> he had really gate-crashed into the movement (which I learnt later) –
> and his people [were] saying, 'Our respected leader, et cetera, et cetera
> . . .' To hell with our respected leader! I realized the workers did not
> have any say anymore.

The workers' lack of agency was the question for Suman. He would not
speak for the workers. He would neither adopt nor support even the slightest
hint of a patronizing position. Explaining how the Kanoria workers were
almost coerced to follow the path of middle-class leadership, he said,

The workers feel kind of intimidated. They're always worried that if they say no, maybe these [city folks] will go away. I don't know. I don't want to underestimate their sagacity. I think they're wiser than all of us. They are the ones who suffer most. They are the ones who toil. They are the ones who are really oppressed and repressed. So . . . what I had told them is that as long as the workers would continue their movement independently, independent of any middle-class leadership, I will be with them, not as a vanguard, but as someone who happens to make music and who's there to entertain them during their struggle.

Suman's opposition to the hypocritical politics of the left movement in West Bengal was only one side of the coin. The other side has been asserting his own class limitations, and confessing its complicity in perpetuating socials ills. 'I am not [Swāmī] Vivekānanda or Che Guevara,' Suman told *Swādhīn Bānglā* (*Independent Bengal*) in 1995. 'I am just a member of the privileged class. I can't even eat heartily when I am outdoors. Feels like there are so many unfed eyes staring at me. I feel an impotent rage, an emasculated frustration within myself. I sing, but all the time it seems I am stuck in the same place!'

Along with this has come his scathing criticism of the right wing, especially the rising Hindu fundamentalism and its intolerant anti-Muslim agenda. In the Spring of 1993 for example, a big procession had been planned in Calcutta by a coalition of Hindu fundamentalist parties. A chariot symbolizing the mythic vehicle of the Hindu God Rāma was to traverse the length of the city, with volunteers shouting anti-Muslim slogans. This was part of a nationwide project undertaken by Hindu fundamentalist parties using processions of chariots to signify the journey of Hinduism to Ayodhyā, Rāma's supposed birthplace. Not all Indian states agreed to give the procession free passage, since it was expressly unsecular and designed to denigrate the minority Muslim population, but the Left Front in West Bengal had. Suman Chatterjee showed up to protest:

[W]e formed a cordon. People came down from their houses, from buses. Not many. But at least a good 50 people. They gathered. It was also not without hazards, because the procession was headed by armed hooligans, you know. Armed with lathis, batons. Wonderful, isn't it!? In a democratic [country]. You can't even imagine . . . what I experienced that day. And . . . not one party belonging to the Left Front government opposed the procession [or got] involved in a resistance.

Among the songs sung on the occasion was Suman's adaptation of Bob Dylan's 'Blowin' in the Wind.' The performative circumstance here was basic – plain human voices, singing in unison. The resistance was finally broken down by the police and the crowd dispersed: 'There's no point in bloodshed. No point in martyrdom. So we withdrew. But at least we put up a resistance for a good three to four hours.' Suman's political position puts him between the recognized 'extremes' of Indian politics – the official left and the right – and places him beyond its visible margins. In actuality, however, Suman proposes an alternate activism that does not tout political colors hypocritically.

Suman, especially after Kanoria, has been a consistent cause for governmental embarrassment, and his songs cause for irritation. The government has made all kinds of attempts to curb his wagging tongue, from trying to grease his palms to direct death threats. Cultural organizations wanting to hire Suman have been threatened and state-owned auditoriums have on many occasions refused to let him perform in their spaces. But Suman's immense popularity among the people, especially the youth, of West Bengal has made it difficult to silence him. Even while his albums flourish in the commercial market, Suman, intent on assaulting complaisant consciences, continues to address, even 'stage,' the life of Calcutta streets.

In December 1996, the Left Front administration launched 'Operation Sunshine,' an urban 'clean-up' project for Calcutta. It was essentially a crackdown on the street hawkers/vendors, erstwhile unemployed people who had found a living through setting up shops on the sidewalks. The hawkers' hatches would have to go. They were issued warnings, but without viable rehabilitation arrangements. Calcutta had to be cleaned up, since its decrepit looks were turning corporate investors, domestic and foreign, away. Turning the hawkers out was an easy way to let the sun gleam on the streets. In response, Suman Chatterjee did what he has always done: made up a song:

> This many people, where do they go?
> Rehabilitation? Where? Do you know?
> (No elections now, that's the good part!)
> The Policemens' watches strike midnight
> Hawkers are booted, their daily bread knocked outta'sight.[4]

This song is, quite literally, about life in the streets. It 'stages' street life while, at the same time, 'streeting' the stage to turn it into an extension of pedestrian life.

Suman's music thus, despite its participation in the commercial mode of production, moves through several modes of dissemination, working at times through the industry, at times outside it. More than the urban folk (song) hero that his politics can easily make him out to be, Suman Chatterjee is a professional musician who produces and sells his craft to earn a livelihood out of an industry that has built itself on the commodification of music. At the same time, he consciously reaches out to audiences through direct communication from both the stage and the street. The corpus of Suman Chatterjee's work as a whole palpably connects the Bengali music industry in an ambivalent, though polydirectional, loop circulating between

109

Stage ↔ Studio ↔ Street

that, as of April 1997, plays on.

Notes

1   From *Suman Caṭṭopādhyāyer Gān* (*Songs of Suman Chatterjee*), Volume III,
    p. 1. All translations from Bengali sources are mine unless otherwise indi-
    cated. The English versions of the songs are part of a larger translation
    project.
2   Bengali words in the essay have been spelled with standard international
    diacritical phonetic marks used for transliterating words from the North
    Indian group of languages.
3   From a private interview conducted in March 1997. All unreferenced
    quotes are from the same interview.
4   Printed in a protest pamphlet circulated by a citizens' group opposing
    'Operation Sunshine.'

References

Chatterjee, Suman (1993) *Suman Caṭṭopādhyāyer Gān* (*Songs of Suman Chatterjee*),
    Calcutta: Swatantra Prakāśanī.
—— (1994) *Suman Caṭṭopādhyāyer Gān, Dwitīya Saṅkalan* (*Songs of Suman Chatterjee,
    Volume II*), Calcutta: Swatantra Prakāśanī.
—— (1996) *Suman Caṭṭopādhyāyer Gān, Tṛtīya Saṅkalan* (*Songs of Suman Chatterjee,
    Volume III*), Calcutta: Swatantra Prakāśanī.
Kanoria Jute Workers' Revolutionary Union (1994) *Kānoriā: Jībaner Jayagān
    (Kanoria: The Victory-Song of Life)*, Calcutta: Kanoria Jute Workers'
    Revolutionary Union.
Rāy, Rabi (ed.) (1994) *Kānoriā Śramik Āndolan Kon Pathe (Whither the Struggle of
    the Workers of Kanoria)*, Calcutta: Social Education and Alternative Research
    (SEARCH).

Chapter 14

Hollis Giammatteo

from ON THE LINE, A MEMOIR

THE WITNESSING OF THE WHITE train carrying nuclear waste occurs in a flash. What happens while waiting, the direct contact with a range of people so central to the experience of touring street theatre, is arguably as important an element of witnessing as the vigils by the tracks.

A word about the peace walk

I walked to Amarillo, Texas from a submarine base on Puget Sound, Washington with seven other women. That was in 1984. It took six months. We walked for peace, although we found, among each other, very little. Above all else, our peace walk was a perambulatory stage. We carried a banner and talked a party line which, like all dogma, reduced complexity to an axiom, a frown, a judgement. Our frowning axioms, however correct and impassioned they might have been, hit up against the complexity of people's lives. The resolve, as often with drama, occurred through the constraint of time – the curtain falls, the day ends, the walkers leave one town to present this wild mix to another.

We walked along the tracks of the White Train, which carried the warheads that arm the Trident submarines. We were eight women ranging in age from twenty-one to thirty-six. Our goal was the Pantex Plant in Amarillo, Texas, the final assembly point for all nuclear weapons in the United States, and then on to Charleston, South Carolina. We walked in order to forge a chain of resistance in towns and cities along the tracks, to speak with railroad officials, to talk nonstop for twenty-seven hundred miles, and to listen.

We carried everything in carts. They had been built especially for us. We covered them with stickers and peace flags and hung them with banners, and they looked not quite of this century and a little bit like ships. This gaiety contradicted the challenges in store.

How could I think of this walk as anything but political? We were launched by the force of the local peace community and sparked by the sharing of brave words: nonviolent resistance, vigilling, civil disobedience, prayer. I am not political. The word conjures *improvised*: shabby offices; skimpy budgets; memos and letters written hastily on the blank sides of outdated news releases; failing equipment; virulent posters and exhausted air. Or, I think of saints, and I am neither.

[. . .]

July 22

Gothenberg was a town of 3,479. We were to share our vigil there with the Methodist minister, Jim, and his wife, Joanna. By late afternoon, exhausted, we walked up to their house. Patty, Maura, and M.A. were swallowed into the cool upstairs for naps. Ellen, Sande, and Rhea sat stiffly in the living room, a line of Huck Finns unaccustomed to upholstery and etiquette and parlor air. About our hosts we knew nothing. Joanna had been gracious in a flash and disappeared as quickly into her kitchen, where she fried pounds and pounds of chicken and chopped vegetables. It wasn't clear whether all this was in our honor, or if our visit coincided with some greater party plans. Jim wasn't home yet.

I was thinking about prayer in the great cave of the house, out of the heat and calmer. I sat by Rhea in the living room under a glossy rubber tree. I thought I could absorb some prayer from her. After all, she was a preacher. But Sande and Ellen were tittering behind me. They were grouped with Rhea conspiratorially on the couch. Their hands fussed with their lips, and they had red faces. 'What's going on?' I said.

'Hsst,' Rhea turned, and jerked her attention from the others. 'Hollis, I think we have a problem here.' She straightened, a long woman who got longer in the serious times. She was still recuperating from heat sickness and her movements seemed, in contradiction to her agitation, languid, more fitting for a Tennessee Williams play. That contrast was enhanced by the rubber trees. 'You're not going to believe what's in there.' She pointed to a closed door across the hall. 'Guns,' she said, close to my face, in a whisper. 'A fucking arsenal.'

I looked at Sande and Ellen. I did not want to be inside their drama, did not want to heap this paradox – weapons in the home of a pacifist – onto an already full platter. I wanted to get ready for the Train, to squat down in coolness and fold my hands.

'Why did you go in there at all?' I snapped.

Sande cleared her throat and looked up at the ceiling. 'Well, you might say that Ellen was doing a little exploring,' she said.

Ellen blew out some air. 'I was looking for a place to nap,' she said, and turned a shade redder.

'A nap,' I said. 'There are bedrooms upstairs.'

'Hollis, that is not the point.' Rhea was leaning into my face again. 'Come and see.' I didn't want to come and see, but before I could protest they were up and off and leading me across the hall. We squeezed inside a small, square room lined with tall cabinetry. 'Open one,' said Rhea.

At attention stood a line of rifles with high-powered sights, all seemingly new, their metal precision good, and their oiled butts gleaming.

[. . .]

Rhea had it all figured out. The man was mad, the minister was mad, and even if the guns were not to mow us down as we held up our fists against the passing Train, they would prod us from our beds at night, and . . .

'You're reading too much Stephen King,' I said. I knew there had to be an explanation.

'I don't think we should stay here, Hollis,' Rhea said.

'You mean we should just leave? Without saying anything? With that lovely woman cooking her heart out in the kitchen?'

'Well, I have to be honest with you, Hollis . . .' I wanted her to stop calling me Hollis like that. It made me feel I had to salute or take on her reality. And then she said, 'I can't, I'm sorry, do that – go into the kitchen and talk. The whole thing makes me sicker.'

'Wait a minute,' I said. 'Do you expect *me* to go out to the kitchen and ask about the guns? You want to leave without saying anything at all, but you won't mind if I take care of it?' I wanted to add, This isn't even my issue, but I knew better.

'I'm not asking you to fix it for me.' Rhea slumped back on the couch. Her weariness seemed elevated, the epaulets of her morality. I wondered if she still thought of the Walk as a vacation. 'I'll sleep in the park,' she said. 'I have no problem with that.'

The front door opened. It was Jim, we guessed. He nodded our way and headed for the kitchen.

'I'm not going to sit here and pretend that nothing creepy's going on.' Sande flung herself off of the sofa. 'I'm going to go out there and talk.' She looked at me. 'Are you coming?'

'Ellen, are you?' I passed.

113

Ellen shrugged. 'It is pretty creepy,' she said.

'Good response,' I said. Rhea sank deeper behind her crossed arms. 'Plus,' she said, 'they are all new. They all have extremely powerful sights. Something's up for sure.'

I turned and followed Sande.

Joanna had achieved luminous piles of golden vegetables and chicken, and still she was sautéing. Jim was leaning against the sink. They looked surprised when we walked in, as if we'd staggered in too soon from naps and they didn't know where to put us.

'We've seen your guns,' Sande said immediately.

[. . .]

Joanna returned the fury. 'Jim works very hard,' she said, 'and I'll be damned if I'm going to listen to you judge what he does for pleasure.' She turned back to the zucchini and then back again. She was leonine in her defense. I thought for a moment that the guns were hers.

'Lady, I don't know what you mean by "pleasure." Guns kill.'

'I like hunting deer,' Jim said in a voice unassociable with killing. He was middle-aged and balding, a slight man, nondescript really, until you looked into his eyes, which were as clear as Sande's.

'God, here we go again,' Joanna said in his direction. 'You know, this man works like the dickens, and then he needs to take time off and go hunt deer, and suddenly his commitment to peace is challenged.' Her exasperation threw itself around him, protecting him from this scene, which had happened, it would seem, before. She turned back with a sigh to her stirring.

Jim pushed himself from the counter slightly. 'I'm a farm boy,' he said. But he knew he could say nothing to appease Sande. 'I've always hunted,' he continued anyway. 'It was my way of loving nature.' He looked at Joanna as if she could convince him that this was so.

Sande's face was the stage for her feelings. She'd never learned to freeze it into one particular expression so that feelings could play themselves out under the surface unobserved. It was like watching Mount Rainier make weather around her top for miles around. Jim knew he couldn't save himself, and he didn't try. I hung out in the impasse until Sande, reaching the high ground of indignation, declared, 'I can't stand this; it is revolting,' and stormed out.

'My name is Hollis,' I said. 'Maybe we can start again.'

[. . .]

'I think what Sande meant was if you really appreciate the beauty, then why kill it?'

'Is she a vegetarian?' he asked.

'Yes.'

'Well now, I can see it from that point of view. I grew up differently, though.'

We talked a while longer and, while I wasn't entirely at ease with the discrepancy between the minister and his closet full of guns, I figured that Jim hadn't gone into my closet, and if he had, well, maybe he wouldn't have been any more comfortable with what he'd have found there.

Sande was hanging on the dark banister of the wide stairway when I left him. 'How could you talk to that man? How could you listen to those lies?'

'I believed him,' I said simply. 'You should have stayed. How could you leave like that? You left me to clean up your mess.' But I'd been amazed at the strength of her feelings, and so I did not say this harshly. She just hadn't managed to make her outrage mine. She only managed to show me how the personal and the political crossed over, the one losing a sense of proportion and the other losing heart. It was as if a rape had happened.

We sat in the park folding peace cranes. The sun shone brilliantly, and the evening had turned beautiful. Joanna's dinner, sadly enough, had been hurried through but friends came and shared it, so the festivity didn't suffer. I wanted to be festive. I had wanted to eat and eat, but sensed the others' impatience to get to the tracks. And so I hurried, too.

The sun poured over the wooden loading platform, and was resplendent on the grain elevator rising like a pepper mill above it. A boldly lettered sign blocked out the town's name with characteristic Nebraska neatness. We sat on a blanket with colored peace cranes strewn around.

Evy and Sande were back from the tavern where they'd gone looking for paper and pens. They wanted to make a sign for the Train. They said how the men had pushed their caps back and rocked on their chair legs when they'd entered. I could see it, how Sande's directness would disarm them, how Evy would be at home in their cap-scratching gazes. So, in this way, the word got out that there were women 'stationed' in the park to see some train.

It was Saturday night. There was a high in the air, as of six-packs and dating, cruising in new cars. Pickups and motorcycles bounced over the railroad crossing. In the direction of town it was the boys we saw, full face, gawking. Back again, we got their girls, blank-faced and pale, in profile. Some stopped, parked the trucks or motorcycles, and came shyly to talk. The town's radical – voluptuous, wild-haired, and on crutches – had adopted us. She sat on our blanket and folded cranes. Her presence made us a little more real to the town, gave us a frame of reference. Jan's presence scaled us down but gave us substance. She was the bridge between gawk and gather.

The Bishop sisters stood at the railroad crossing. Their sign was stretched between them, facing Texas. Sande's face was a gulp, and Evy's was a strangle. They had gone into a private place of grief and images, as if laying their hearts, like ears, to the track to catch the Train's vibration. The sign said, 'The White Train Passes Through Here,' and they held it between them as if it would tear through the paper and then right on through their lives.

We had called the local newspaper, and Peggy, its reporter, came. The Department of Energy (DOE), *legally* bound to inform the authorities in every town of the Train's passing, hadn't. They sat, when they came, in their gray, official car at the edge. Patty walked over. They seemed annoyed and surprised, as if she'd blown their cover. The Gothenberg cop had gotten word of the Train from Peggy. They were married. Nothing of how it was handled endeared the DOE or the Train to Gothenberg.

I went to listen to Peggy interviewing Jim. He was describing his involvement with various peace committees, a long list and history, and I had the urge to signal Sande and Rhea. He spoke candidly and bravely against the MX and the Train.

'If this stuff gets printed,' he turned to me, 'the story won't sit well with my parish. Second week on the job here, too.' He turned back to Peggy. 'Print it.'

It was dark. We put away the cranes and folded up the blanket. The Train was late by two hours. 'Surely any minute,' we thought, lining up along the tracks with our placards of Hiroshima and Nagasaki, our banners and signs. We squinted down the tracks. A pinpoint of light pricked the distance. The gate fell down in front of us. We breathed in all at once and held it, attuned to the distant roar. The funnel of light widened and drew us closer.

'Stand back,' I shouted to Evy, who was leaning in too close, in a kind of willful innocence of the danger. M.A. moved to stand behind her. And then it was on us. We were nicked by the cinder and blasted by its hot air. As long as our breath took to exhale, it lasted; in a flash it receded, and then it was gone. The air quivered like a rip, and the ground's quake was faded, and in the comparative quiet we began to cry.

The Train had passed at sixty-five miles per hour. We expected it to tarry as it had at Bangor and slow to a decorous roll, acknowledging the flowers, the keening, the kneeling, and the signs. The Train hadn't even seen us. It was on the books to go no faster than thirty-five, and it had gone through Gothenberg at sixty-five, and in its draft our tiny line was scattered like dry leaves. How could love stop the Train when it was going so fast? How could it obey the laws of God when it couldn't even obey the speed limit?

The train's 'invisibility' was understandable now. Our judgement softened against towns professing never to have seen it, against people professing ignorance. In darkness it had passed, its eerie sidelights off, its whiteness not evident, like every other freight train that barreled through every other town. Big deal. Big fucking deal.

PART THREE

INTEGRATION

Introduction

PRACTITIONERS OF THE CASE STUDIES described in this section abandon formal separation of actors and spectators and insert performance into everyday life. The essayists here suggest that such direct, individual experience can lead to political change. Augusto Boal, the first contributor in the section, has contrasted what can be achieved at mass political rallies with the one-to-one contact that his 'invisible theatre' engenders:

> Big rallies are for people who are already convinced. You make a manifestation of force and many people see that you are strong, and by seeing the support those who are undecided may join along. The other way, like doing invisible theatre, reaches very few people. But it modifies people's opinions. That man whose opinion was changed goes home and talks to his family, and he goes to a bar and talks to his friends . . .
> (Cohen-Cruz 1994: 232)

Some practitioners merge performance with everyday life in response to the devaluing of formal theatre's political possibilities. For others, it is a way to disguise politically engaged work under an oppressive regime. Or use of performance techniques interactively in public may deepen the exchange that takes place there, establishing personal as well as political connections. During the 1970s, Los Angeles was a center for feminist theatre practitioners who inhabited other personas off the stage largely for reasons of personal growth (Roth 1983). Whether consciously or not, those who integrate performance into everyday life are picking up the torch of life/art experimentation that has interested avant-gardists throughout the twentieth century.

References

Cohen-Cruz, Jan (1994) 'Theatricalizing Politics: An Interview with Augusto Boal,' in Mady Schutzman and Jan Cohen-Cruz (eds) *Playing Boal*. London: Routledge.

Roth, Moira (ed.) (1983) *The Amazing Decade: Women and Performance Art in America, 1970–1980*, Los Angeles: Astro Artz.

Chapter 15

Augusto Boal

INVISIBLE THEATER

BOAL IS THE BRAZILIAN CREATOR of Theatre of the Oppressed, an arsenal of dramatic techniques that function as rehearsals for personal and social change. He created *invisible theater* to stimulate debate on political issues while living in Argentina in the 1970s, when overt political theatre was impossible. Answering the charge of manipulation, Boal emphasizes that the consequences of invisible theatre are real. He does, nevertheless, add a safety net: 'warmer-uppers' get people involved in invisible theatre, and 'cooler-downers' guard against unforeseen danger in doing these acts as reality in public.

Invisible theater . . . consists of the presentation of a scene in an environment other than the theater, before people who are not spectators. The place can be a restaurant, a sidewalk, a market, a train, a line of people, etc. The people who witness the scene are those who are there by chance. During the spectacle, these people must not have the slightest idea that it is a 'spectacle,' for this would make them 'spectators.'

The invisible theater calls for the detailed preparation of a skit with a complete text or a simple script; but it is necessary to rehearse the scene sufficiently so that the actors are able to incorporate into their acting and their actions the intervention of the spectators. During the rehearsal it is also necessary to include every imaginable intervention from the spectators; these possibilities will form a kind of optional text.

The invisible theater erupts in a location chosen as a place where the public congregates. All the people who are near become involved in the eruption and the effects of it last long after the skit is ended.

A small example shows how the invisible theater works. In the enormous restaurant of a hotel in Chiclayo, where the literacy agents of ALFIN[1] were staying, together with 400 other people, the 'actors' sit at separate tables. The waiters start to serve. The 'protagonist' in a more or less loud voice (to attract the attention of other diners, but not in a too obvious way) informs the waiter that he cannot go on eating the food served in that hotel, because in his opinion it is too bad. The waiter does not like the remark but tells the customer that he can choose something *à la carte*, which he may like better. The actor chooses a dish called 'Barbecue à la pauper.' The waiter points out that it will cost him seventy *soles*, to which the actor answers, always in a reasonably loud voice, that there is no problem. Minutes later the waiter brings him the barbecue, the protagonist eats it rapidly and gets ready to get up and leave the restaurant, when the waiter brings the bill. The actor shows a worried expression and tells the people at the next table that his barbecue was much better than the food they are eating, but the pity is that one has to pay for it. . . .

'I'm going to pay for it; don't have any doubts. I ate the 'barbecue à la pauper' and I'm going to pay for it. But there is a problem: I'm broke.'

'And how are you going to pay?,' asks the indignant waiter. 'You knew the price before ordering the barbecue. And now, how are you going to pay for it?'

The diners nearby are, of course, closely following the dialogue – much more attentively than they would if they were witnessing the scene on a stage. The actor continues:

'Don't worry, because I *am* going to pay you. But since I'm broke I will pay you with labor-power.'

'With what?,' asks the waiter, astonished. 'What kind of power?'

'With labor-power, just as I said. I am broke but I can rent you my labor-power. So I'll work doing something for as long as it's necessary to pay for my "barbecue à la pauper," which to tell the truth, was really delicious – much better than the food you serve to those poor souls. . . .'

By this time some of the customers intervene and make remarks among themselves at their tables, about the price of food, the quality of the service in the hotel, etc. The waiter calls the headwaiter to decide the matter. The actor explains again to the latter the business of renting his labor-power and adds:

'And besides, there is another problem: I'll rent my labor-power but the truth is that I don't know how to do anything, or very little. You will have to give me a very simple job to do. For example, I can take out the hotel's garbage. What's the salary of the garbage man who works for you?'

The headwaiter does not want to give any information about salaries, but a second actor at another table is already prepared and explains that he and the garbage man have gotten to be friends and that the latter has told him his salary: seven *soles* per hour. The two actors make some calculations and the 'protagonist' exclaims:

'How is this possible! If I work as a garbage man I'll have to work ten hours to pay for this barbecue that it took me ten minutes to eat? It can't be! Either you increase the salary of the garbage man or reduce the price of the barbecue! . . . But I can do something more specialized; for example, I can take care of the hotel gardens, which are so beautiful, so well cared for. One can see that a very talented person is in charge of the gardens. How much does the gardener of this hotel make? I'll work as a gardener! How many hours work in the garden are necessary to pay for the "barbecue à la pauper"?'

A third actor, at another table, explains his friendship with the gardener, who is an immigrant from the same village as he; for this reason he knows that the gardener makes ten *soles* per hour. Again the 'protagonist' becomes indignant:

'How is this possible? So the man who takes care of these beautiful gardens, who spends his days out there exposed to the wind, the rain, and the sun, has to work seven long hours to be able to eat the barbecue in ten minutes? How can this be, Mr. Headwaiter? Explain it to me!'

The headwaiter is already in despair; he dashes back and forth, giving orders to the waiters in a loud voice to divert the attention of the other customers, alternately laughs and becomes serious, while the restaurant is transformed into a public forum. The 'protagonist' asks the waiter how much he is paid to serve the barbecue and offers to replace him for the necessary number of hours. Another actor, originally from a small village in the interior, gets up and declares that nobody in his village makes seventy *soles* per day; therefore nobody in his village can eat the "barbecue à la pauper." (The sincerity of this actor, who was, besides, telling the truth, moved those who were near his table.)

Finally, to conclude the scene, another actor intervenes with the following proposition:

'Friends, it looks as if we are against the waiter and the headwaiter and this does not make sense. They are our brothers. They work like us, and they are not to blame for the prices charged here. I suggest we take up a collection. We at this table are going to ask you to contribute whatever you can, one *sol*, two *soles*, five *soles*, whatever you can afford. And with that money we are going to pay for the barbecue. And be generous, because what is left over will go as a tip for the waiter, who is our brother and a working man.'

Immediately, those who are with him at the table start collecting money to pay the bill. Some customers willingly give one or two *soles*. Others furiously comment:

'He says that the food we're eating is junk, and now he wants us to pay for his barbecue! . . . And am I going to eat this junk? Hell no! I wouldn't give him a peanut, so he'll learn a lesson! Let him wash dishes. . . .'

The collection reached 100 *soles* and the discussion went on through the night. It is always very important that the actors do not reveal themselves to be actors! On this rests the *invisible* nature of this form of theater. And it is precisely this invisible quality that will make the spectator act freely and fully, as if he were living a real situation – and, after all, it is a real situation!

It is necessary to emphasize that the invisible theater is not the same thing as a 'happening' or the so-called 'guerrilla theater.' In the latter we are clearly talking about 'theater,' and therefore the wall that separates actors from spectators immediately arises, reducing the spectator to impotence: a spectator is always less than a man! In the invisible theater the theatrical rituals are abolished; only the theater exists, without its old, worn-out patterns. The theatrical energy is completely liberated, and the impact produced by this free theater is much more powerful and longer lasting.

Note

1   Ed. note: ALFIN stands for Operación Alfabetización Integral, or Integral Literacy Operation.

Chapter 16

Adrian Piper

from XENOPHOBIA AND THE
INDEXICAL PRESENT II: LECTURE

CONCEPTUAL ARTIST ADRIAN PIPER TOOK to the
streets to confront 'interpersonal manifestations of racism rather than
institutional ones.' This text was delivered as an illustrated lecture, which
explains Piper's occasional reference to slides.

My area of interest is xenophobia and racism. Xenophobia is defined as the
fear of strangers, but it actually is not just the fear of strangers as such; for
example, xenophobia does not apply to people in one's family, relatives
whom one happens not to have met, or to neighbors, or to other inhabitants
of one's small town. Xenophobia is about fear of the other considered as an
alien – someone who does not look the way that one takes to be normal.
It's about the violation of boundaries, and I think that this perhaps has
increasing resonance now in the European context, because of the demo-
graphic changes and waves of immigration that you are experiencing from
Eastern Europe, Asia, and Africa. My topic is racism because in the United
States the analogue of your problem is the problem of racism and the integration of the slave population from Africa that has been in the United States
for the last four hundred years.

Kant tells us in the *Critique of Pure Reason* that in order for us to make
sense of experience at all, we have to categorize those experiences in terms
of certain basic categories, which Kant thinks of as being innate. He says that
categorizing experience in that way is a necessary condition for having a

unified and internally integrated sense of self, so that if we did not categorize our experiences, we would be confronted with total chaos. We would
experience cognitive overload and perhaps enter a state of cognitive psychosis.
We just wouldn't be able to make sense of anything.

He also says that if perceptual data are presented to us that do not
conform to the categories of experience, then we can't have any experience
of that perceptual data at all. So what that means is that we essentially have
to repress or ignore or dismiss anomalous objects that do not conform to
our presuppositions of what experience should be like.

In the natural sciences we see this kind of attitude when scientists are
confronted by new data that don't conform to prevailing theories. For
example, scientists are very uncomfortable with the suggestion that psychic
phenomena might be real, that mental powers have causal efficacy, because
we have no way of explaining how that could happen. The result is that the
data that seem to confirm those extrascientific theories are just ignored.

In the social sphere we see exactly the same phenomena, that is to say,
individuals who do not conform to these categories of what a person looks
like, what a person should be like; such individuals are systematically disregarded or exterminated or sent back to their countries of origin, or demeaned
in various ways.

I would suggest that the basic tendency that gives rise to all of these
areas of repression is the same. I think that Kant is right about this; there is
an innate tendency to categorize, and if we did not do that, we would experience total chaos. So the basis of xenophobia is innate. It is hard-wired, and
it is impossible to escape.

However, what counts as alien, what counts as fearful and unfamiliar,
is entirely a matter of social context. If one is raised in a social context that
has lots of different kinds of people in it, is very cosmopolitan, then one will
not experience fear of other people, no matter how they look. If one is
raised in a situation that is very provincial, very homogeneous, in which
everyone looks more or less the same, then it is much harder, because any
variation in appearance or dress or conventions or behavior will be cause for
fear until one can grow accustomed to someone who has that anomalous or
different appearance.

I would suggest that xenophobia does not arise only in these contexts
but also arises in the most basic relations between human beings, that is to
say, intimate relations. Kant also says in the first *Critique* that it is impossible
to be a subject at all without dependence on the object of perception. So
there is a kind of mutual dependence between subjects insofar as they perceive
one another and conditions for the identity are established. There is often a
period when we go into a relationship with someone, where we think that
the person meets all of our highest expectations, our most romantic expectations about what our partner should be like. She is perfect, she is beautiful,
he is handsome, he is everything we could possibly wish. That period may

last for a few months, a few weeks maybe, and as we get to know the person better, the difference between us and our partner becomes more and more salient. We start realizing that in fact he does not conform to our expectations. She behaves in ways we did not expect and do not particularly like, and we have to adjust to those idiosyncrasies, differences in behavior and temperament that may completely violate our expectations about what our partner would be like. My suggestion would be that this is not simply *like* xenophobia. This *is* a case of xenophobia, where we find ourselves reacting negatively to someone with whom we are trying to establish an intimate relationship. Exactly the same sense of fear, the sense of boundary-violation that may occur in one case in the international context, in a geographical context, also can occur in terms of physical boundaries – the boundaries of the body, also the boundaries of the self. Becoming intimate with someone means in a sense merging, it also means dealing with areas of difference, and of course this is where relationships either stand or fall. If we cannot achieve the acceptance and the tolerance of the other person, then the relationship is over; and of course many relationships *are* over.

But there is a kind of conversation that we have probably all had with our partners in intimate relationships where we are not referring to something outside ourselves, we are not referring to something external, to the situation, say, to the price of tea in China, or to the nature of abstract numbers, or to Medieval art in the thirteenth century; we are referring to the here and now: What is going on at this minute between you and me. We have these conversations that take a certain form, a very familiar form: 'You are not paying attention to me.' 'You are not hearing what I am saying.' 'Stop trying to pigeonhole me.' 'Don't tell me what I think.' These are very familiar utterances, and I would be very surprised if there were anyone in this room who did not have that experience at some point, of feeling as though she were being turned into an alien object somehow, that communication had broken down.

I am a methodological individualist, and so I believe that forms of institutional oppression ultimately devolve into individual relationships, specific concrete relationships between you and me. After all, institutions are not abstract objects; institutions are run by individuals, they are staffed by individuals, individuals make policy decisions that determine the lives of others, and so ultimately individuals have to be held accountable for any form of social oppression, and that is why my work, although mostly not autobiographical, is very individual. It is very personal. It concerns the immediate relationship in the indexical present – that is, the present of the here and now – between the art object and the viewer as a kind of medium for social relations.

My training is in minimal art, and although it is very hard for me to talk coherently about motivations, it seems to me not an accident that one of the major drives of minimal art is the idea of repudiating abstract aesthetic theory and focusing attention on the individual, specific, unique object, reducing that object to a set of properties that reveal it simply as what it is: as an object in space and time, and not something that is full of external associations, suppositions, and preconceptions. If you think that xenophobia can be overcome by focusing on the specific, unique, concrete qualities of individuals, then it would make sense to think of minimal art decision-making as a kind of aesthetic strategy for drawing attention to the concrete, specific, unique qualities of individuals, and that is what my work does.

[. . .]

In the [. . .] series [. . .] called *Catalysis*, [. . .] the basic idea was that an object can be a catalytic agent and can make a change in other sorts of objects without undergoing change itself. This was done on Fourteenth Street in Union Square in New York, and I really did paint my clothes with wet, sticky, oil paint and simply walk down the street. One important aspect of this format was that I never violated any codes of behavior in these pieces. The idea was to behave normally and simply alter my physical appearance in the way that one would sculpturally alter an object with respect to material. As you can see here, I was, in the immortal words of Michael Fried, 'activating the space around me'; people were making wide circles as I walked through. Here's another one in that series. There I am sitting on the Second Avenue bus with a towel stuffed in my mouth. In fact, although I was still thinking very formalistically and abstractly at this point, I think that the symbology of these pieces had a lot to do with my emerging sense of myself as a woman, as having been silenced in various ways, as having been objectified and as being a black person as well.

This is another series of street performances that I started in 1973; this is called the *Mythic Being* series. In this series I dressed in drag as a young black male; as you can see, I am wearing an Afro and a moustache. I basically invaded various contexts within New York cultural life. I went to the opera; I did all the sort of things I normally did except with the masculine guise. I was thinking a lot about specific alterations in physical subjectivity, particularly as a way of bringing out aspects of my own identity that are not readily available – not only the fact that I am black, because many people do not realize that, but also that I have a very strong masculine component to my character. I wanted to be able to explore that. It was just great to be able to take the subway late at night and not worry about being mugged or raped. To be able to sit on the subway, the way guys often do, with their legs wide apart, kind of making room for their genitals. They take up a lot of space. Whereas we women don't. We scrunch up and crouch in. So it was really great to be able to make room for my genitals in that way. That part was really wonderful; the sense of freedom that I experienced in doing this work was a real revelation to me. The bad part was that I got to experience what it is like for visibly black Americans to simply move through the world in

Figure 16.1 Catalysis IV.

any social context that is primarily populated by white people, and because I was showing certain visual cues of a black person, I was responded to in that way and it was truly horrible: I felt objectified over and over again in subtle ways that I, to this day, believe people have no control over. I do not think that anyone intentionally rejects or dismisses or ignores or objectifies another person. I do believe that it is completely an innate uncontrollable fear impulse, and if you are not used to seeing black people in your environment, that is the way you are going to react. There is just no other solution but to bring black people into your environment so that they will not seem so strange. That was very much a conclusion of doing this work, for me.

[. . .]

This, *The Mythic Being: Getting Back*, is a continuation of that series of performances; it was done in 1975. I had left New York in 1974 and had moved to Cambridge, Massachusetts, to do a Ph.D. in philosophy at Harvard. This was on the Cambridge Commons. This is a friend of mine who is a collaborator and does not realize what is about to happen. The piece is called *Getting Back*. Essentially, I mug him and run off with his wallet.

Here is another one; this was done in Harvard Square. This one is called *Cruising White Women*. As you can see, there I am, cruising white women. Again, the idea is to not actually violate conventions of behavior but simply to set myself up as an altered object of perception and explore those differences.

[. . .]

This is a piece from 1986. It is a business card. It is two by three inches and it is called *My Calling (Card) Number One: A Reactive Guerrilla Performance for Dinners and Cocktail Parties.*[1]

> Dear Friend,
>   I am black.
>   I am sure you did not realize this when you made/ laughed at/agreed with that racist remark. In the past, I have attempted to alert white people to my racial identity in advance. Unfortunately, this invariably causes them to react to me as pushy, manipulative, or socially inappropriate. Therefore, my policy is to assume that white people do not make these remarks, even when they believe there are no black people present, and to distribute this card when they do.
>   I regret any discomfort my presence is causing you, just as I am sure you regret the discomfort your racism is causing me.

This is a piece that I started doing when I realized that there was no easy solution to the problem of how to deal with the kind of dissonance and disorientation I was causing, because I identify myself as a black person and to many people do not look black. White people have often made racist remarks in my presence, not realizing that a black person is present. They make a remark thinking that they are among themselves. This is, of course, very disturbing for me. One thing that I tried doing was simply confronting the person verbally and saying, 'You know, I am black and you are insulting me.' The problem with that is that first of all it really ruins everybody's evening. I am a nice middle-class person. When I get asked to a dinner party, I try to be nice and I try to make the evening go smoothly as everybody does, so the thought of disrupting everyone's evening by introducing something like this, by being the one to disrupt the convention that remarks like that are acceptable, is just too much for me. I tried it once, and it was just too upsetting. Another strategy that I tried was raising the issue in the abstract without identifying myself as black, but just saying, 'Well you know, that is a racist remark, and it is not nice and black people are not really jungle bunnies,' and so forth. The problem with raising it in the abstract is that it then enables people to have an abstract discussion about whether the remark was really a racist remark, what their intentions were in making it; maybe it was a back-handed compliment, is it a terrible thing to be a jungle bunny? One can go on like that without really addressing the issue. So that did not work. I have also had friends try announcing in advance to the guests that there will be a black person present. The problem with that is that then everyone spends the whole evening making politically correct remarks and wondering who the black person is. That just did not work at all. What is nice about the card is that the only people whose evenings are ruined are mine and the person who made the remarks. Everyone else gets to carry on as usual, and if that person then wants to initiate a dialogue with me that is fine, but then the responsibility of ruining the evening is on them, it is not on me. Actually no one who got this card ever initiated a dialogue with me. They just read the card, did a double take, and withdrew. That surprised me.

I got the idea for this piece from an interview I saw with Esther Williams on *Entertainment Tonight*. The interviewer asked Esther Williams if she still swam, and Esther Williams started complaining about how she was always getting the same question all the time. She showed the interviewer this card she'd had made up – a small, gold-embossed business card that said, 'Yes, I still swim.' And she talked about how the next time she was at dinner, Henry Kissinger was sitting next to her, and he turned to her and started to ask, 'Do you still sw–' and she just gave him the card. I really liked that idea a lot. I stopped doing this piece a couple of years ago. I was at a party and got introduced to someone who looked at me for a long moment and said, 'You know, I'm trying to think of a racist remark so I can get one of the cards.' So that was the end of that!

Here is one for bars and discos, *My Calling (Card) Number Two: Reactive Guerrilla Performance for Bars and Discos*. This was about wanting to reclaim as a woman the freedom I'd experienced dressing in drag as a man as the Mythic Being, the freedom to just go into a public social space and be anonymous and undisturbed, to go to a bar and just sit and nurse my beer and read the newspapers, or go to a disco and just stand on the sidelines and watch people without being hit on. People assume that if a woman is alone in a public social space it's because she wants to be hit on. That's a really peculiar idea when you think about it. Actually this card was not as successful in bringing dialogue to an end. It tended more to encourage dialogue. Ultimately, I stopped going to bars and discos, and that solved the problem.

Here is an installation shot of those pieces from my retrospective when it first opened in 1987. The cards are printed up without my name on them, and the sign says, 'Join the struggle, take some for your own use,' which means that people can just take them and use them in any situation they encounter of this kind. I am very proud to report that at the end of every day at my retrospective these little card containers were empty, which means that there are lots of people all over the world, lots of white people giving out these cards in uncomfortable social situations. I understand that in New York members of the gay community have printed up similar cards for use in situations when people make homophobic remarks about gay people. I really like this. I wanted to disseminate this idea as far as possible. [. . .]

Note

1   Ed. note: Text from *Adrian Piper's MY CALLING (CARD) NUMBER 1*, 1986. Guerrilla performance with printed calling card, 2 × 3½″. Reprinted by permission of Adrian Piper.

Chapter 17

Lauren Berlant and
Elizabeth Freeman

from QUEER NATIONALITY

BERLANT AND FREEMAN FOCUS ON the gay and lesbian
political organization Queer Nation and its creative challenges to public
spaces that claim neutrality but are, in fact, heterosexual and white. Earlier
in the essay excerpted below, they locate Queer Nation's origins at an ACT
UP New York meeting in 1990. Its aim was 'to extend the kinds of democratic counter-politics deployed on behalf of AIDS activism for the
transformation of public sexual discourse in general' (198).

Outside: politics in your face

On February 23, 1967, in a congressional hearing concerning the security
clearance of gay men for service in the Defense Department, a psychiatrist
named Dr. Charles Socarides testified that the homosexual 'does not know
the boundary of his own body. He does not know where his body ends and
space begins.'[1] Precisely: the spiritual and other moments of internal consol-
idation that we have described allow the individual bodies of Queer Nationals
to act as visibly queer flash cards, in an ongoing project of cultural pedagogy
aimed at exposing the range and variety of bounded spaces upon which heterosexual supremacy depends. Moving out from the psychological and physical
'safe spaces' it creates, Queer Nation broadcasts the straightness of 'public
space,' and hence its explicit or implicit danger to gays. The queer body –
as an agent of publicity, as a unit of self-defense, and finally as a spectacle

of ecstasy – becomes the locus where mainstream culture's discipline of gay citizens is written and where the pain caused by this discipline is transformed into rage and pleasure. Using alternating strategies of menace and merriment, agents of Queer Nation have come to see and conquer places that present the danger of *violence* to gays and lesbians, to reterritorialize them.

Twenty-three years after Dr. Socarides's mercifully brief moment of fame, New Yorkers began to display on their chests a graphic interpretation of his fear for the national defense. The T-shirt they wore portrays a silhouette of the United States, with the red tint of the East Coast and the blue tint of the West Coast fading and blending in the middle. Suddenly, the heartland of the country is a shocking new shade of queer: red, white, and blue make lavender. This, Queer Nation's first T-shirt, extends the project of an earlier graphic produced by Adam Rolston, which shows a placard that reads 'I Am Out, Therefore I Am.' But Queer Nation's shirt locates the public space in which the individual Cartesian subject must be out, transforming that space in order to survive. Queer Nation's design maps a psychic and bodily territory – lavender territory – that cannot be colonized and expands it to include, potentially, the entire nation. This lamination of the country to the body conjoins individual and national liberation: just as Dr. Socarides dreaded, the boundaries between what constitutes individual and what constitutes national space are explicitly blurred. 'National Defense' and 'Heterosexual Defense' become interdependent projects of boundary-maintenance that Queer Nation graphically undermines, showing that these colors *will* run.

While the Queer Nation shirt exploits heterosexist fears of the 'spread of a lifestyle' through dirty laundry by publicizing its wearer as both a gay native and a missionary serving the spread of homosexuality, not all of its tactics are this benign. The optimistic assertion that an army of lovers cannot lose masks the seriousness with which Queer Nation has responded to the need for a pseudomilitia on the order of the Guardian Angels. The Pink Panthers, initially conceived of at a Queer Nation meeting but eventually splitting off into a separate organization, provided a searing response to the increased violence that has accompanied the general increase of gay visibility in America. The Panthers, a foot patrol that straddles the 'safe spaces' [. . .] and the 'unsafe spaces' of public life in America, not only defend other queer bodies but aim to be a continual reminder of them. Dressed in black T-shirts with pink triangles enclosing a black paw print, they move unarmed in groups, linked by walkie-talkies and whistles. In choosing a uniform that explicitly marks them as targets, as successors of the Black Power movement, and as seriocomic detectives, the Panthers bring together the abstract threat implicit in the map graphic described above, the embodied threat implicit in individual queers crossing their subcultural boundaries, and the absurdity that founds this condition of sexual violence.

Their slogan is 'Bash Back.' It announces that the locus of gay oppression has shifted from the legal to the extralegal arena, and from national-juridical to ordinary everyday forms.² The menace of 'Bash Back' reciprocates the menace of physical violence that keeps gays and lesbians invisible and/or physically restricted to their mythically safe neighborhoods. But rather than targeting specific gay-bashers or lashing out at random heterosexuals, the Panthers train in self-defense techniques and travel unarmed: 'Bash Back' simply intends to mobilize the threat gay-bashers use so effectively – strength not in numbers, but in the presence of a few bodies who represent the potential for widespread violence – against the bashers themselves. In this way, the slogan turns the bodies of the Pink Panthers into a psychic counterthreat, expanding their protective shield beyond the confines of their physical 'beat.' Perhaps the most assertive 'bashing' that the uniformed bodies of the Pink Panthers deliver is mnemonic. Their spectacular presence counters heterosexual culture's will-to-not-recognize its own intense need to reign in a sexually pure environment.

While the rage of 'Bash Back' responds to embodied and overt violence, Queer Nation's 'Queer Nights Out' redress the more diffuse and implicit violence of sexual conventionality by mimicking the hackneyed forms of straight social life. 'Queer Nights Out' are moments of radical desegregation with roots in civil rights era lunch counter sit-ins; whereas the 1960s sit-ins addressed legal segregation, these queer sorties confront customary segregation. Invading straight bars, for example, queers stage a production of sentimentality and pleasure that broadcasts the ordinariness of the queer body. The banality of twenty-five same-sex couples making out in a bar and the silliness of a group of fags playing spin-the-bottle efface the distance crucial to the ordinary pleasures straight society takes in the gay world. Neither informational nor particularly spectacular, Queer Nights Out demonstrate two ominous truths to heterosexual culture: one, that gay sexual identity is no longer a reliable foil for straightness, and, two, that what looked like bounded gay subcultural activity has itself become restless and improvisatory, taking its pleasures in a theater near you.

Queer Nights Out have also appropriated the model of the surprise attack – which the police have traditionally used to show gays and lesbians that even the existence of their subcultural spaces is contingent upon the goodwill of straights. Demonstrating that the boundedness of heterosexual spaces is also contingent upon the (enforced) willingness of gays to remain invisible, queers are thus using exhibitionism to make public space psychically unsafe for unexamined heterosexuality. In one report from the field, two lesbians were sighted sending a straight woman an oyster, adding a Sapphic appetizer to the menu of happy hour delights. The straight woman was not amused.³ Embarrassment was generated – the particular embarrassment liberals suffer when the sphere allotted to the tolerated exceeds the boundaries 'we all agree upon.' Maneuvers such as this reveal that straight mating techniques, supposed to be 'Absolutely Het,' are sexual lures available to any brand of pleasure: 'Sorry, you looked like a dyke to me.'⁴ This political transgression of 'personal space' can even be used to deflect the violence it provokes. Confronted by a defensive and hostile drunk, a Queer Nation gayboy addresses the room: 'Yeah, I had him last night, and he was terrible.'

In this place of erotic exchange, the army of lovers takes as its war strategies 'some going down and butt-fucking and other theatricals.'[5] The genitals become not just organs of erotic thanksgiving, but weapons of pleasure against their own oppression. These kinds of militant-erotic interventions take their most public form in the Queer Nation kiss-in, in which an official space such as a city plaza is transfused with the juices of unofficial enjoyment: embarrassment, pleasure, spectacle, longing, and accusation interarticulate to produce a public scandal that is, as the following section will reveal, Queer Nation's specialty.

Hyper-space: 'Try me on, I'm very you'

In its most postmodern moments, Queer Nation takes on a corporate strategy in order to exploit the psychic unboundedness of consumers who depend upon products to articulate, produce, and satisfy their desires.[6] Queer Nation tactically uses the hyper-spaces created by the corporeal trademark, the metropolitan parade, the shopping mall, print media, and finally advertising, to recognize and take advantage of the consumer's pleasure in vicarious identification. In this guise the group commandeers permeable sites, apparently apolitical spaces through which the public circulates in a pleasurable, consensual exchange of bodies, products, identities, and information. Yet it abandons the conciliatory mode of, for instance, Kirk and Madsen's plan to market 'positive' (read 'tolerable') gay images to straight culture.[7] Instead, it aims to produce a series of elaborate blue-light specials on the queer body. The Queer National corporate strategy – to reveal to the consumer desires he/she didn't know he/she had, to make his/her identification with the product 'homosexuality' both an unsettling and a pleasurable experience – makes consumer pleasure central to the transformation of public culture, thus linking the utopian promises of the commodity with those of the nation.

One particular celebrity oscillates between local/embodied and corporate/abstract sexual identification: the bootleg 'Queer Bart' T-shirt produced by Queer Nation in the summer of 1990. Queer Bart reconfigures Matt Groening's bratty, white, suburban anykid, Bart Simpson, into the New York gay clone: he wears an earring, his own Queer Nation T-shirt, and a pink triangle button. The balloon coming out of his mouth reads, 'Get used to it, dude!' Like all bodies, Queer Bart's body is a product that serves a number of functions. In the first place, he provides a countertext to the apparent harmlessness of the suburban American generic body: Queer Nation's Bart implicitly points a finger at another bootleg T-shirt in which Bart snarls, 'Back off, faggot!' and at the heterosexuality that Normal Bart's generic identity assumes. In the second place, the original Bart's 'clone-ness,' when inflected with an 'exceptional' identity – Black Bart, Latino Bart, and so on – not only stages the ability of subcultures to fashion cultural insiderhood for their members, but also reinscribes subcultural identity into mainstream style. The exuberant inflection of Bart Simpson as queer speaks to the pleasures of assuming an official normative identity, signified on the body, for those whom dominant culture consistently represents as exceptional.

Queer Nation's reinflection of Bart's body, which, precisely because it *is* a body, readily lends itself to any number of polymorphously perverse identities, graphically demonstrates that the commodity is a central means by which individuals tap into the collective experience of public desire. Queer Bart, himself a trademark, is a generic body stamped with Queer Nation's own trademarked aesthetic, which then allows consumers to publicly identify themselves as members of a trademarked 'nation.'[8] Thus he embodies the nonspaces we will discuss in the following paragraphs: his own unboundedness as a commodity identity exploits the way that the fantasy of being something else merges with the stereotype to confer an endlessly shifting series of identities upon the consumer's body.[9]

The genealogy of the Queer Bart strategy extends from the gay pride parades of the 1970s, when for the first time gay bodies organized into a visible public ritual. In addition to offering gays and lesbians an opportunity to experience their private identities in an official spectacle, the parades also offered flamboyant and ordinary homosexuality as something the heterosexual spectator could encounter without having to go 'underground' – to drag shows or gay bars, for voyeuristic pleasure or casual sex.[10] In the last twenty years, the representation of 'gayness' in the gay pride parade has changed, for its marching population is no longer defined by sexual practice alone. Rather, the current politicization of gay issues in the metropolitan and civic public spheres has engendered broadly based alliances, such that progressive 'straights' can pass as 'queer' in their collective political struggles.[11] As a result, the gay pride parade no longer produces the ominous gust of an enormous closet door opening; its role in consolidating identity varies widely, depending on what kind of communication participants think the parade involves. While gay pride parades have not yet achieved the status in mainstream culture of, for instance, St. Patrick's Day parades (in which people 'go Irish for a day' by dressing in green), they have thus become pluralistic and inclusive, involving approval-seeking, self-consolidating, saturnalian, and transgressive moments of spectacle.[12] Although Queer Nation marches in traditional gay pride parades, it has updated and complicated the strategy of the parade, recognizing that the planned, distanced, and ultimately contained nature of the form offers only momentary displacement of heterosexual norms: after all, one can choose not to go to a parade, or one can watch the scene go by without becoming even an imaginary participant.

In parades through urban American downtowns, Queer Nationals often chant, 'We're here, we're queer, we're not going shopping.' But shopping itself provides the form of a tactic when Queer Nation enters another context: the Queer Shopping Network of New York and the Suburban Homosexual Outreach Program (SHOP) of San Francisco have taken the relatively bounded spectacle of the urban pride parade to the ambient pleasures of the shopping mall. 'Mall visibility actions' thus conjoin the spectacular lure of the parade with Hare Krishna-style conversion and proselytizing techniques. Stepping into malls in hair-gelled splendor, holding hands and handing out fliers, the queer auxiliaries produce an 'invasion' that conveys a different message: 'We're here, we're queer, *you're* going shopping.'

These miniature parades transgress an erotically, socially, and economically complex space. Whereas patrons of the straight bar at least understand its function in terms of pleasure and desire, mall-goers invest in the shopping mall's credentials as a 'family' environment, an environment that 'creates a nostalgic image of [the] town center as a clean, safe, legible place.'[13] In dressing up and stepping out queer, the network uses the bodies of its members as billboards to create what Mary Ann Doane calls 'the desire to desire.'[14] As queer shoppers stare back, kiss, and pose, they disrupt the antiseptic asexual surface of the malls, exposing them as sites of any number of explicitly sexualized exchanges – cruising, people-watching, window-shopping, trying on outfits, purchasing of commodities, and having anonymous sex.[15]

The inscription of metropolitan sexuality in a safe space for suburban-style normative sexual repression is just one aspect of the network's critical pedagogy. In addition, mall actions exploit the utopian function of the mall, which connects information about commodities with sensual expressivity, and which predicts that new erotic identities can be sutured to spectacular consuming bodies. The Queer Shopping Network understands the most banal of advertising strategies: sex sells. In this, though, sex sells not substitutions for bodily pleasures – a car, a luxury scarf – but the capacity of the body itself to experience unofficial pleasures. While the network appears to be merely handing out another commodity in the form of broadsides about homosexuality, its ironic awareness of itself as being on display links gay spectacle with the window displays that also entreat the buyers. Both say 'buy me'; but the Queer Shopping Network tempts consumers with a commodity that, if they could recognize it, they already own: a sexually inflected and explicitly desiring body. Ultimately, the mall spectacle addresses the consumer's own 'perverse' desire to experience a different body and offers *itself* as the most stylish of the many attitudes on sale in the mall.

Queer Nation exploits the mall's coupling of things and bodies by transgressively disclosing that this bounded safe commercial space is also an information system where sexual norms and cultural identities are consolidated, thus linking it with Queer Nation's final frontier, the media. As it enters the urban media cacophony, Queer Nation scatters original propaganda in the form of graffiti, wheatpasted posters, and fliers into existing spaces of collective, anonymous discursive exchange. While the mall circulates and exchanges bodies, print media circulates and exchanges information in the most disembodied of spaces. Queer Nation capitalizes on the abstract/ informational apparatus of the media in a few ways, refunctioning its spaces for an ongoing 'urban redecoration project' on behalf of gay visibility.[16] First, it manipulates the power of modern media to create and disseminate cultural norms and other political propaganda: Queer Nation leeches, we might say, onto the media's socializing function. Second, Queer Nation's abundant interventions into sexual publicity playfully invoke and resist the lure of monumentality, frustrating the tendency of sexual subcultures to convert images of radical sexuality into new standards of transgression.

In addition to manufacturing its own information, Queer Nation's mass mediation takes on a more ironic Madison Avenue mode, 'queering' advertisements so that they become vehicles of protest against and arrogations of a medium that renders queerness invisible, sanitary, or spectacularly fetishized. More ambiguous than the tradition of political defacement from which it descends – feminist spray-painting of billboards with phrases like 'this offends women,' for example[17] – Queer Nation's glossy pseudoadvertisements involve replication, exposure, and disruption of even the semiotic boundaries between gay and straight. The group's parodies and reconstructions of mainstream ads inflect products with a sexuality and promote homosexuality as a product: they lay bare the queerness of the commodities that straight culture makes and buys, either translating it from its hidden form in the original, or revealing and ameliorating its calculated erasure. In short, the most overtly commercial of Queer Nation's campaigns, true to the American way, makes queer good by making goods queer.

One form this project takes is an 'outing' of corporate economic interest in 'market segments' with which corporations refuse to identify explicitly. The New York Gap series changes the final *p* in the logo of stylish ads featuring gay, bisexual, and suspiciously-polymorphous celebrities to a *y*. For the insider, these acts 'out' the closeted gay and bisexual semicelebrities the Gap often uses as models. But the reconstructed billboards also address the company's policy of using gay style to sell clothes without acknowledging debts to gay street style: style itself is 'outed,' as are the straight urban consumers who learn that the clothes they wear signify gay.

Whereas the Gap ads confront both the closetedness of a corporation and the semiotic incoherence of straight consumer culture, another series addresses the class implications of advertising's complicity in the national moral bankruptcy. A series of parody Lotto ads exposes the similarities and differences between the national betrayal of poor and of gay citizens. The 'straight' versions of a series of advertisements for New York's Lotto depict generic citizens of various assimilated genders and ethnicities who voice their fantasies about sudden wealth underneath the caption: 'All you need is a dollar bill and a dream.' The ads conflate citizenship and purchase, suggesting that working-class or ethnic Americans can realize the American dream through spending money. One of Queer Nation's parody ads shows an 'ordinary citizen' in one of the frank, casual, head and shoulders poses that characterize the real ads. The caption reads, 'I'd start my own cigarette company and call it Fags.' The Queer Nation logo appears, along with the slogan, 'All you need is a three-dollar bill and a dream.' Again, the ads link citizenship with capitalist gain, but the ironized American dream cliché also establishes the group's resistance to a liberal 'gay business' approach to social liberation, in whose view capitalist legitimation neutralizes social marginality. Queer Nation recognizes that the three-dollar bill remains nonnegotiable tender. The transformed caption reveals that the lottery's fundamental promise does not hold true for the nation's gay citizens in terms of the freedom to pursue sexual pleasure, which costs more than any jackpot or bank account has ever amassed.

In posing as a countercorporation, a business with its own logo, corporate identity, and ubiquity, Queer Nation seizes and dismantles the privileges of corporate anonymity.[18] It steals the privilege that this anonymity protects, that of avoiding painful recrimination for corporate actions. As it peels away the facade of corporate neutrality, Queer Nation reveals that businesses are people with political agendas, and that consumers are citizens to whom businesses are accountable for more than the quality of their specific products: abstracting itself, Queer Nation embodies the corporation. The Lotto ad finally promises an alternative to the capitalist dream-machine: its Queer Nation logo, juxtaposed against the 'All you need is a three-dollar bill and a dream' caption, appeals to the consumer to invest in its own 'corporate' identity.

The Queer Nation logo itself, then, becomes a mock-twin to existing national corporate logos: just as red, white, and blue 'Buy USA' labels, yellow ribbons, and flag icons have, by commodifying patriotism, actually managed to strengthen it, so does the spread of Queer Nation's merchandise and advertising expand its own territory of promises.[19] Because Gap clothes and lottery fantasies confer identities as much as flag kitsch does, Queer Nation has the additional power to expose or transform the meaning of these and other commodities – not simply through the reappropriation that camp enacts on an individual level, but through collective mimicry, replication, invasion of the pseudoidentities generated by corporations, including the nation itself.

Queer Nation's infusion of consumer space with a queer sensibility, and its recognition of the potential for exploiting spaces of psychic and physical permeability, are fundamental to its radical reconstitution of citizenship. For in the end, an individual's understanding of her- or himself as 'American' and/or as 'straight' involves parallel problems of consent and local control: both identities demand psychic and bodily discipline in exchange for the protection, security, and power these identities confer. If the official nation extracts public libidinal pleasure as the cost of political identity, queer citizenship confers the right to one's own specific pleasures. In the final analysis,

America, understood not as a geographic but as a symbolic locus in which individuals experience their fundamental link to 250,000,000 other individuals, is the most unbounded of the hyper-spaces we have been describing. The official transformation of national identity into style — of flag into transvestite 'flagness' — offers Queer Nation a seamless means of transforming 'queerness' into a camp counternationality, which makes good on the promise that the citizen will finally be allowed to own, in addition to all the other vicarious bodies Queer Nation has for sale, his or her mighty real, very own national body.

Notes

1   John D'Emilio, *Sexual Politics, Sexual Communities* (Chicago: University of Chicago Press, 1983), 216.

2   John D'Emilio, 'Capitalism and Gay Identity,' in Ann Snitow, Christine Stansell, and Sharon Thompson, eds, *The Powers of Desire* (New York: Monthly Review Press, 1983), 108.

3   Guy Trebay, 'In Your Face,' *Village Voice*, August 14, 1990, 36.

4   The 'Absolutely Het' series, parodies of the ads for Absolut vodka, were produced by the anonymous group OUTPOST.

5   Trebay, 'In Your Face,' 39.

6   The quote in the title to this section is from Deee-Lite, 'Try Me On, I'm Very You,' *World Clique*, Elektra Entertainment, 1990.

7   Marshall Kirk and Hunter Madsen, *After the Ball: How America Will Conquer Its Fear and Hatred of Gays in the '90s* (New York: Doubleday, 1989). Kirk and Madsen advise the gay community to present nonthreatening images of homosexuality to straight culture, a 'marketing campaign' designed to win mainstream approval for the bourgeois homosexual at the cost of eliminating drag queens, butch lesbians, transsexuals, and so on, from visibility.

8   For a discussion of the relationship between the trademark, commodity identification, and the colonized American body, see Lauren Berlant, 'National Brands/National Body: Imitation of Life,' in Hortense J. Spillers, eds, *Comparative American Identities: Race, Sex, and Nationality in the Modern Text*, Selected Papers from the English Institute (Boston: Routledge, 1991), 110–40.

9   A powerful and extensive exploration of the role of this 'stereotyped fantasy body' in the black gay voguing subculture is provided by Jenny Livingston's documentary *Paris is Burning*. See also Berlant, 'National Brands/National Body.'

10 On the history of the gay pride parade, see D'Emilio, *Sexual Politics*.

11 See Andrew Ross, *No Respect: Intellectuals and Popular Culture* (New York: Routledge, 1989).

12 See Richard Herrell, 'The Symbolic Strategies of Chicago's Gay and Lesbian Pride Day Parade,' in Gilbert Herdt, ed., *Gay Culture in America* (Boston:

Beacon Press, 1993). Herrell discusses how Chicago politicians annually assume at the parade psuedo-Irish last names such as 'Mayor Richard O'Daley.' The stigma attached to certain cultural groups might well be discerned by such a litmus test: the unthinkable prospect of 'Mayor Richard Gayley' suggests that there is as yet no such thing as 'honorary' symbolic homosexuality in the realm of the civic.

13 See Anne Friedberg, 'Flaneurs du Mal(l),' *PMLA* 106 (May 1991): 419-31. Whereas Friedberg analyzes the mall as a theater, an illusory and ultimately nonparticipatory realm, we would argue that 'mall erotics' extend beyond the consumer/commodity exchange she describes to include visual consumption of other people as products.

14 Mary Ann Doane, *The Desire to Desire* (Bloomington: Indiana University Press, 1987).

15 A letter in *Raunch* reveals that Southglenn Mall in Denver, Colorado, where guess-which-one-of-us hung out every Saturday for her entire adolescence, also used to contain one of the best arrays of glory holes in the country. Imagine my delight. Boyd McDonald, *Raunch* (Boston: Fidelity, 1990)

16 We first heard this phrase at Queer Nation Chicago, Spring 1991.

17 See Jill Posener's photoessay on the British and Australian feminist billboard spray-painting movement, *Louder Than Words* (New York: Pandora, 1986).

18 Paradoxically, actual corporations have in turn exploited Queer Nation/Gran Fury's recognizable style to produce mock-gay ads such as the Kikit billboard that portrays two 'lesbians' – actually an androgynous heterosexual couple – kissing.

19 The *New York Times* devoted a full section to paid advertisements supporting the Persian Gulf invasion and to commercial ads linking patriotism with purchase. Included were an ad for a Steuben glass flag paperweight, a Bloomingdale's spread saluting fathers' 'devotion to family and country alike,' and – in the most sinister pun of our times (apart from, perhaps, 'Saddamize Hussein') – a Saks Fifth Avenue ad captioned: 'A woman's place is in the home of the brave and the land of the free' (*New York Times*, June 9, 1991).

Chapter 18

Nelly Richard

from THE DIMENSION OF SOCIAL EXTERIORITY IN THE PRODUCTION OF ART

T HE CHILEAN ARTISTS THAT RICHARD describes left
institutional contexts to redefine 'the conditions of their creative participation in the behavior and discourses of everyday life.' They wanted to raise
the consciousness of would-be spectators and thus emphasized '. . . the *incompleteness* of the work . . . to solicit the viewer's intervention to complement
its meaning.' Note the resonance with Boal who wrote that the bourgeoisie
can present finished images of their world because it exists; those dissatisfied
with this world will make a theatre that is unfinished, a rehearsal for reality
(1979).

The various attempts to exceed the spatial limits of art by moving away
from the format of painting (the pictorial tradition) towards the use of
the landscape (the social body as a support for artistic creativity), represents
one of the most dynamic transformation of Chilean art over the last twenty
years.

The gradual shift in creative thinking from traditional formats and
supports to the use of the social landscape was anticipated, it must be said,
in the work of Francisco Brugnoli, or that of his students at the University
of Chile,[1] as well as in the work of the Brigadas Muralistas (Mural Artists
Brigade), comprising artists such as Balmes, Perez, Nunez and Matta. This
organisation, formed in the beginning as propaganda for Salvador Allende's
1958 and 1964 electoral campaigns, later on developed (and especially the

Brigada Ramona Parra of the Young Communists) a popular form of graphics to illustrate the political program of the Unidad Popular. Even though the Brigadas Muralistas were among the first to challenge the individualistic and fetishised type of pictorial gesture, and despite the fact that they used the city as background for their collective performances, they did not question the relationship between art and its power to reorganise society; they remained within a tradition of realism by making the image subservient to an ideological message. They treated the painted wall as a monument portraying the saga of the popular movement, by means of precoded figures which *addressed the social imaginary through the program of political representation*. In other words, here the function of art continued to express a pre-fabricated reality by *illustrating* its discourse or by dressing up its stated aims. This mural art neither reformulated the urban experience by relocating the parameters for reading walls as a text of the city, nor modified the casual perception that most citizens have of them given their restricted trajectory through a grid of monuments and institutions.

Despite the claims of the group CADA (Colectivo de acciones de arte – Collective for Art Actions),[2] which acknowledged the Brigadas Ramona Parra as 'their closest antecedent,' the actual performances carried out by them were different. The relationship between their art and its urban subject no longer took the form of a mural narrative of popular events. Rather, the group *redefined the conditions of their creative participation in the behavior and discourses of everyday life*. With CADA's 'art actions,' unlike the work of the Brigadas, the Chilean in the street no longer sees the ornamented walls as a space for graffiti or political propaganda, he is no longer a passive spectator of images but actively involved in the creative process: he becomes part of the living material of the work through his own interaction with it, by being urged to intervene in the whole network of social conditioning in which he is ensnared.

It was from Vostell, whose works were exhibited in 1977 at the gallery Epoca,[3] and his concept of 'found lives' or the aesthetic reprocessing of the coordinates of social existence, that the Chilean artists inherited their desire to confront the dead time of the museum picture with the *living time of an art that works with vital experiences*.

After the *Exposición de los derechos humanos* (Exhibition of Human Rights) at the Museum of St. Francis in 1978, the new work that evolved was based on a different dynamic of space and time, leaving the artwork unfinished. All the works of Rosenfeld, Castillo, Parada, the Taller de Artes Visuales, Codocedo and Jaar have open structures; they use biography or community events as living material so as to guarantee the *incompleteness* of the work and to solicit the viewer's intervention to complement its meaning.

The work which became the primary model for the new Chilean art after 1979 was *Para no morir de hambre en el arte* (Not to Die of Hunger in Art). This work came from the group CADA, which was initially composed of the artists Lotty Rosenfeld and Juan Castillo, the sociologist Fernando Balcells, the poet Raul Zurita and the novelist Diamela Eltit (hence the group's interdisciplinary composition and approach).

Para no morir was constructed from actual social events. It diagnosed the wants of the national body by using the symbol of milk to denounce poverty, hunger or other economic deprivations.

> The overall panorama of malnutrition or the lack of basic consumer or cultural goods is presented by this work in the following manner:
> – The CADA artists distribute powdered milk amongst families living in a shanty town on the edge of Santiago.
> – A blank page of the magazine *Hoy* is made available as another support for the work: 'Imagine that this page is completely blank / imagine that this blank page is the milk needed every day / imagine that the shortage of milk in Chile today resembles this blank page.'
> – A text recorded in five languages is read in front of the United Nations building in Santiago, thus portraying the international view of Chile as precarious and marginal.
> – In the art gallery Centro Imagen there is placed an acrylic box containing some of the bags of powdered milk, a copy of the *Hoy* issue, and a tape of the text read in front of the UN. The milk is left in the box until it decomposes. A statement on top of the box reads: 'To remain here until our people receive the proper amount of food. To remain here as a symbol in reverse of our deprived social body.'
> – Ten milk trucks parade through Santiago from a milk factory to the Museum, thus highlighting for the passerby the general lack of milk.
> – A white sheet is hung over the entrance to the Museum, both as a symbolic closing down of the establishment and as a metaphorical denunciation of continuing hunger.

Thus the interventions staged by this work, and documented with photography and video, tried to modify both the customary perceptions of the city, by the unexpected sight of a parade of milk trucks and by altering the facade of the Museum to attract attention to the social landscape and the way that it is continually covered up or remains unnoticed – and the social norms which regulate the behaviour of the citizen, by intervening in the field of social productivity: simultaneously, in the milk industry, in the networks controlling the distribution of magazines, in the institutional space of art discourse, in the interrelationship of signs of 'art' and 'life.' Another collective work performed by CADA in 1981 was *Ay Sudamerica!* (O, South America!). Here they again used the concept of interfering in the models of everyday life prescribed by society, but this time by using a 'social sculpture'[4] to designate the degree to which their art practices could reappropriate interpersonal relations in the community in new aesthetic terms.

Ay Sudamerica! involved three aeroplanes dropping leaflets over poor sectors of Santiago. These leaflets included the following statement: '. . . the work of improving the accepted standard of living is the only valid art form / the only exhibition / the only worthwhile work of art. Everyone who works, even in the mind, to extend his or her living space is an artist.'

The proposition contained in the leaflet was also stated in the magazine *Apsi*. Again, art forces the gaze to unlearn what the press habitually teaches it. Through this new poetics of word and image, the discourse of the imaginary is able to collide with the discourse of political contingency.

Both *Para no morir* and *Ay Sudamerica!* were shaped by the *multiple social dimensions of their artistic framework*. The Chilean subject postulated by them is inserted in everyday community activities, while the works themselves incorporate this subject in their own procedures for socially and politically redefining the real.[5]

These two works from the group CADA significantly influenced the new work of artists like Castillo, Donoso, Saavedra and Parada, with their selection of the city and its social landscape as a support for art. Such artists operated in a space that provided an alternative to that of the art institution.[6] Hence their critique of the museum or galleries, which were accused of endorsing 'the bourgeois ideological space and the way that it separates art from reality' and 'the elitism assigned to artworks by the authorities' (Balcells).

This questioning of the official status of the museum and its discourse on art was formulated, for example, in the 1981 performance piece *Tránsito suspendido* (No Through Traffic) by Carlos Altamirano. But CADA's metaphorical closing down of the sanctuary of art best epitomizes the attempt to challenge such patrimony or preservation of the past from outside the museum through the interweaving of creative and social space–times. In the work of CADA *the city becomes its own museum, but only in the sense that its repressive structure is revealed by altering the landscape through art actions*.

The institution of the Museum is based on material structures which ideologically condition the value of artworks, in particular those which endorse their ahistoricity and give them the illusion of eternity, placing them outside time by neutralising all trace of the concrete historical circumstances under which they were produced. These were the sort of structures which CADA's 'art actions' tried to dismantle, by reasserting the subject's actual physical participation in the construction of the artwork; the actions refused to become trapped in the past under the *extemporaneous gaze* of the museum visitor. Thus for these works, to question the Museum meant that they also had to question the rituals of perception consecrated by it in the ceremonial hanging of works, as well as the effect of confinement imposed on them by its institutional apparatus.

Both the Museum and the Gallery are inherently criticized by works displayed outside, and which contest 'the private ownership of the salon work' or 'the increasingly ritual nature' of its contemplation in those privileged areas[7] defined by CADA as a 'concealed bomb': 'the gallery is therefore absolutely analogous to that certain spatial notion we have of ourselves.' It is not insignificant that one text from the group CADA condemning the *self-referentiality* of the gallery space, published on the occasion of an exhibition by Codocedo at the gallery Sur in 1983, was called *Contingencia* (Contingency). This radical critique of the art concentrated in galleries happened to coincide with the celebration of ten years under the military regime (September 1983). At this time, collective works emerged in which the artists 'chose to address the walls of the city and voice their protest with the brief and simple cry, No †, which encouraged others to fill in the missing word: for instance, no more hunger, no more pain, no more death' (*Hoy*, September 1983). The walls, whose use was forbidden throughout the regime, were reconquered by the CADA artists as places for a popularly committed art, but in a way that linked up with the earlier political *testimonials* of the Brigadas Muralistas, thus eradicating the difference between the two. This phase of production corresponding to the work of urban intervention came to an end because of the absence of new propositions and because, after 1982, the young artists returned to painting and to the gallery circuit. The retreat of art practice once more to the picture or to institutionalized spaces also coincided with the failure of democracy, and destroyed any illusion of change. The *private*, or the subjective pictorial imaginary, replaced *the public* as the scene of art production. After all that effort to establish the outside as a place for art, the return to the picture protected the artists against their *personal disillusionment* with History. Thereafter, only a few works were concerned with the social space: for example, the 1983 *Paisaje* (Landscape) by Francisco Brugnoli and Virginia Errazuriz, or the 1984 *¿Qué hacer?* (What to Do?) by Gonzalo Diaz and Justo Mellado, tried to *invert* this space by theoretically relating the outside (the social) to the inside (the gallery, whose discourse of art about art is tautological). These works attempted to metaphorically redefine the conventions of the gallery, either by parodying its architecture or by calling its visual topology a 'landscape.'

On the other hand, Lotty Rosenfeld, who has insistently remained outside the protected spaces of the institution, continues to desecrate the cult of art and its market fetish by utilizing the streets. Since 1979, she has traced crosses on the road as a way of altering the codes of urban movement: in the desert of Northern Chile, in front of the White House in Washington, on the border between Chile and Argentina, on the Pacific Coast, etc.

> The dividing lines on the street are traversed by a white cloth to form a cross or chain of crosses in order to transgress the road signs which regulate the traffic.
>
> (Balcells)

By rearranging the marks which regulate the social landscape, the work of Rosenfeld exposes the ideal expressed by a linear system of urban transportation. Her work not only symbolically alters this space by converting the minus sign into a plus sign, *thus contravening the one-way traffic of meaning*, but it also violates the grammar of order imposed by the inner network of social communication. She brings the road sign and its legibility into crisis by reconjugating the vertical and horizontal lines as a (feminine) act of dissidence.

The crosses of Rosenfeld take as their premise the fact that the road sign seems the most inoffensive of signs, and submit it to inversion. This not only makes the traveller alert to the possibility of violating the geography of transportation, but also has an even greater metaphorical impact in the Chilean context. Her gesture of *intersecting the code* is disobedient in that it provides a basis for the rearticulation of meaning.

Notes

1   'The mural work by college students was just as relevant . . . Some of Fernan Meza's students from the School of Architecture in Santiago, and those of Francisco Brugnoli from the School of Fine Arts, were the ones who went out into the city and intervened in its visual codes, along with their teachers and tutors.' Osvaldo Aguilo, *Plastica Neovanguardista* [pamphlet, privately published in Santiago].

2   CADA editorial in *Ruptura* (August 1982).

3   After years of being ignored internationally because of the ban by the left on the Chilean military regime, and given that most of the cultural production going on inside Chile was suspected, both by the left and by the Chilean exiles, of complicity with the administration, Vostell was perhaps the first avant-garde artist of any international standing to accept an invitation to visit Chile. Undoubtedly his favorable response to the invitation issued by Ronald Kay was due to this personal contact, and to the fact that he was assured that he would not be involved in any official matters. Even so, one should stress the courage of his decision to bring to Chile works that ran the risk of being misinterpreted by the left.

4   'We understand by social sculpture a work or art action that tries to organise, by means of intervention, the time and space in which we live, firstly to make it more visible, and then to make it more livable. The present work (*Para no morir de hambre en el arte*) is a sculpture since it organises the material of art in terms of volume, and it is social to the extent that such material is our collective reality.' *La Bicicleta*, 5 (December 1979).

5   'Their proposal is to rescue the latent creativity of the landscape and its social use, and to provide mechanisms for a possible reappraisal of it . . . thus creating an essential basis for experiencing what until now has escaped our attention.' Fernando Balcells, 'Acciones de arte hoy en Chile' (Art Actions in Chile Today), *La Bicicleta*, 8 (December 1980).

6   '. . . we are witnessing the construction of an "art gallery" in the street, or inversely the destruction of that concept by the use of open and public spaces as markers or receivers of the artwork, whose ultimate aim is not personal profit but to remain in the eye and memory of the passerby who moves daily through the open landscape. The landscape is thus transformed into a creative space which forces the passerby to change his point of view, which obliges him by and large to question his surroundings and the conditions of his own becoming.' Diamela Eltit, 'Sobre las acciones de arte: Un nuevo espacio crítico' (Concerning Art Actions: A New Critical Space), *Umbral* (1980).

7   'One thinks of the Gallery as a conventional place. Outside the Gallery . . . art generates its pre-history, that is its most transgressive history, which it doesn't even have the words to express. This pre-history is the gesture, the physical and also emotional work from which the photo album or the gallery always profits. Every photo album is the non-savage part of the savage, its most innocent exhibition.' CADA, 'Una bomba cerrada' (A Concealed Bomb), catalogue, Galeria Sur, 1983.

Work cited

Boal, Augusto (1979) [1974] *Theater of the Oppressed*. New York: Urizen.

Chapter 19

Cindy Rosenthal

LIVING ON THE STREET

Conversations with Judith Malina and Hanon Reznikov, co-directors of the Living Theatre

I N THIS INTERVIEW, ROSENTHAL QUERIES Malina and Reznikov about the company's three decades of street performance.

Founded by Julian Beck and Judith Malina in 1947, the Living Theatre is internationally known as the longest extant avant-garde theatre company, committed to creating political (pacifist, anarchist) theatre that is also poetical. After Beck's death in 1985, Hanon Reznikov became co-director of the company with Malina.

ROSENTHAL: Judith, when we spoke on the phone about this interview, you wanted it understood that from your perspective, 'street theatre is not inside theatre work done on an outside platform.' How does that statement reflect on the Living Theatre's creation of and participation in street theatre?

MALINA: The street is a great mystical venue. It belongs to everybody, it belongs to nobody. The street is a passageway from one place to another where people don't want to stop. The street has its own rules. Each street is different from every other street as one person is different from another person. Each street has its own political and spiritual ambiance. When we come to bring an idea to the street we come saying, 'We are now infringing on your territory because we want to tell you about the possibility of peace, of not having a tyrannical government, of finding other ways to organize our lives, of getting rid of some serious abuses. We want to bring this message to you.'

The aesthetic of street theatre is based on trying to understand the language of the people on that street. We need to create plays that can speak on many levels to many people. Perhaps the most outrageous example of this is when we did street theatre in Brazil. We had to make a theatre that spoke of revolution to the people but would not be comprehensible as such to the authorities. Brazilian revolutionaries used to say, 'The success of the revolution depends on the stupidity of the police.'

No one is really going to stop and hear the whole story. In the play we're doing now, *Not in My Name* – I like to talk about what we're doing now – we play in the middle of Times Square on an island between one side of 46th Street and another and there's an enormous amount of traffic surrounding us. We play on this triangle, the hypotenuse of which is a walk-through, and people who want to, stop. Very few people watch the whole play. People watch from one traffic light to the next. Some people stay a couple of traffic lights. But many see the words EXECUTION TONIGHT and ABOLISH THE DEATH PENALTY on our large banners and some see a group of people in black clothes singing (from Eugene Debs) 'where there is a lower class, I am of it,' ending with 'while there is a soul in prison I am not free.' Others might hear the story of the man who is being killed that night, who he is, how old he is, what the sentence was, what he is accused of, what his mother said, what his sister said, and then they might cross the street. Many people say abusive things. Some people stop and add to our play by shouting, 'Burn 'em all. Burn 'em all!' But what happens or may happen afterwards is much more important than what can be developed in that moment on the street. We end the play by going up to strangers saying, 'I swear to you I will never kill you. Can you promise me the same?' We get a wide range of reactions from 'Fuck Off' to 'I want to see those people dead' to 'You have no compassion for the victims' families.' Sometimes these people stand around and talk to each other. Then they go home and they talk to other people. Our hope is that this leads to further dialogue. And that is why we stand in the middle of the street – to initiate, to provoke that dialogue.

ROSENTHAL: Where did the idea for *Not in My Name* come from?

MALINA: Hanon has long thought that the death penalty is socially structured in such a way as to be a fundamental apology for killing. Everyone is taught that it is all right to kill. It's the same with War. Everyone who kills feels that she/he is justified. The death penalty supports all the excuses people make for killing each other. And focusing on the death penalty – rather than war – is an important revolutionary strategy for peace. It is the one we could *win*. We can stop the death penalty. If we say you've got to stop poverty, or you've got to stop war – and of course you've got to say both those things all the time – people feel helpless. How could we possibly stop war? But doing away with the death penalty *is* possible, it's economically desirable – we *can* protect ourselves from people we're afraid of without resorting to murder. And we need a victory. Our greatest victory right now is in the field of vegetarianism. So many young people are waking up to the fact of this kind of killing. So, getting back to your question, Hanon felt this was a very important idea to explore, he said he was going to write it, but he didn't write it, and finally he said to me, 'You write it.' I wrote it after many months of discussions with the company. It was part of the collective creation process.

ROSENTHAL: Why do you perform *Not in My Name* in Times Square?

MALINA: We play it in Times Square where we have the least attentive, the most hostile and the most transient audience. We could do it in a park such as Washington Square – where we get more attention. But the intention – although it is not at this point being fulfilled – is when people are killed by the state, to go to the center of your city and demonstrate against it. If you want to use our text, or any part of it, we'll send it to you. It's free for anyone to use, to rewrite, to rework – come to the center of your city, anytime the state commits capital punishment.

ROSENTHAL: Can you say more about this one-to-one connection you're striving for?

MALINA: For me, very personally, the goal is to diminish the difference between public and private utterance, between what I would say to you in our most private moment and what I would say in public. I say to diminish it, because of course this difference exists, but the goal is to overcome it. My personal relationship with you, whether you are a stranger I have never seen before or my close friend, is a political act. Good politics should be about constantly evaluating our relationship to each other. There's so much bread – shall we ship it there or ship it there – what about the people that are eating it, making it, transporting it, what are their feelings about it, what are their needs, what are their desires? The same questions you would ask your lover you must ask socially. It's always just you and I – this is the basis of Buber's *I and Thou*. It's always human to human, one to one.

ROSENTHAL: Where do these one-on-one dialogues in *Not in My Name* go?

MALINA: We work hard to sharpen our one-on-one discourse. Company members have questions they don't know how to answer and they bring them back to the group. For instance, 'You know this guy said to me, 'My brother was murdered by some crazy guy and if I found him . . .' What should I say to such a person?'

ROSENTHAL: What should you say?

MALINA: I think you have to show a certain sympathy to such a person. And first reassure him that you do understand his suffering, but the only way to end the suffering so that other people will not have to suffer as he suffers is to stop this idea that's it's all right to kill sometimes. Because an unbearably gruesome thing happened, this man now thinks he can do another gruesome thing and that this in some way equalizes that. It really doesn't. It just sets up a climate of fear and anger. It sets up two classes, a criminal class and a victim class.

ROSENTHAL: So when you come to the moment in the play when you as individual actors ask direct questions to individual spectators – 'I swear I will never kill you. Can you promise me the same?' – how many in the company are doing the asking? How many spectators do you approach, or need to find?

REZNIKOV: Anywhere from eight to twelve, usually. Maybe twenty to fifty people stop to watch it at any given moment. I think as many as 500 people are aware of it, if you count vehicles passing by. For me as holder of the banner, it's very important that people see this being announced publicly and being made the subject of some kind of dramatic presentation in the middle of Times Square. Even people who don't hear a word of it, understand that there's a group of people out there motivated by opposing the fact that it's happening tonight.

ROSENTHAL: How do people join the *Not in My Name* company?

REZNIKOV: We did a series of workshops announced in various media in the downtown scene and at colleges, and through the War Resister's League. The notice would read something like, 'Join the Living Theatre in a workshop leading to the performance of a street play to protest the death penalty.' It was seeking people who were interested in a theatrical protest against the death penalty. It was not reaching out to theatre people as much as it was to activists. A few who joined us were theatre students who are politically minded, because there happen to be, thank God, some of those.

ROSENTHAL: Looking back on the Living Theatre's work on the street, which piece or project connects most directly to *Not in My Name*?

MALINA: The General Strike for Peace was the street theatre project we've been involved with that has had the most impact. The first call for the General Strike for Peace took place in '61, and the Living

Theatre organized it. A genuine call for a strike that resulted in a week-long, world-wide series of actions for peace. There were demonstrations in Mexico, in Germany, in Asia. Julian Beck and I and one or two members of the strike committee traveled all over the world to organize it about two years ahead of time so that it was a coordinated action. The General Strike for Peace was a precursor of the die-ins and the be-ins of the sixties. Bread and Puppet was also working on the theatricalization of protest at the time, as was the San Francisco Mime Troupe.

ROSENTHAL: Tell me about the actions of the General Strike for Peace.

MALINA: We got together five thousand dollars for a full page in the *New York Times* which printed in small letters the program of the First General Strike for Peace. We distributed a six-language leaflet, which was written by a very talented literary committee much influenced by the style of Paul Goodman who gave us our slogan, 'Do not be discouraged that we are few, we shall be many.' Anybody could go on strike, you could go on strike a thousand different ways. We suggested the various actions that people could take. We asked people to send in strike pledges at the bottom of the leaflet.

ROSENTHAL: How many did you receive?

MALINA: About 1200 or so. We had actions in all parts of the city. We ended with a huge party in the Village called 'The Declaration of Peace' at which Bob Dylan sang 'Blowin' in the Wind' for the first time as his contribution. There was a great deal of enthusiasm for this kind of non-violent dramatic expression of outrage.

Not all the street theatre we've done was like the General Strike and *Not in My Name*. *Not in My Name* derives from demonstrations, and has certain earmarks: You have to have a leaflet explaining what you're doing; you have to have a sign saying what you're doing or you'll be misrepresented in the press, if not misunderstood by passersby. You have to have a very specific, issue-oriented commitment in a demonstration. *The Legacy of Cain* was in a simple sense a protest but in a much more theatrical form. *The Legacy of Cain* comes from Sacher Masoch's name for his oeuvre about our legacy as dominants and submissives. In the Living Theatre's *Legacy of Cain* we did many different kinds of plays; only a few of them took demonstration form.[1]

In Brazil, in the *favelas*, or shanty-towns, above Rio de Janeiro, *The Legacy of Cain* plays were performed in a clandestine manner, out of necessity. Everything that was performed had to be approved beforehand by the cultural commission. Hence, in the favelas we did not present a script. We came in, performed and left before the authorities could find us. The police were actually reluctant to enter the favelas – they are very much a people's enclave. For the favela work we went in and asked the people one simple question: 'Tell me something about your life here in the favela.' The people spoke to us and we recorded them. At the beginning of our play, we amplified this tape of their voices. All the people in the community gathered around to hear their own voices and the voices of their relatives and neighbors. We used this device to get the people's opinions. We needed to move in and out quickly. We would also do theatrical exercises without words – we began one revolutionary play by scrubbing the floor of the piazza with actual soap suds.

In the schools we did present a script (*Six Dreams about Mother*, 1971). There the tactic was different. When a child, tied to his or her mother and teacher with crepe paper bands, flew through the air into the arms of dancing children and the crepe paper bands broke in mid-air – the teacher understood what it meant, the mother did not. The authorities did not.

ROSENTHAL: Could you talk a little bit about the development of your street work in Pittsburgh? About how you used the street as a research site –

MALINA: We came to Pittsburgh after I compiled, with the help of Karen Malpede, an intricate history of the labor movement in Pittsburgh, which the whole company studied. Groups of three to five people in our company went together into various sections and organizations of the city: boys' sports club, the children's school, the local jail, the women's clubs, I joined the police league. Each group would try to learn what they could and bring back information. This went on for a year.

ROSENTHAL: The two venues where you performed in Pittsburgh – outside the steel mills and inside the urban ghettos – how were those performances different?

REZNIKOV: There was a particular challenge, or thrill, performing at the gates of the big steel mills when the shift was changing. People came out of the gates and all of them saw some of the play and maybe ten percent or 200 people stuck around for the whole forty minutes or whatever it was and talked with us afterward. In the poor, black community there was a parallel involvement but it was more like a street fair/festival atmosphere. Actually, we were like a spaceship from Mars landing there with *The Money Tower*.

ROSENTHAL: So how was audience response different?

MALINA: In front of the steel mills, we constructed a forty-foot tower very rapidly and were able to take it down very rapidly and skillfully while singing songs . . .

REZNIKOV: The dismantling was the denouement of the play.

MALINA: The dismantling, this denouement, was done with great grace and skill. The steel workers – who regularly use their bodies in a physical way – had a certain respect for us.

REZNIKOV: In *The Money Tower* each of these audience groups was represented within the play itself. The worker level was a steel mill. The biomechanical representation of proletarian labor we did was based on etudes devised with the help of people who knew steel-making very well. There was a Plexiglas furnace in the middle of the steel-making level. An elevator ran up the tower. Part of the workers' job was to pull the elevator up and down. The elevator brought raw materials out of the mines, which was the bottom level, where the black people and the poor people of the Third World were trapped in a place where they couldn't stand up.

MALINA: It was too small to stand. But at the same time, they had to hold up the whole tower.

ROSENTHAL: And this was meant to represent the Third World.

REZNIKOV: The poor and unemployed.

ROSENTHAL: What was on top?

REZNIKOV: Me (laughter). Me and Mary Mary as the capitalist class. The least numerous and most powerful in silver jumpsuits and tails manipulating a Plexiglas world bank. The stuff coming up the elevator was transformed from raw materials on the bottom level into goods by the steel workers. The middle-class level packaged it, the military level protected it, we got it and it turned into cash. And we would stuff this Plexiglas world bank with it.

ROSENTHAL: Could you compare the response from the blue collar workers at the steel mills to the spectators in the ghetto?

REZNIKOV: I think the poor people were much more available, more like the Brazilians. And the steel workers, although there were some progressive ones among them, were often what we called a 'redneck' crowd – very suspicious of long-haired hippies . . .

MALINA: I don't know. I was standing down there among them. You were up there on the tower. They were interested and attentive. They weren't like the people in Times Square. They weren't hostile to us.

REZNIKOV: Steve Ben Israel (Living Theatre company member) heard some rednecks say they were going to get their guns and blow away some heads.

MALINA: I thought they said they were going to get some gasoline and burn us.

REZNIKOV: One way to measure audience participation in Pittsburgh was the scene in *Six Public Acts* in which we stuck our fingers with surgical lances and smeared our blood on a monument or wall of an institution that we protested. We invited the audience to join us and –

MALINA: A lot of people gave their blood on the street. You couldn't do that now.

ROSENTHAL: It seems that the work in Brazil was more participatory – having the children enact their dreams as you did, for instance . . .

REZNIKOV: Those were workshop-type performances.

ROSENTHAL: Can you talk about *Waste*, which was the largest, longest street performance of the Third Street period [New York City, 1989–91]? Where did you perform *Waste*?

REZNIKOV: Mostly around the neighborhood of the theatre (East Third Street, between Avenues A and B) but also in community gardens and public parks.

ROSENTHAL: Was it done, as in *Six Public Acts*, in stations, in processional style?

REZNIKOV: No. It was done on two facing platforms with an open space in between. We alternated the stages scene by scene, sometimes using both of them.

ROSENTHAL: *Waste* had a positive critical response, yes?

REZNIKOV: Because it was the only big street play, it was the only one we invited press to. We also did *Turning the Earth*, about creating a community vegetable garden out of vacant land – both in Pittsburgh and on the Lower East Side. And we did *Tumult or Clearing the Streets*, which was a response to two events that happened more or less at the same time – the massacre at Tiananmen Square and the closing of Tompkins Square Park [in New York]. *Tumult* was about the use of public spaces.

ROSENTHAL: What is the difference between performances in the park and on the street?

REZNIKOV: There's an Artaudian feel to performing on the sidewalk or on a street that's quite unlike the protected feel of the park, which is a *homo ludens* space, a play space.

ROSENTHAL: By Artaudian, you mean –

Figure 19.1 The Living Theatre performs *Six Public Acts*. Ann Arbor, May 1975 (photo by Ron Blanchette).

REZNIKOV: You're doing something that runs counter to the accepted or expected notion of what a sidewalk is for. There's a tension produced by your passage through it that the audience perceives, that excites them. Sometimes it puts them off and makes them want to walk a little bit faster and move to the other side of the street. Depending on their mood, or what part of their biorhythm they're in – and how well we're doing our job, as well.

MALINA: The most important thing is that the LT was there, was open, as were many other community centers, during the struggle for Tompkins Square Park, during the crisis. Speaking of timing, street theatre beckons.

ROSENTHAL: There is an execution tonight?

MALINA: There is an execution tonight and we will be out in the street.

Note

1   *The Legacy of Cain* was first performed in Brazil (1970–71), then in the US (1973–75) and finally in Europe (1975–80).

Chapter 20

Alice Cook and Gwyn Kirk

from TAKING DIRECT ACTION

T HE 'DIE-INS' DESCRIBED BY Cook and Kirk are remi-
niscent of US civil rights movement 'sit-ins' – efforts by African
Americans to integrate lunch counters in the 1950s by literally sitting down
and attempting to order food until being dragged away by police. Indeed,
the history of non-violent direct action from Leo Tolstoy through Gandhi,
Martin Luther King, Jr., the Greenham women and beyond, is an abundant
source for further research into street performance.

In August 1981 a group of women, children and a few men, marched from
Cardiff to Greenham Common in protest at NATO's decision to site cruise
missiles at Greenham. Much of South Wales is within a 200-mile target area
based on Greenham Common, and it was women living in Wales who initiated
the march. Some stayed and set up the peace camp. Other women in Wales
decided to take supportive action, telling people about the peace camp and
the issue of cruise missiles.

[. . .]

The first large action initiated by Greenham women in London was the
die-in outside the Stock Exchange on 7 June 1982, coinciding with President
Reagan's visit. Helen John from Greenham spoke to a massive CND rally in
Hyde Park the day before, and invited women present to participate in an
action in London the next day:

'You're within the 200-mile area where these weapons are going to be put and that makes you not a defended area, but a target for certain. We're taking an action tomorrow. We're going to institute a die-in. That's a very simple thing to do – you just lie down and die, because that's exactly what's going to happen if these missiles come here.'

Many of the women who responded to this invitation had not been associated with Greenham before. However, it was clear to them that larger and larger demonstrations were not actually changing anything.

Groups of six or seven women met in Hyde Park to discuss the action, what we felt about participating, the legal consequences, and what each woman would do – who would actually 'die', hand out leaflets or act as observers and peacekeepers. By the end of the afternoon about eighty women had gone through this process. Many women had arrived knowing no one, and by the end had a strong sense of being included within a small and supportive group. Early the next morning, those who had decided to do the action met again in Jubilee Gardens, and the overall feeling was of strength and confidence mixed with varying degrees of apprehension. The police had gathered in large numbers in Jubilee Gardens and followed our small groups to the underground station.

The aim was to lie down and 'die' across five roads around the Stock Exchange, thus effectively blocking all traffic going through the City. The Stock Exchange – one of the world's financial centres – was chosen to highlight the connection between the vast sums of money spent on nuclear weapons and the consequences in human lives. The road each group of women would lie across had been decided beforehand, and when we arrived at the Stock Exchange, women quickly lay down. In each group there were women handing out leaflets and trying to talk to passing office workers, explaining why the action was taking place: that the women were lying down to symbolise the one million who would be killed instantly in a nuclear attack on London. It was an attempt to confront people going to work, doing their job, with the realities behind the nuclear threat.

Reactions of passers-by to this action were predominantly hostile. Most people resented their morning routine being disrupted in this unforseen way. One man snatched a woman's bundle of leaflets, tore them up and proceeded to stamp on them. The leaflet read:

In front of you are the dead bodies of women.

Inside this building men are controlling the money which will make this a reality, by investing our money in the arms industries who in turn manipulate governments all over the world and create markets for the weapons of mass destruction to be purchased again with our money.

President Reagan's presence here today is to ensure American nuclear missiles will be placed on our soil. This will lead to you lying dead.

> As women we wish to protect all life on this planet. We will not allow the war games, which allegedly protect some whilst killing others, and lead to nuclear war which will kill us all.

Motorists shouted and swore at the women. It was hard for the leafleters to keep calm and keep talking. Some people, however, took the leaflets and showed support for what was happening.

The police, arriving on the scene rather late because their vans had been held up by the traffic jams, found the whole situation rather confusing. They stood about for some time, giving women conflicting stories: some were told they were arrested, others just dragged away. In the end nine women were arrested, seemingly at random. The police obviously believed that they should make some arrests, and it did not seem to matter whom they chose.

We had planned a time limit of fifteen minutes on the action. As it happened, we had underestimated the scale of disruption that seventy well-organised women could create by peacefully lying down in London streets. Once the action was over, it was possible to quietly disperse back into the rush-hour crowds. We made our way back to Jubilee Gardens in small groups, because it was important to meet together afterwards to make contact with each other again and to learn how to be more effective in the future.

If one person on their way to work had suddenly made the connection between the money spent on arms and the deaths of millions, then the action had been a success.

[. . .]

[Testimony of Susan Lamb, April 1983]
When we heard that the women from the march to Greenham Common had stayed there and set up a peace camp outside the main gate, we decided to let people know what was happening by mimicking their action: we decided to live on the streets at Porth Square, Rhondda Valley, Wales. The press should be getting information about nuclear weapons across to people, but it's obvious that other people have to do their job for them. We must cut across all the misinformation which, either by accident or design, we are given. On the first day at Porth Square we didn't know what to expect. But we were in the street, and quite soon people's curiosity got the better of them and they started reading our leaflets and talking to us, even if at first they thought of us as a loony bunch of women. We went carrying four flasks. By the end of the first day we had twenty-five flasks lined up that had been given us. A man across the street brought us a bottle of whiskey; his wife had not let him go to sleep until he brought something to keep us warm. Old people and children were the first to respond to us being there. Several old people came up and blessed us, saying they'd lost brothers in the first world war, sons in the second, and thank God someone was doing something to stop there being another war which would kill us all. We went out

of desperation and we came away knowing we could do it, because of the response of people – the way they opened their minds and talked. Every night people would come and talk to us. Perhaps they wouldn't go to meetings, but they could easily approach an individual and talk about their fears and what they could do. We can't leave everything up to committees, we must take action for ourselves. Women are often intimidated by organisations like CND [Campaign for Nuclear Disarmament]. They could identify with us and would come and talk. Local people were very supportive. The action started a chain of letters to papers, and opened up discussion. The fact that people knew us all reinforced this.

PART FOUR

UTOPIA

Introduction

Utopia is a critique of the official history of a society . . .
Carnival is an old and persistent way of acting out utopia.

Michael Bristol

THE ESSAYS IN THIS SECTION describe performances that
critique official social organization by offering the experience of an alternative mode. They merge desire with reality by staging themselves in streets and other public venues and transforming would-be spectators into participants. So, for example, the Chinese pro-democracy movement occupied Tiananmen Square, the seat of the Chinese government. Hitler chose the medieval city of Nuremberg, associated with Germany's former mercantile strength and boasting old Teutonic architecture, to stage his annual party rallies.

Mikhail Bakhtin resuscitated the idea of carnival as a critique of the status quo. Describing such events as playful, non-hierarchical and sensorily excessive, Bakhtin conjectures that

> The carnivalesque crowd in the marketplace or in the streets is not merely a crowd. It is the people as a whole, but organized in their own way . . . outside of and contrary to all existing forms of the coercive socio-economic and political organization, which is suspended for the time of the festivity. The festive organization of the crowd must be

first of all concrete and sensual . . . The individual feels that he is an indissoluble part of the collectivity.

(1968: 255)

Lest we over-romanticize the utopian, however, this section begins with an essay on the Nazi Nuremberg Party rallies. While hardly carnivalesque in the utter order enacted at the yearly Party gatherings between 1923 and 1939, they were as much an enactment of utopia as were the anarchistic impulses of 1960s counter-cultural French, Americans and Brits, also represented here.

The inevitable question raised by carnival in the context of social change is what happens after the celebration? Is carnival, or any acting out of utopia, just a letting off of steam? Is there a way to capture that energy, stay grounded in that longing, make permanent change? In his essay in this section, Richard Schechner concludes that carnival can critique but not replace the status quo. But the last piece in the section suggests another possibility. Welfare State International, one of a number of theatre companies who, after years of wanderings and 'one night stands,' put down roots in a community, is following a different model than carnival as a temporary suspension of the status quo. They are looking to weave celebrations into the everyday life of their towns. The jury is still out.

References

Bakhtin, Mikhail (1968) *Rabelais and His World,* trans. Helene Iswolsky, Cambridge, MA: MIT Press.
Bristol, Michael (1973) 'Acting Out Utopia,' *Performance* 6, May/June.

Chapter 21

David Welch

from *TRIUMPH DES WILLENS* (*TRIUMPH OF THE WILL,* 1935)

WELCH'S ESSAY IS AN IMPORTANT reminder that radical performance encompasses left- and right-wing politics. Broadcasting the Aryan ideal to the masses present as well as thousands of others who saw Riefenstahl's film, the 1934 Nuremberg Party rally is a paradigm of street theatre as media opportunity.

In December 1941, at the height of Germany's military success, Goebbels modestly informed his officials in the Propaganda Ministry about the services he had rendered over the years towards the Party's current triumphs. Two factors that he stressed were, first: 'the style and technique of the Party's public ceremonies. The ceremonial of the mass demonstrations, the ritual of the great Party occasions', and, secondly, that through his 'creation of the Führer myth Hitler had been given the halo of infallibility, with the result that many people who looked askance at the Party after 1933 had now complete confidence in Hitler.'[1] Referring to the leader cult in National Socialism, Walter Hagemann has said that the relationship between the leader and those he leads can be 'that of a father, of a comrade, of a despot and of a demi-god.'[2] This total identification of the led and their leader was the main objective behind Goebbels's manipulation of the Führer cult in Nazi propaganda throughout the Third Reich.

[. . .]

In her published account of the filming, Leni Riefenstahl revealed that 'the preparations for the Party Convention were made in connection with the preparations for the camera work.'[3] Siegfried Kracauer concluded that 'this illuminating statement reveals that the Convention was planned not only as a spectacular mass meeting, but also as spectacular film propaganda.'[4] Riefenstahl's staff consisted of sixteen cameramen, each with an assistant. Thirty cameras were used to film the events together with four complete sound-equipment trucks. Altogether, 120 assistants were assigned for the filming, and new techniques of wide-angle photography and telescopic lenses were employed to scan the crowd's reactions. The result was a transfiguration of reality which purported to assume the character of an authentic documentary. Not only were scenes rehearsed beforehand, but it was not a direct record as the sequence of events in the film are manipulated in order to build up an image of leader worship. Its political mission was to show, as the *Völkischer Beobachter* put it, 'the order, unity, and determination of the National Socialist movement . . . a documentary record of the unanimous loyalty to the Führer and therefore to Germany.'[5]

The ritual of the mass meetings was an important element in the projection of the Führer cult. They also served as means of demonstrating the sense of national community and the desire for order. Hitler knew this, as the extract from *Mein Kampf* shows:

> Mass assemblies are necessary for the reason that, in attending them, the individual . . . now begins to feel isolated and in fear of being left alone as he acquires for the first time the picture of a great community which has a strengthening and encouraging effect on most people. . . . And only a mass demonstration can impress upon him the greatness of this community . . . while seeking his way, he is gripped by the force of mass suggestion.[6]

The importance of the visible display of power as an intermediary between the persuasiveness of emotional appeals and pressures through the evoking of fear is reflected in the Nuremberg rallies.[7] For in a totalitarian state, as Ernst Bramsted observed, 'it is not enough to have power, it has to be advertised continuously. In other words, the possession of power is nothing without its display.'[8] Eugen Hadamovsky, who was later to become the Third Reich's National Broadcasting Director, wrote in 1933: 'All the power one has, even more than one has, must be demonstrated. One hundred speeches, five hundred newspaper articles, radio talks, films, and plays are unable to produce the same effect as a procession of gigantic masses of people taking place with discipline and active participation.'[9]

[. . .]

In projecting the image of the strong leader to an audience that had come to associate the Weimar Republic and the Treaty of Versailles with national ignominy, *Triumph des Willens* represented the triumph of self-realization over the hegemony imposed by foreigners. Hence, the opening of the film begins with a slow fade-up of the German eagle and the title *Triumph des Willens*, with the caption:

Twenty years after the outbreak of the First World War,
Sixteen years after the beginning of Germany's time of trial,
Nineteen months after the beginning of the rebirth of Germany,
Adolf Hitler flew to Nuremberg to muster his faithful followers . . .

The Nazi ethos was, as we have seen, anti-individualist and therefore anti-democratic. *Völkisch* thought had always been preoccupied with myths and symbols. The irrationality that was central to *völkisch* experience led to a belief in magic, represented by the old German gods of the *Volk*.[10] The leadership ideal became part of this complex *völkisch* thought, in which a revolutionary leader would emerge and bring about a *völkisch* revolution. According to Hitler, this meant that the nation should also make 'sacrifices for their great men as a matter of course. It's the great men who express a nation's soul.'[11] The strength of the nation was therefore seen to lie in the submergence of the individual will in the will of the nation, as expressed by Adolf Hitler. William Shirer witnessed the 1934 Nuremberg Rally and noted the willingness of the audience to surrender their independence of thought and action:

'We are strong and will get stronger,' Hitler shouted at them through the microphone, his words echoing across the hushed field from the loudspeakers. And there, in the flood-lit night, jammed together like sardines, in one mass formation, the little men of Germany who have made Nazism possible achieved the highest state of being the Germanic man knows: the shedding of their individual souls and mind – with the personal responsibilities and doubts and problems – until under the mystic lights and at the sound of the magic words of the Austrian they were merged completely in the Germanic herd.[12]

Leni Riefenstahl has stated that the 'triumph' depicted in the film was twofold: the triumph of a strong Germany and the triumph of the will of the Leader.[13] These themes were conveyed by distinct stylistic device, each commanding the guise of documentary 'reportage.' The text of the film consists of policy speeches made by Hitler and his Party Leaders and oaths of loyalty from his faithful supporters. [. . .] The monumental style of *Triumph des Willens* was meant to show Hitler, in Erwin Leiser's words, 'as a new Siegfried and his supporters as extras in a colossal Wagner opera, an anonymous mass completely under his sway.'[14]

Although the sequence of events was changed, *Triumph des Willens* is structured in the literal documentary narrative and yet it avoids the monotony of describing such uniform events. By her skillful use of ordinary cinematic devices, Riefenstahl successfully orchestrates the motifs that are to be highlighted. These motifs include: ancient buildings, statues, icons, the sky and clouds, fire, the swastika, marching, the masses, and Hitler. As one critic has observed, the central theme they develop is that 'Hitler has come from the sky to kindle ancient Nuremberg with primeval Teutonic fire, to liberate the energy and spirit of the German people through a dynamic new movement with roots in their racial consciousness.'[15]

The opening sequence of the film celebrates the apotheosis of Hitler. It is worthy of particular attention as it is a statement of the key theme in *Triumph des Willens*. Through a break in the clouds we see an aeroplane waving through the white masses and suddenly appear in a clear sky. Medieval Nuremberg with its towers and spires wrapped in the mist appears below. As the plane becomes more defined the overture to *Die Meistersinger* slowly merges into the Horst Wessel Lied, just as the old Germany has given way to the new. By means of magnificent aerial photography the streets of Nuremberg are lined by thousands of marching Germans all in perfect formation, creating the first geometric pattern of humanity to be shown in the film. The plane eventually makes contact with the earth and taxis to a halt. The German people await their leader. Hitler emerges, in uniform, to acknowledge the cheers of the crowd who surge forward to greet him.

Throughout the film, Hitler is always seen in isolation photographed from below so that he appears to tower above the rest of the proceedings. Furthermore, it is not without symbolic meaning that the features of Hitler invariably appear against a backdrop of clouds or sky. The triumphant journey from the airport through Nuremberg is used to juxtapose the essential loneliness of the Führer with shots of the masses. The camera is placed behind Hitler, concentrating on his arm extended in the Nazi salute. There follows a montage sequence of Hitler's arm and individual faces that are picked out of the crowd together with the close-ups of Nuremberg's great statues looking on approvingly. As if to reinforce the message that the Saviour has descended from the heavens and is among his people, Hitler's car stops for a mother and her little girl to present flowers to the Führer.

Whenever Hitler is shown in the film he is depicted as a lone figure whereas the individuality of the people is submerged in the symmetry and order that characterizes the mass scenes. Riefenstahl conveys this idea of *Ordnung* (Order) by a whole series of rigidly straight columns of marching units surging across the screen in a succession of different patterns and combinations. An important element in the creation of this ritual is the use made of banners and flags in Nazi pageants. Throughout all the ceremonies flags proliferate, but there is one scene of special significance that encapsulates the mysticism and the linking of past and future that was so typical of the Movement. It concerns the ceremony of the 'blood flag,' the official flag stained with the blood of the Nazi martyrs during the abortive Munich beer-hall *putsch* of November 1923.[16]

The ceremony starts in the Luitpold Stadium where columns of the SA (97,000) and the SS (11,000) form giant rectangles beneath a sea of banners and flags. The camera is placed high up on one of the special towers constructed for the film. Stephen Roberts, who was in the stadium, observed what happened next:

> Before addressing them, Hitler solemnly marched up to the sacrificial fires that paid homage to those who had died for the movement. It was the only moment of quietness in the whole week. For what seemed an interminable time, three men – Hitler, Himmler, and Lutze – strode up the wide path that clove the brown mass in twain and, after saluting the fire, marched back. It was a superbly arranged gesture. Those men represented individualism as against the solid anonymity of the massed Brownshirts; they stood for leadership as against the blind obedience of the people.[17]

Considering that the rally was taking place only a few months after the Röhm purge, in which the SA were brought to heel, it is not surprising to discover that the occasion was used to emphasize the unity of the Party. At this solemn moment Lutze (the new head of the SA) moves towards the rostrum on which Hitler is standing and reiterates that the Party's troubles are now over:

> LUTZE: My Führer, just as in the old days we carried out our duties, so we shall wait upon your orders in the future. And we cannot do anything other than follow the orders of our Führer, Adolf Hitler, Sieg Heil! Sieg Heil!

Hitler then speaks. He stands alone on the rostrum, silhouetted against the sky:

> HITLER: Men of the SA and SS, a few months ago a black cloud rose over the movement, but our Party knew how to overcome it as it knows how to overcome everything else. So it will be with every rift that appears in the fabric of our movement. It stands as solid as this block of stone and there is nothing in Germany that can break it . . . Only a madman or a confirmed liar can think that I or anyone else could have any intention of destroying the links that we joined over the years with such difficulty. No, comrades, we stand firm together here in Germany, and we must stand firm together for Germany. Now I hand over the new flags to you, convinced that I am handing them over to the most faithful hands in Germany . . . And so I greet you as my old, faithful men of the SA and SS. Sieg Heil!

The ceremony comes to an end with the consecration of rows of banners and flags as Hitler solemnly touches these new flags with the old 'blood flag'

Figure 21.1 Labor Service Day ceremonies at the Nuremberg Party Rally of 1938. National Socialism was promoted among industrial labor by inviting thousands of workers from all over Germany to attend at the party's expense.

– a form of ritualistic baptism. Cannons are fired as he presents each new flag to the storm-troopers. The scene ends with a seemingly endless procession of flags passing down the stadium and up past both sides of the rostrum where Hitler stands saluting them.

What is so remarkable about this episode with the parade of flags, and also a similar scene where they are borne into the Congress Hall for the final speeches, is that one rarely glimpses those people who are bearing them. Close-up plunges the viewer into the midst of the forest of flags that seem to move of their own accord, and in the longer shots the camera angle obscures any human presence. Furthermore, this feeling of being caught in almost constant motion has a hypnotic effect. An impartial British observer at the Rally later wrote: 'It was at times a struggle to remain rational in a horde so surcharged with tense emotionalism.'[18]

On the previous evening the Party leaders came forward to pay their tribute to Hitler. Goebbels's speech is of particular interest because it reveals his attitude towards propaganda and elucidates his fear that such films (like *Triumph des Willens*) could crystallize latent opposition to the manifest crudities of National Socialism:

> GOEBBELS: May the bright flame of our enthusiasm never be extinguished. It alone gives light and warmth to the creative art of modern political propaganda. It arose from the very heart of the people in order to derive more strength and power. It may be a good thing to possess power that rests on arms. But it is better and more gratifying to win and hold the heart of the people.

Bismarck once stated that 'enthusiasm cannot be pickled like herrings,' but he did not foresee the extent and power of the mass demonstrations that the Nazis incorporated in their art of pageantry. Intrinsic in the ritual of the mass demonstrations were the quasi-religious liturgical responses. An excellent example of this can be found in *Triumph des Willens* in the sequence where 52,000 *Arbeitsdienst* (members) have gathered on the Zeppelin Field, holding spades, to affirm their faith in Hitler. Marshaled in ranks beneath the great German eagle mounted over the stadium, the ceremony is conducted like a religious service:

> HIERL [*leader of the Labour Front*]. My Führer, I announce that 52,000 workers have answered the summons.
>
> HITLER. Hail, worker volunteers!
>
> CORPSMEN. Hail, Our Leader! Corps, Take up arms! [*drumrolls*]
>
> CORPSMEN. Where do you come from, comrade? – I come from Friesia. And you, comrade? From Bavaria. And you? From Kaiserstuhl.

175

And you? From Pomerania . . . from Königsberg, Silesia, Baltic, Black Forest, Dresden, Danube, from the Rhine, and from the Saar . . .

CORPSMEN. [*in unison*]. ONE PEOPLE, ONE FÜHRER, ONE REICH!

ONE. Today we are all workers together and we are working with iron.

ALL. With iron.

ONE. With mortar.

ALL. With mortar.

ONE. With sand.

ALL. With sand.

ONE. We are diking the North Sea.

ALL. We greet you, German worker.

ONE. We are planting trees.

ALL. Forests everywhere.

ONE. We are building roads.

ALL. From village to village, from town to town.

ONE. We are providing new fields for the farmer.

ALL. Fields and forests, fields and bread – for Germany!

SONG. We are true patriots, our country we rebuild. We did not stand in the trenches amidst the exploding grenades but nevertheless we are soldiers.

VARIOUS. From one end of Germany to the other. Everywhere, in the north, in the west, in the east, in the south, on the land, on the sea, and in the air. Comrades, down with the Red Front and reaction.

ALL. You are not dead, you live in Germany!

HITLER. My comrades, you have now presented yourselves to me and the whole German people in this way for the first time. You are representatives of a great ideal. We know that for millions of our countrymen work will no longer be a lonely occupation but one that gathers together the whole of our country. No longer will anybody in Germany consider manual labour as lower than any other kind of work. The time will come when no German will be able to enter the community of this nation without first having passed through your community. Remember that not only are the eyes of hundreds of thousands in Nuremberg watching, but the whole of Germany is seeing you for the first time. You are Germany and I know that Germany will proudly watch its sons marching forward into the glorious future.

SONG. We are the soldiers who work.

ALL. Sieg Heil!

This affirmation of faith in the Führer reaches its crescendo in the closing ceremony held in the Conference Hall. Once again the camera links the crowd to the key icons in Nazi ritual and to Hitler himself. This technique is used throughout the film to relate the masses to specific symbolic objects. Riefenstahl frames the crowds which are dominated by huge banners and then moves deftly from the swastikas to eagles and then back to the people. The effect is one of total identification between leader and led. A massive demonstration of individuality submerged in wave after wave of fanatical devotion. In his final speech of the Rally, Hitler builds up his audience to a point of exultant fanaticism; he is both calm and impassioned: 'The nervous century has reached its end. There will not be another revolution in Germany for the next 1,000 years.' He is loudly acclaimed as the camera pulls back to reveal waves of outstretched arms hailing their Führer. Rudolf Hess, the Deputy Leader, comes forward, waiting for the applause to stop. Eventually he brings the 1934 Rally to a close by declaring: 'The Party is Hitler. But Hitler is Germany, just as Germany is Hitler. Hitler! Sieg Heil!'

Banners are raised once again and the Horst Wessel Lied swells up on the sound-track. *Triumph des Willens* ends with a dissolve from a large swastika to marching storm-troopers who represent its power incarnate. The marching columns are shot from an angle which juxtaposes them not merely against the sky, but leading up to it. The final image is the subliminal ascension of the German nation to the heavens from which the Führer came in the beginning. It symbolizes the final consummation of the triumph of the will, and in the process Leni Riefenstahl achieved the definitive obliteration of the division between myth and reality.[19]

[. . .]

Uniforms, bands, flags, and symbols were all part of the Nazi propaganda machine to increase the impact of strong words with powerful deeds. This is the fundamental rationale behind the constant display of Nazi symbols in a film like *Triumph des Willens*. The determination to be and feel united was not enough; the Nazis had to give public testimony to this unity. The Nuremberg Rallies were carefully staged theatrical pieces devised to create such an effect. 'I had spent six years in St. Petersburg before the war in the best days of the old Russian ballet,' wrote the British Ambassador to Germany, Sir Nevile Henderson, 'but for grandiose beauty I have never seen a ballet to compare with it.'[20] The nature of the Nazis' message was such that concrete demonstrations of physical strength gave a visible reinforcement to the spiritual message the propaganda was trying to instill. Such emotional manipulation worked best at these ceremonies where the individual participant in the ritual, fanatically moved by Hitler's rhetoric and swayed by the crowd, underwent a metamorphosis – in Goebbels's famous phrase – 'from a little worm into part of a large dragon.'[21]

Notes

1   R. Semmler, *Goebbels, The Man Next to Hitler*, entry of 12 December 1941, pp. 56–7.

2   W. Hagemann, *Vom Mythos der Masse* (Heidelberg, 1951), p. 63, quoted in E. K. Bramsted, *Goebbels and National Socialist Propaganda 1925–45* (Michigan, 1965), p. 203.

3   L. Riefenstahl, *Hinter den Kulissen des Reichsparteitagfilms* (Munich, 1935).

4   S. Kracauer, *From Caligari to Hitler. A Psychological History of the German Film* (Princeton, 1947 and 1973), p. 301.

5   *Völkischer Beobachter*, 2 September 1933. This included an interview with Riefenstahl.

6   A. Hitler, *Mein Kampf* (London, 1939), pp. 397–8.

7   The stage-management of the Party Congresses has been well analysed by H. T. Burden, *The Nuremberg Party Rallies, 1923–39* (London, 1967). Bramsted, p. 451

9   E. Hadamovsky, *Propaganda und nationale Macht, Die Organisation der öffentlichen Meinung* (Oldenburg, 1933), p. 2.

10   For a more detailed discussion see, G. Mosse, *Nazi Culture: Intellectual, Cultural and Social Life in the Third Reich* (London, 1966), pp. xxvii–xxviii.

11   H. Trevor-Roper, *Hitler's Table Talk, 1941–44* (London, 1973), p. 206.

12   W. Shirer, *Berlin Diary 1934–41* (London, 1972), p. 25.

13   Riefenstahl, p. 102.

14   E. Leiser, *Nazi Cinema* (London, 1974), p. 25.

15   See K. Kelmann, 'Propaganda a Vision – Triumph of the Will,' in *Film Culture*, Spring, 1973, p. 162–4.

16   The 'blood flag' was in fact the bullet-riddled flag that Andreas Bauriedl had allegedly held until he was struck down at the Feldherrnhalle in 1923.

17   S. Roberts, *The House that Hitler Built* (London, 1937), p. 140.

18   E. Amy Buller, *Darkness Over Germany* (London, 1943), p. 166.

19   Cf. Kelmann, p. 164. It is ironic therefore that such a powerful film could be ridiculed as easily as it was in Charles Ridley's Movie-Tone newsreel, *Germany Calling* (1941).

20   N. Henderson, *Failure of a Mission* (London, 1940), p. 71.

21   J. P. Goebbels, *Der Kampf um Berlin. Der Anfang*, (Munich, 1932), p. 18.

Chapter 22

Jean-Jacques Lebel

NOTES ON POLITICAL STREET
THEATRE, PARIS: 1968, 1969

THE 'EVENTS OF MAY' 1968 in Paris, initiated by students against conservative university policies, spread to workers striking for higher wages and better working conditions. Lenora Champagne captures its utopia-like atmosphere:

> The events of the Barricades, where a festive spirit reigned and collective decision making and animated discussion took place; the formation of action committees which solved problems as groups and aided striking workers and their families; the instances of anonymous collective creation of wall posters [. . .] – these provided the crucible of action where themes and structures of the May Movement could be tested. There was a briefly-lived utopia, which took the form of an 'anti-society' or 'counterculture' opposed to existing social relations and proposing new ones.
>
> (*Sub-stance* 18/19, 1977: 59)

Here Jean-Jacques Lebel, one of the key players in student street actions, emphasizes the connectedness of casting off (social) oppression and (personal) repression.

From the early twenties, when the Paris Dadaists enacted the *Trial of Maurice Barrés* in the St. Julien le Pauvre Park, to the recent theatrical events of a political nature performed in the streets, there is a long story of militant outsiders and anti-artists for whom the cultural industry is just another aspect of capitalism and, as such, must be destroyed. On the other hand there are non-political Fluxus-type events, arty-farty happenings, and street shows such as those organized by the Groupe de Recherche de l'Art Visuel which claim to be 'unintentional' and not aimed at the destruction of the existing social structure. These events are still concerned with the history of art, of theatre, or of culture in general and tend to be quickly absorbed into the art market, the 'avant-garde' department of Madison Avenue, and wind up as the latest form of entertainment for Jackie Onassis. It is important not to confuse the art of revolution with its commercial and bourgeois imitation.

1968

The May Revolution dynamited the limits of 'art' and 'culture' as it did all other social or political limits. The old avant-gardist dream of turning 'life' into 'art,' into a collective creative experience, finally came true. All of a sudden the corruption and stupidity of the old world's 'cultural specialists' became obvious to everyone. Along with the rest of the power elite – the bankers, the army chiefs, the managers and tycoons – the cultural industry moguls are the first to be eliminated by any liberation movement. They should know when to disappear.

Exciting socio-dramatic events occurred in the streets of Paris in May, primarily because the 22nd of March Movement made it clear to everybody that 'power is in the streets' – or, as the Motherfuckers put it: 'the streets belong to the people.' The first stage of an uprising (the barricades, the mass demonstrations, the street fighting between the government forces and the radicals, as well as such events as the burning down of the Stock Exchange, which occurred on May 24th), the first stage of *any* revolution, is always theatrical. The May uprising did not turn into a full-blown civil war or a traumatic blood bath comparable to what happened in Mexico in October when the grenaderos murdered at least 200 students. Nevertheless it certainly was a surprising chapter in a class war which most people thought long over and finished. The May uprising was theatrical in that it was a gigantic fiesta, a revelatory and sensuous explosion outside the 'normal' pattern of politics. Ten million workers went on strike in mid-May. It was the largest general strike in the history of industrial civilization and the one that came the nearest to upsetting the entire economic structure. Most plants were occupied by the workers, the universities by the students, and, at one point, the government and the ruling class were powerless. Then the so-called 'Communist' party and its unions came to de Gaulle's rescue and accepted a ridiculous compromise. The workers were persuaded to go back to work by their bureaucratic 'leaders.' One by one the factories were re-occupied by the police and their 'rightful owners.' Once again the social-democratic and counter-revolutionary 'Communist' party had saved the capitalist system from collapsing under the pressure of the workers and students. It was a very close shave – and the living proof that a full-scale economic and social revolution is possible in any industrial country, regardless of what the reformist and Stalinist theoreticians pretend.

Such was the context of the deep psychic change experienced by hundreds of thousands in May. The results of this individual as well as social change were immediate: human relations were freer and much more open; taboos, self-censorship, and authoritarian hangups disappeared; roles were permutated; new social combinations were tried out. Desire was no longer negated but openly expressed in its wildest and most radical forms. Slavery was abolished in its greatest stronghold: people's heads. Self-management and self-government were in the air and, in some instances, actually worked out. The subconscious needs of the people began to break through the ever present network of repressive institutions which is the backbone of capitalism. Everywhere people danced and trembled. Everywhere people wrote on the walls of the city or communicated freely with total strangers. There were no longer any strangers, but brothers, very alive, very present. I saw people fucking in the streets and on the roof of the occupied Odéon Theatre and others run around naked on the Nanterre campus, overflowing with joy. The first things revolutions do away with are sadness and boredom and the alienation of the body.

Street theatre as such started to pop up here and there in mass demonstrations, such as the 13th of May, which gathered more than a million people. Large effigies appeared of the CRS (French riot police), of de Gaulle and other political clowns. Short, funny theatrical rituals were performed around them as they burned. When the officially subsidized Odéon Theatre was occupied by the movement, many small groups of students and actors began to interpret the daily news in the street in short comic dramas followed by discussions with the passing audience.

1969

The main problem, then as now, is to propagandize the aims and means of the revolutionary movement among those millions who, while not actually being hostile, have not yet taken part in the action. Since the mass media are totally controlled by the State, all they pour out are lies befitting the State's psychological warfare. French public opinion is manipulated into submission with techniques similar to those used by Franco or Stalin, if more 'liberal' (i.e., clever). Communication is strictly one way: from the top down. Newspapers, leaflets, handmade or printed posters, and movies (modestly distributed because of police censorship) proving insufficient to inform people, let alone to help them *express themselves*, we are trying to use street theatre as a means to provoke encounters and discussions among people who usually shut themselves off from each other.

The project we have just worked on was the preparation of the anti-imperialist week preceding Dirty Dick Nixon's visit to de Gaulle. The mass of the French people are unaware of the political and economic penetration of American capitalism in Europe and in the Third World; so we devised a campaign on this subject. Some groups destroyed obvious symbols of what Malcolm X called *dollarism*: the offices of IBM, American Express, Pan American Airways, TWA, etc. By coincidence the composer Xenakis, who works for IBM, came to lecture at Vincennes a few days before Nixon's arrival. 'All I am interested in is beautiful music,' said he. Rotten tomatoes took care of him. But no music, however 'modern,' goes anywhere near the beautiful noise of an expensive computer used by the army being broken to bits by a bunch of happy kids. Other groups gathered around the idea of using street theatre to provoke free discussions and awaken people to the fact that imperialism is present in their daily life. Besides, we had been tired of the more conventional militant means of expression ever since we realized that the revolution, even in its less glorious preparatory work, must be fun to do.

Our group was made up of about forty students from Vincennes University. One had some previous experience in 'theatre,' two or three had worked in movies. All the others were totally inexperienced and were brought together mostly by their desire to work out some different means of political activity. Our orientation was agit-prop, yet we wanted to be creative and not just limited to old political clichés – above all we considered 'theatre' only as a means of breaking down the Berlin Wall in people's heads and helping them out of their state of passive acceptance. We didn't give a shit about 'art' – we were interested in sabotaging capitalism by helping to blow its arsenal of images, moods, perceptual habits, and tranquilizing illusions of security.

Most of the students involved were bored by the sociology, the philosophy, and the economics they were more or less studying and were certainly hip to the meaninglessness of the 'knowledge' they were supposed to be acquiring. So we started out by having several long talks on the political and personal state of emergency we were, and are, living in. A few of us had heard of experiments in political street theatre made in Frankfurt by the German SDS or by other such groups in London, New York, Rome, and San Francisco. Nobody had actually seen any 'guerrilla theatre' though. Some were familiar with the Living Theatre but criticized it as too 'arty' or 'not directly political enough' or 'non-violent' (the company was admired more as an anarchist community than as a theatre group). Actually no one had a definite idea of how or where to start and it took some time to work up the idea of theatrical cartoons on the subject of imperialism. Finally we cut four archetypal characters out of our mental storybook:

The Third World Peasant (the immediate victim of imperialism).
The Guerrillero (the peasant turned revolutionary).
The Ugly White Man (Nixon, the Ruler, the Wall Street King).
The Army Officer (General Motor, the capitalist cop).

Then we stuck together a synopsis of straightforward actions – not really a storyline but a series of simple ideograms – something like frame-by-frame shots. No dialogue since we would be working in noisy subway stations and streets, but we wrote some phrases and words on pieces of cardboard which were brought out during certain actions or yelled out during a demonstration. When needed, the costumes were exaggerated and funny. The general outline, which varied according to circumstances and mood, usually ended with General Motors being killed by the Guerrillero and the Ugly White Man being killed by the rebelling peasant, who seizes the UWM's money and burns it or distributes it to everyone (the bystanders yelling: 'Long live the Workers' Councils! Long live libertarian socialism!' etc.).

While the four actors are performing, about five others kneel in a circle around them to clear the small space which they need. Meanwhile about ten other people are busy putting up posters and painting slogans on as many walls as possible in the immediate vicinity. Six or eight others stand by to participate in the discussions or to protect the actors in case of trouble with the police. The group has on occasion used collective self-defense so as not to let any of its members get busted – in such cases it also depends on the help of the audience and bystanders – since it is politically important not to let the police interfere with the 'play' or discussions. As I write this the piece has been performed eight times in the subway and once in the street. The piece lasts only about two minutes but it is not uncommon for the discussions to go on for more than an hour, vigorously and passionately. These free discussions enable many who would not 'normally' dare to do so to transgress the law of silence and accomplish direct communication (similar to what happened in May when the streets were liberated for a while of the Police State's rule). We consider this a modest but valid answer to the problem of information and communication since the people who partake in these impromptu discussions usually blast off on their particular experiences in whatever here and now situation they are alienated by: *their* factory, *their* office, *their* school, how the union bureaucrats betrayed *them*, how *they* think *they* should get rid of the owners and run the factory. The debate often centers on reform vs. revolution, on whether to work within the system or to overthrow it. The conversations often get quite technical. It is interesting that such a large number of the working population actually is aware of the revolutionary movement, its motivations and problems. This indicates that more people expect another revolution, soon, than one would think: 'But this time it will be a real one, we will go all the way, we will take it into our own hands, we won't let the social-democrats and the bureaucrats fuck it up, we won't give back the factories we occupy . . .' These words spoken by a young steelworker after one of our performances last week made us think that even theatre can lead to revolution – if that's what you really want it to do.

Chapter 23

Eugenio Barba

from LETTER FROM THE SOUTH OF ITALY

THE BARTERING OF PERFORMANCE THAT Barba describes is utopian in the non-hierarchical value it places on local culture. These exchanges were radical in the deeper level of contact that they facilitated, in contrast to the status quo, and to the extent that the company used them as stepping stones to more long-lasting change.

In Spring 1974, Odin Teatret left its home in Denmark and settled in Carpignano, a small village in southern Italy. This new geographical and cultural environment had a shattering impact on the group, throwing it into many unexpected circumstances. With this sojourn, which lasted five months, began Odin Teatret's 'open' period, its open air performances and its awareness of itself as a micro-culture which could be 'bartered.'

[. . .]

One evening, after about a month in Carpignano (until then we had lived in almost total isolation, concentrating on our work) we decided to visit some friends from the University of Lecce who had come to stay in the same village. We took our musical instruments and left our quarters.

It was the first time that we had appeared in the village in a compact group with musical instruments and the multicolored clothing we used in our training. It was also the first time, in so many years of theatre work, that we found ourselves face to face with people on the street. Previously,

Figure 23.1 Odin Teatret actor in southern Italy (photo by Tony D'Urso).

we had been alone in our work rooms or at seminars among a few attentive and interested persons.

People immediately began to follow us, asking us to play. We arrived
at our friends' house but they were not in. Without intending to, we found
ourselves in the open, in a public square, surrounded by many people waiting
for us to do something. We had our backs to the wall and so began to play:
Scandinavian folk songs mingled with vocal improvisations as used by our
actors in their training.

We sang and played for about an hour. And what surprised us most, at the end, was not the long applause of the public ('What had Odin actors become: a casual group of musicians?'), but the fact that some people said to us: 'Now you must hear *our* songs.' They began to sing: work songs, songs with the special rhythm that accompanies the movement of the tobacco and olive harvests, and also songs of unhappy love and of death. From this improvised situation was born our idea of the 'barter.'

[. . .]

When rumors of a foreign theatrical group spread to other localities around Carpignano, young people came and asked us to go to them. We answered frankly that we were not philanthropists, that no one likes to work for nothing, that we wanted compensation, but that we did not want money. We wanted them to present themselves to us in the same way we presented ourselves to them, with their songs and their dances. These young people often answered that they did not know how to sing, nor did they know the songs of the place. Sometimes they said that there were no traditions in the locality. We then asked them to seek out the old people, suggesting that they go to the taverns where the old people meet and learn songs from them, or else invite the old people themselves to come into the village square to sing.

[. . .]

During the five months of our stay in Carpignano, 'barter' enlivened the entire region. If we brought our songs, our dances, our parades to a village, they were able to give us in exchange something of the same kind, or else a group of them would come to us in Carpignano, or maybe go to another place, where another group had to reciprocate or go elsewhere in their turn. The last three months were a lively 'barter' among peasants, workers, and students who went to present themselves reciprocally in the village squares with their own culture.

There was no professional theatre. Yet the theatrical situation existed: a point in time that permitted a gathering together, the occurrence of situations involving unknown people who made an impact and attracted other people to them.

A small group of foreign actors, seemingly not well grounded in social and political questions, had destroyed the theatre, but they had brought to light the ore hidden in the mine.

But can one go further? Can one transform the 'barter' from a cultural phenomenon into something that will leave a mark on the political and the social situation of the place? After many experiences, the 'barter' reminded me of the body of an octopus without tentacles, a little pulsating sack that emits coloring material which momentarily seems to change the color of the water, but then vanishes, disperses. How can tentacles be given to this little sack, tentacles capable of clinging to a small piece of rock and breaking it off?

Thus it was that in the following year, in 1975, returning to Carpignano and later moving to the mountains of Sardinia, we tried to make tentacles grow that would take hold and remain after our parting. We demanded not only a 'barter,' we asked the group that had invited us which problem in their village they most wanted to solve. The answers were many and varied.

Then, as a condition of our presence, we insisted on mobilizing more than musicians or people who sang. In Monteiasi, near Taranto, in southern Italy, a group of young people had rented a room at their own expense and had brought some of their own books there with the intention of creating a library for everyone, something that had always been lacking.

When we went to Monteiasi, in addition to the 'barter,' we asked the people who wanted to attend our dances to bring a book. It was paradoxical: why not pay in money instead of coming with a book? What were these written pages, which were alien to the peasants, yet which now permitted them access to the entertainment? It was our desire to support those who wanted to make their village aware of the usefulness of something that was apparently superfluous. The books were brought to the library at the end of the evening. That dark little room now became something very clear in the memory of many who attended. But in doing this, where were we going?

And we who are not missionaries, what did we really receive in exchange? How can theatre tangibly affect something which is outside of theatre? How can it open a breach – in deed, not in words – in the wall which divides us from others, but nevertheless protects us and allows us to live freely?

To do this, we must resort to humble crafts: things on which we can really make our mark are always much smaller than those we can discuss. Even so, trying always to break out, we run the risk of losing our way.

[. . .]

At Gavoi, a small village in the interior of Sardinia, a group of young, leftist workers and shepherds told us how they lacked money to publish information on the condition of the workers in a nearby factory. We told the population that, in addition to the 'barter,' we were interested in knowing more about their living conditions and had asked the group of young people to gather material about the place. We asked the population to help them discharge their obligation to us. In this manner, the villagers cooperated toward the collection of this information, which was then distributed among them.

In every place there was a different form of compensation, adapted to what the people of the place felt as a need, which they would then try to fulfill even after the theatre had left.

Revolutions do not happen in this way, nothing apparently changes. But it is the only possibility that the little sack of the theatrical octopus has to grow a tentacle that grasps, hoping that other tentacles will begin to grow, take a hold on the rock and finally succeed in shaking it.

At Ollolai, a village even smaller than Gavoi, they told us of their wish to open a small archive of the local traditions that seemed threatened by extinction, and collect old musical instruments, local legends and biographies of the old people. So we knew what to ask for barter. In these unknown places, among these uncelebrated people, will the actors lose the drive they seem to possess? Will they lose the intransigent commitment to their own art that seems to give them bearings and which allows them to present themselves to others only at the summit of their work, of their own experience?

In our last production it was as if seven young people had abandoned the skin of their being as actors. As crabs who have lost the shelter of their shells, they were nevertheless able to survive the panic of becoming a parcel of white and rosy flesh, at the mercy of pain that could be inflicted at the slightest touch. Their almost unnatural nudity drew our looks and made us want to trample on them and to protect our hands. They were shaken by their passions, by the memory of a security now lost, and by a longing for a new one. On their bodies, the slightest tensions could be distinguished. The interior volcano, seeking to be rid of its fire, made them palpitate, seemed to want to burn their fragile flesh. However, despite the embarrassment, almost the horror these crabs roused, we felt extremely close to them: paradoxically strangers in this unknown landscape, in a group and yet in deep solitude, they moved forward as if they wanted to become human.

[. . .] If you came here now, into the mountains of Sardinia, you would see the actors of the Odin running through the streets and squares, like figures imagined by a bizarre painter. Are they players on tour only for their daily bread and for the applause of the audience, or are they *Alvars*?

The Hindu *Alvars* profess that divinity does not exist, that hope does not exist, that all is illusion. In the search for a truth beyond all this, they perform acts disapproved by all society, which make a scandal of them and isolate them. But they are the *fools of God*, and their conflicting passions in search of a unity fall into a realm which society respects: religion.

Within the realm of theatre, the actors present themselves as strolling players, as tightrope-walkers, as beings of ridicule, and the people laugh and applaud. But sometimes their laughter freezes, when the player abandons the show of his virtuosity and almost shamelessly disowns the existence of any divinity, disowns his profession, seeks to go amok, as if controlled by a searching will that refuses to be walled up by the applause of the encircling audience.

Now, dances and parades: the masks are like crusts on the faces of our actors. Soon, in their new production, the layers that cover them will melt again. The mad horse will be left free to fly and fall, pursuing its visions.

Chapter 24

Abbie Hoffman

AMERICA HAS MORE TELEVISION
SETS THAN TOILETS

Abbie Hoffman, who personally embodied
the playful and anarchic aspects of carnival, here refigures the media
as America's main street, the conduit of symbolic action capable of reaching
the most people.

Valentine's Day had special significance. For its celebration I concocted a gift
of love, compliments of the counterculture. Three thousand persons selected
at random from the phone book were sent a well-rolled marijuana cigarette
with a card saying: 'Happy Valentine's Day. This cigarette contains no harmful
cancer-causing ingredients. It is made from 100 percent pure marijuana.'
Directions followed on how to smoke it, so the recipients could cut through
all the baloney and make up their own minds. A postscript warned: 'Oh, by
the way, possession of the item you now hold in your hand can bring up to
five years in prison. It matters not how or from whom you got it.'

The press reacted as if a plague of killer-weeds had descended on the
defenseless Big Apple. Special squads of narcotics agents, they reported, had
been dispatched from Washington to ferret out the perpetrators. Newscaster
Bill Jorgensen, then of Channel five, played the perfect straight guy. Midshot:
'Good evening, this is Bill Jorgensen with the evening news. This (*dramatic
pause*) is a reefer. It is made from an illegal substance, marijuana. Thousands
of unsuspecting citizens of New York received them today with the following
Valentine message,' he said, straight-faced. 'The police have set up a special

number to process complaints' (the number flashed across the screen). 'We are now going to call that number.' News and commercials filled the next twenty minutes while much of New York waited with bated breath. Near the end of the show, the announcer invited two trench-coated men, playing 'Dragnet' clones, to come onto the set:

ANNOUNCER: You're the police?

POLICE: That's right.

ANNOUNCER: I received this in the mail.

POLICE: Approximately what time of day was that?

ANNOUNCER: It came in the morning mail.

POLICE: What's your name and address?

ANNOUNCER: Bill Jorgensen.

POLICE: Do you have any identification?

ANNOUNCER (*puzzled*): Why, I'm Bill Jorgensen. See the sign? This is the Bill Jorgensen news show.

POLICE: We still have to see some ID.

ANNOUNCER: What about what it says here (*pointing*) about me – holding this reefer could earn me a prison sentence? Is that true?

POLICE: That's not our department. You'll have to ask the DA's office.

ANNOUNCER: (*even more puzzled, faces the camera*) Well, that's all we have time for on the news tonight.

All this actually took place on New York television. A New Jersey radio station went so far as to report Bill Jorgensen had been arrested for possession of marijuana while delivering the evening news. Of course no one, including sourpuss Bill, took a fall on the prank, but for days the most amazing stories circulated. Trying to separate news from gossip has been a lifetime endeavor and I'm unconvinced there's any difference. All is subjective, all is information molded by distortion, selection, exaggeration, emphasis, omission, and every other variable of communication. Walter Cronkite just leans over the country's back fence and tells his stories. There's a lot of bias.

Broadcasters report 'news,' the enemy engages in 'propaganda.' Our 'soldiers' and allies must kill to defend freedom, their 'terrorists' kill for criminal reasons. (Remember, no terrorist bombs from a jet plane, therefore only enemies of imperialism can earn that label.) Unions are to blame for strikes, never management. Murders are newsworthy, corporate price-fixing too 'abstract.' Even the newscaster I most respect, Cronkite, is prone to using cold-war imagery. In covering the Vietnam War, for years he described it as 'our American way of life' or 'the Free World battling Communism.' Home-grown culture versus foreign ideology. No US broadcaster or reporter can ever speak of 'capitalism' or 'imperialism' being 'our way of life,' with 'cooperation' being the social dynamic of communist countries. It's our 'leaders' against their 'rulers.' Our 'free press' compared with their 'party-line.' Our government, their regime.

On domestic news, I heard of many cases where an editor would tell a reporter, 'Ten thousand at that rally? That's too many. Make it three thousand.' The reporter would say, 'Sure,' then go out and get drunk. When you turn on the telly or pick up a newspaper you are tuning in on the boss's gossip and propaganda. If you believe America has a free press it just means you haven't thought about it enough. Everyone who makes and reports the news knows what I'm talking about. (In case you're curious, Jimi Hendrix financed the entire marijuana mailing.)

Theater of protest expanded from the streets to the television studio and into the home. Keep in mind, there was a television rule that they only invited a person with any kind of radical ideas on a show for ridicule. Knowing that, I approached talk shows as you would enter a war zone. I brought every conceivable kind of verbal ammunition, prepared for any situation, and before every appearance I spent hours studying the show's format.

It was very tricky business. What I lost by going on these shows was a reinforcement of the idea that America is a free and open society. One of the first questions I'd be asked would be, 'If you're so censored how come you're sitting here with me on nationwide TV?' I was also allowing myself to be edited, to fulfill a personality role in a play designed by the producers of American society. 'He's just another pretty face.' Keeping all these pitfalls in mind, television was nevertheless an enormously successful vehicle for making statements to a mass audience, and I used it as a form of theatrical warfare. Readers should understand television interviews are edited to make the interviewer, not the interviewee, look good. They are 'based' on reality, just as all other fiction in the media.

Invited on the David Susskind Show, we were ready for America's star performing intellectual's attempt to neutralize us by forcing explanations. 'How do you eat?' queried the Skeptic, and we passed out sandwiches to the audience. 'But what *is* a hippie?' pressed the emissary of New York's literati. A box opened as if by magic. 'Why don't you ask him, David, if he's a hippie?' I said and a duck flew out of the box. Around its neck was a sign saying I AM A HIPPIE. Susskind exploded, 'Catch that damn duck!' the duck, scared out of its wits, kept flying into the klieg lights. Chaos, the intellectual's nightmare, broke loose. Staff tried to grab the elusive duck. Each time the duck took off he crapped in midflight. Hippie-duck shit-bombs fell on the audience.

'That duck goes,' screamed Susskind. 'Hold the cameras!'

'David, you're television's worst C-E-N-S-O-R' (a particularly low blow). 'No duck, no hippies,' we shot back. Negotiations. The duck will stay, the duck shit goes. Later, when the show was aired, Susskind reneged and cut the entire scene. For a week he got late night calls: 'Quack, quack, quack!'

The goal of this nameless art form – part vaudeville, part insurrection, part communal recreation – was to shatter the pretense of objectivity. The calm, patriarchal voice of reason, embodied in an Eric Sevareid or a David Susskind, could be a greater danger than shrill Red-baiting. We learned to sneak onto the airwaves with Conceptual Art pieces that roused viewers from their video stupor.

To do that, we had to study the medium of television. At first we aimed at the human-interest slot near the end of each news program called the 'Happy Talk' segment, offering some freaky tableau to contrast with the nightly news blur. We infiltrated news by entering through the back door and slowly worked our way up to the lead news items. To find us in *Time* and *Newsweek* you had to turn to the back pages. Of course, any clever student of mass communication knew most people read those two magazines backwards anyway. Everyone paid attention to Happy Talk because in being personal it deviated from the prepared script.

The things about television you weren't supposed to take seriously I took very seriously and vice versa. Everybody knows that studio audiences are primed to laugh, applaud like crazy, and look generally ecstatic, but it's easy to forget how contrived and manipulated the situation is. I used this distortion of reality to my own advantage on the David Frost Show, pumping reverse responses out of the studio audience.

During the commercial break I got out of my seat, already creating a little chaos because guests aren't supposed to get out of their seats on talk shows unless the host tells them to get up ('How 'bout a song?' 'Yes, sir'). I walked right up to the audience and started conducting them:

'Come on, you're not angry enough! I'm a gook. I'm a nigger, I'm a kike – come on, get it off your chest!' They started yelling and getting up out of their seats, enraged and shaking their fists at me. It was a symphony of hate. By the time the commercial break was over I was back in my seat, smiling like an innocent lamb, while Frost worked me over and the audience roared and snarled. Then I jumped up and played hate conductor again. It came off very effectively.

On the same Frost Show I waited until the camera was on me while I was talking, and near the end of my rap I mouthed some words soundlessly, putting in the word 'fuck' for those who were up to a little lip reading. People watching said, 'Oh my God. They've censored him. They blipped him right there! I saw it!'

To practice this reverse manipulation you had to be very much in control. People weren't supposed to do these things in the television studio. The point was to give the home audience a different message, one closer to reality. I mean, who really gives a fuck about how hard it is for actors to get up at 5 A.M. to powder their noses?

Radio needed another frame of mind. I studied how it was different, always preferred it to TV, and felt I was better on the radio because the listener couldn't see what was going on and respond to certain visual images I had to create. One night I was being interviewed by a hostile host live on New York radio station WNEW. I picked up my host's pack of cancerettes and said, 'Can I have a cigarette?'

'Sure, help yourself,' he said, and I took one and dragged on it slurpily. 'Hey, this is really good stuff here, man,' I said, imitating the stereotyped stoned musician. The host got all flustered and announced, 'Ladies and gentlemen, he's just smoking a plain Marlboro cigarette.' 'Tell them that – tell them it's just a cigarette, man,' I agreed, then apologized profusely. 'Oh my God, ah shoudna done it. . . . I'm sorry, I don't wanna blow your gig. So cool, though, man disguisin it as a cigarette.' There was no way the host could get out of the little trap with just words. He completely lost his composure, but he had me back.

On another talk show, I got a call-in death threat. I said over the air that I'd be leaving the studio at 5 o'clock and went on to describe myself, only using the appearance of the host. 'I got horn-rimmed glasses and a brown and white-checkered sports jacket.' Most of the time I'd talk about the war or other social issues, using humor as a hook. I would use the opportunities to advertise upcoming demonstrations. It was free space and effective. Before Disco, people actually talked on radio. Now it seems like everyone, disc jockeys, broadcasters, newsmen, are all hopping to the same monotonous beat. One-two-three. One-two-three.

I practiced talk shows and press conferences just as singers and comedians practice their routines. You train to improvise. Most TV dialogue is canned, but I never read prepared lines. Talk show questions are sometimes given, often requested, from guests. Press conferences by politicians are carefully orchestrated. What viewers are led to believe is that all is 'totally unrehearsed.' Yet most, if not 'rehearsed,' is certainly 'arranged.' For example, take a presidential press conference. Only mainstream (controllable) reporters are allowed in the White House press corps. The safest, most controllable (TV commentators) are recognized for the first questions. Jumping from reporter to reporter, from question to question, lends the appearance that a free and open exchange is taking place. As one who has played both sides of the Q and A, I know that no format lends itself more to burying the truth beneath public relations gloss. Everyone on TV works on a media 'presence.' From the White House briefings to *The Gong Show*, entertainment rules the tube. The similarities between Rona Barrett and Walter Cronkite are far more interesting than the differences. And, if we are talking of accuracy, Ms. Rona is far ahead of most so-called news reporters. Obviously there is *some* freedom in the US media, but rather than pay it unbending homage is it not better to educate the public in the ways it is *not* free? Like not being free to suggest an alternative to our economic system.

My television act was close to my everyday life. Close, in fact, to my unconscious world. I personalized the audience. I think aloud. Recognizing the limited time span of someone staring at a lighted square in their living room, I trained for the one-liner, the retort jab, or sudden knock-out put-ons. I practiced with friends, waiters, people on the street, cab drivers, mayors, movie stars, cops, reporters, and relatives. When no one was around to practice with, I turned on the TV set and played each character, internalizing their questions and answers. What I'm trying to say was I didn't practice at *all*; that all communication is the same – face-to-face or face-to-camera.

I read *Variety*, *Show Business*, *Billboard*, and other trade papers far more probably than any radical organizer in history. It would be little problem for me to recite the ten top-rated TV shows or movies of the week. I tried to study things such as the effect of looking at the camera as opposed to the host (it depends) or whether or not to wear makeup. No makeup, although visually handicapping, gave me a bottom-line edge; if I was accused of being phony I could respond: 'It's funny, Dick, people who say that to me are always wearing makeup.' Immediately the audience at home could 'see' the difference between us and have their consciousness raised about television information. There is nothing more radical you can talk about on TV than TV itself.

In analyzing word communication, I've arranged a list of the ten most acceptable words. The most popular word in the American language is 'free,' 'new' is second. The word 'less' is more acceptable than 'more.' The potential customer is suspicious of 'more'; he knows the maxim – you pay more, get less. Television advertising is the height of fantasy manipulation. I tried writing commercials for revolution to learn the medium.

My work in TV was a long way from accepting its format. I entered the world of television to expose its wasteland. The top one hundred corporations control eighty percent of all network air time. Robert Hutchins once said: 'We can put television in its proper light by supposing that Gutenberg's great invention had been directed at printing only comic books.'

Later a group of us performed a guerrilla theater piece which adequately summed up our attitude toward television. While Nixon addressed the nation on the need for invading Cambodia, we set a twenty-four-inch receiver on a pedestal and before twenty thousand angry protesters pick-axed the flickering image. Electronic voodoo. Sometimes the proper intellectual argument is 'FUCK YOU!'

Chapter 25

Richard Schechner

from THE STREET IS THE STAGE

IN HIS MUCH LONGER ORIGINAL essay, Schechner uses the lens of the carnivalesque to examine six events: the Chinese pro-democracy movement centered in Tiananmen Square; the fall of the Berlin Wall; an anti-Vietnam War demonstration in Washington, D.C.; the Mardi Gras of New Orleans and the Gasparilla celebration of Tampa; and Ramlila of Ramnagar in northern India. I include this excerpt on Tiananmen Square in response to numerous colleagues who, perusing earlier drafts of this anthology, felt it was incomplete without an essay on that event.

> . . . old authority and truth pretend to be absolute, to have an extra-temporal importance. Therefore, their representatives . . . are gloomily serious. They cannot and do not wish to laugh; they strut majestically, consider their foes the enemies of eternal truth, and threaten them with eternal punishment. They do not see themselves in the mirror of time, do not perceive their own origin, limitations, and end; they do not recognize their own ridiculous faces or the comic nature of their pretensions to eternity and immutability. And thus these personages come to the end of their role still serious, although their spectators have been laughing for a long time . . . time has transformed old truth and authority into a Mardi Gras dummy, a comic monster that the laughing crowd rends to pieces in the marketplace.
>
> Mikhail Bakhtin (1984: 212–13)

The role of the revolutionary is to create theatre which creates a revolutionary frame of reference. The power to define is the power to control. . . . The goal of theatre is to get as many people as possible to overcome fear by taking action. We create reality wherever we go by living our fantasies.

Jerry Rubin (1970: 142–3)

[. . .]

Festivals and carnivals – almost but not quite the same – are comic theatrical events: comic in desire, even if sometimes tragic in outcome. When people go into the streets *en masse*, they are celebrating life's fertile possibilities. They eat, drink, make theatre, make love, and enjoy each other's company. They put on masks and costumes, erect and wave banners, and construct effigies not merely to disguise or embellish their ordinary selves, or to flaunt the outrageous, but also to act out the multiplicity each human life is. Acting out forbidden themes is risky so people don masks and costumes. They protest, often by means of farce and parody, against what is oppressive, ridiculous, and outrageous. For one to join the many as a part(ner), is not just a sexy act, it is also a socially and politically generative activity. Festive actions playfully, blasphemously, and obscenely expose to the general eye for approval and/or ridicule the basic (and therefore bodily) facts of human life and death. Such playing challenges official culture's claims to authority, stability, sobriety, immutability, and immortality.

Sometimes street actions bring about change – as in Eastern Europe in 1989. But mostly such scenes, both celebratory and violent, end with the old order restored. Frequently, the old order sponsors a temporary relief from itself. Obeying strict calendars, and confined to designated neighborhoods, the authorities can keep track of these carnivals and prepare the police. But despite such preparations, rebellions swell to almost musical climaxes around sacralized dates – anniversaries of the deaths or funerals of heroes and martyrs or of earlier popular uprisings (as in China) or the Christmas season and the approach of the New Year (as in Eastern Europe). To allow people to assemble in the streets is always to flirt with the possibility of improvisation – that the unexpected might happen.

Revolutions in their incipient period are carnivalesque. Written on a Sorbonne wall in 1968, 'The more I make love, the more I want to make revolution – the more I make revolution, the more I want to make love' (Baxandall 1969: 65). This is because both revolution and carnival propose a free space to satisfy desires, especially sexual and drunken desires, a new time to enact social relations more freely. People mask and costume or act in ways that are 'not me.' These behaviors are almost always excessive relative to ordinary life. Sometimes people drink, fuck, loot, burn, riot, and murder: or practice rough justice on those they feel have wronged them. But sooner

or later, either at a defined moment – when the church bells ring on Ash
Wednesday, when school begins again after Spring Break, when a new government is firmly in power – the liminal period ends and individuals are inserted
or reinserted into their (sometimes new, sometimes old but always defined)
places in society. 'Festivity, ceremonial form, and the transgression of social
boundaries are animated with the strongest possible feeling of solidarity and
community affiliation' (Bristol 1985: 30).[1]

[. . .]

Roger Caillois regarded modern European carnivals 'as a sort of mori-
bund echo of ancient festivals . . . a kind of atavism, a heritage of the times
in which it was felt vitally necessary to reverse everything or commit excesses
at the time of the new year' (Caillois 1959: 123). As Bristol points out, in
modern times state apparatus takes over from festivity the function of guar-
anteeing social solidarity. Rectangular and linear parades replace the more
vortexed and chaotic choreography of carnivals. The state fears unregulated
traffic. Over time in Europe and Europeanized America, festivals were cut
to size, hemmed in by regulations, transformed into Chamber of Commerce
boosterism, coopted by capitalism's appetite for profit, relatively desexualized
(Miss America at least has to pretend to 'innocence'), and served up as
models of social order and conformity. With rare exceptions, today's festivals
and carnivals are not inversions of the social order but mirrors of it. 'Lords
of Misrule' in the Mardi Gras or Gasparilla are rarely drawn from the lower
or oppressed classes or enabled to rule (even for a day). For example, New
York's Halloween parade, originating in the 1960s as a display of (mostly
gay) cross-dressers, maskers, and costume buffs, meandering its noisy way
through Greenwich Village's small streets, has been regularized over time,
tamed and contained by police watchfulness, and rerouted on to wide main
streets where it is more a parade and less an infiltration.

But unofficial culture worms or bullies its way back into public outdoor
spaces. If there is a tradition (and not only in the West) of constructing grand
monuments specifically to present performances – arenas, stadiums, and
theatres – so there is as well a long history of unofficial performances 'taking
place' in (seizing as well as using) locales not architecturally imagined as
theatres (see Carlson 1989 and Harrison-Pepper 1990). A big part of the
celebration is experiencing the transformation of work space, or traffic space,
or some kind of official space into a playfield. Over the past thirty years,
performance experimenters, an art branch of unofficial culture, have used
outdoor spaces – courtyards, streets, walls, beaches, lakes, rooftops, plazas,
and mountainsides – for a number of overlapping purposes – aesthetic,
personal, ritual, and political. And while Western dramatists from Ibsen,
Strindberg, and Chekhov to Miller, Pinter, Shepard, and Mamet abandoned
the public squares of Renaissance theatre for the living room, kitchen,
bedroom, motel, and office, the emerging festival theatre – liminoid rather

than liminal – repositioned itself in places where public life and social ritual have traditionally been acted out.[2] Doubtless, there has been a mutually fruitful exchange between art performances and symbolic public actions. By the 1960s, these actions constituted a distinct liminoid-celebratory-political-theatrical-ritual genre with its own dramaturgy, *mise-en-scène*, role enactments, audience participation, and reception. This theatre is ritual because it is efficacious, intending to produce real effects by means of symbolic causes. It is most theatrical at the cusp where the street show meets the media, where events are staged for the camera.

[. . .]

Tiananmen Square is no European Piazza. More than 100 acres in size, and capable of holding hundreds of thousands of people, it is the center of a city of ten million people, which is the capital of the People's Republic of China, Beijing. It is the symbol of China and Chinese government in the same way that Red Square and the Kremlin symbolize the USSR, and Washington with its white monuments the USA. . . . [In] Tiananmen Square is situated the huge Monument to the People's Heroes and the Mausoleum of Mao Zedong. On the west side of the Square is the Great Hall of the People, the meeting pace for government bodies. . . . On the east side of the Square is the Museum of Chinese History, which is attached to the Museum of the Revolution. At the north end of the Square is the reviewing stand which stands over the entrance to the Forbidden City, now the Palace Museum. To the west of the Forbidden City is the Zhongnanhai compound for senior government and party personnel. . . . Running east–west . . . through the north end of the Square is [Beijing's] major thoroughfare, Changan Avenue.

(Mok and Harrison 1990: xi–xii)

But until 1949 this version of Tiananmen Square did not exist. Earlier photos show a smallish open space in front of the Gate of Heavenly Peace, the southern entrance to the Forbidden City.

Until China's last dynasty fell in 1912, it was through this gate that the main axis of the Emperor's power was believed to run, as he sat in his throne hall, facing south, the force of his presence radiating out across the courtyards and ornamental rivers of the palace compound, passing through the gate, and so to the great reaches of the countryside beyond.

(Spence 1981: 17)

After the communist triumph,

the crowded alleys in front of the gate were leveled, and a massive parade ground was created; in the center of the vast space rose the simple monument to the martyrs of the revolution. . . . During the Cultural Revolution of 1966 [to 1976] the gate, dominated now by an immense colored portrait of Chairman Mao Zedong, became a reviewing stand in front of which marched the Red Guards, a million or more strong.

(Spence 1981: 17–18)

Clearly, the creation of Tiananmen Square was intended to refocus ceremonial – that is, theatrical – power from behind the Forbidden City's walls to the big open space, a more fitting symbol of what the new order promised. Mao, the new emperor, no longer sat on a throne behind the Gate, but was mounted in front, gazing out over the Square and from there to all of China. Power was no longer to radiate from secret forbidden places but be displayed for all people to see and share. The nation itself was renamed The People's Republic of China. And what the students who came to Tiananmen Square in 1978, 1986, and 1989 demanded, more than anything, was what they called 'transparency' – defined as an openness in government operations corresponding to the open square that symbolized the new China. In occupying Tiananmen Square the students were challenging the government, actualizing the students' belief that the government was not living up to its promises. There were precedents for such actions in the dramatic May 4th Movement of 1919 and the more recent democracy movements in 1978 and 1986 – all of which focused on Tiananmen Square. Joseph Esherick and Jeffrey Wasserstrom argue strongly that the 1989 democracy movement was political theatre.

First of all it was street theater: untitled, improvisational, with constantly changing casts. Though fluid in form, it nevertheless followed what Charles Tilly (1978) calls a historically established 'repertoire' of collective action. This means that, even when improvising, protesters worked from familiar 'scripts' which gave a common sense of how to behave during a given action, where and when to march, how to express their demands, and so forth. Some of these scripts originated in the distant past, emerging out of traditions of remonstrance and petition stretching back for millennia. More were derived (consciously or unconsciously) from the steady stream of student-led mass movements that have taken place [in China] since 1919.

(Esherick and Wasserstrom 1990: 839)

The struggle in China, before it became violent, was over controlling the means and style of information. As Esherick and Wasserstrom note, state rituals, the funerals of leaders (in 1989 that of Hu Yaobang, a former General Secretary of the Communist Party who the students highly regarded), and anniversaries of earlier demonstrations or uprisings are of great importance.

In 1989 the question became: would official culture or the student-led democracy movement write the script? The theatrical stakes were even higher in May because fortune laid ceremony atop ceremony. Hu Yaobang died on 15 April, close to the anniversary of the May 4th Movement; Soviet President Mikhail Gorbachev was set to arrive in Beijing on 15 May, possibly healing decades of bad relations between China and the USSR. Clearly, the leadership wanted to impress Gorbachev. The students also wanted to impress him, but with a different show. They admired the Soviet President's policies of *glasnost* and *perestroika*. If Chinese officials wanted Gorbachev to see an orderly China under their control, the students wanted him to see a powerful and seething people's movement akin to those in Eastern Europe and his own country. On 15 May about 800,000 people gathered in Tiananmen Square even as Chinese officials steered Gorbachev around Beijing pretending that this vast spectacle at the very core of power was not occurring. Instead of greeting Gorbachev in the Square, official public ceremonies were held at the Beijing airport, a nonplace historically.

Within the overall dramaturgy of the 1989 demonstrations, [. . .] Esherick and Wasserstrom describe as 'one of the best acts' that

> put on by Wuer Kaixi in the May 18th dialogue with Li Peng. The costuming was important: he appeared in his hospital pajamas [on hunger strike]. So, too, was the timing: he upstaged the Premier by interrupting him at the very start. And props: later in the session, he dramatically pulled out a tube inserted into his nose (for oxygen?) in order to make a point. Especially for the young people in the nationwide television audience, it was an extraordinarily powerful performance.
>
> (1990: 841)

Then there was the dramatic meeting the next day, 19 May, between hunger-striking students and Communist Party Secretary Zhao Ziyang. This encounter had the quality of a tragic *perepeteia* (reversal) and *anagnorisis* (recognition). Speaking through tears, Zhao said 'I came too late, I came too late . . . [but] the problems you raised will eventually be solved.' And, of course, on 30 May the 'Goddess of Democracy and Freedom' – a multivocal figure resembling the Statue of Liberty, a Bread & Puppet Theatre effigy, a 'traditional Bodhisattva, . . . [and] the giant statues of Mao that were carried through the Square during some National Day parades of the sixties' (Esherick and Wasserstrom 1990: 841). The Goddess was a big hit. Before her appearance the crowds had been sagging, but she brought many back to the Square. Earlier, on 25 May in Shanghai, a more exact replica of the Statue of Liberty had come onto the streets – thus ideas for effigies and banners, staging, all kinds of information were circulating through the movement's various parts. Students freely adapted costumes and slogans from non-Chinese sources, including 'We shall overcome.' Across China the democracy movement was 'connected,' a single organism. Serious in their demands and aspirations, the Chinese students still found plenty of time to celebrate, to dance, to enjoy the freedom of the streets. At the same time, the government was getting its forces together, bringing in troops and key leaders from the far reaches of the country.

Esherick and Wasserstrom theorize that the struggle in Tiananmen Square was between official ritual and student theatre:

> there is always the chance that people will turn a ritual performance into an act of political theater. Central to the notion of ritual is the idea that only careful adherence to a traditionally prescribed format will ensure the efficacy of a performance. With any departure from a traditional script, a ritual ceases to be ritual. . . . Theater, by nature, is more liberated from the rigid constraints of tradition, and provides autonomous space for the creativity of playwrights, directors, and actors. This gives theater a critical power never possessed by ritual. . . . Educated [Chinese] youths have repeatedly managed to transform May 4th rituals into May 4th theater.
>
> (1990: 844–5, 848)

Such a distinction between theatre and ritual is too rigid (in fact, Esherick and Wasserstrom do not always stick to it). As Victor Turner has emphasized, and as I have pointed out, the relation between ritual and theatre is dialectical and braided; there is plenty of entertainment and social critique in many rituals (see Turner 1969 and 1982, Schechner 1974 and 1988). Conversely, theatre in its very processes of training, preparation, display, and reception is ritualized. The struggle in Tiananmen Square before the entrance of the tanks was not between rigid ritual and rebellious theatre, but between two groups of authors (or authorities) each of whom desired to compose the script of China's future and each of whom drew on both theatre and ritual. The students improvised in public, while the officials, as always, rehearsed their options behind closed doors. The students took Tiananmen Square, the center stage and ritual focus of Chinese history. Official culture was literally upstaged. When Deng Xiaoping, Li Peng, and the generals of the People's Liberation Army felt their authority slipping, they radically shifted the basis of the confrontation from theatre and ritual to military force. But even after the slaughter of 3–4 June, there were moments of high theatre such as when an unarmed man, his fate since unknown, stood his ground in front of a column of tanks.

For their stage the students claimed not just any old spot, but the symbolic and operational focus of Chinese political power. And despite the orderliness of their demonstrations and the seriousness of their intentions, the students acted up a carnival. Their mood of fun, comradeship, irony, and subversion

Figure 25.1 Beijing University students dance in Tiananmen Square during demonstrations, 1989.

enraged and frightened China's officialdom. Students camped out willy-nilly all over the place in patterns as different as can be imagined from the rigid rectangles and precise lines of official gatherings. The students sang and danced, they spoke from impromptu 'soap boxes,' and granted interviews to the world press. They unfurled sarcastic, disrespectful banners including one depicting hated Premier Li Peng as a pig-snouted Nazi officer. 'Flying tigers' – students on motorbikes – carried news to and from various parts of Beijing, linking the Square to the city and the rest of China. Even the hunger strike, in which thousands participated, had the feel of melodrama rather than the sanctity of one of Gandhi's laydowns (though certainly the Mahatma knew his political theatre – and how sanctity would play in India and Britain).

[. . .]

This [student] radicalism the Chinese government called *luan*, or chaos, a word which in certain of its uses implies dissipation and drunkenness. Because of the 'tigers' – and world media [. . .] – the Chinese leadership feared the virus of luan would spread from Tiananmen Square to the rest of Beijing and China. After all, it was from the Square that official power radiated. Had the students turned inward, not attempting Chinawide and worldwide communication, the government might have waited them out. But Tiananmen Square is not an inwardly focused place: it is a consciously designed, very bright stage, visible all over China. From the government's point of view, luan acted out in Tiananmen Square could not be ignored any more than the Nixon administration could, nineteen years earlier, ignore the ever more carnivalesque anti-Vietnam War demonstrations invading Washington. Meaningful theatrical luan is a potent weapon.

[. . .]

In [what I call] 'direct theatre' large public spaces are transformed into theatres where collective reflexivity is performed, and fecund and spectacular excesses displayed. Parades, mass gatherings, street theatre, sex, and partying – everything is exaggerated, ritualized, done for show. Masquerading encourages experimenting with behavior, identity slippage, and acting as if one were someone else. Rulers are either exalted as at Mardi Gras, Gasparilla, and Ramlila or challenged as in America and China or overthrown as in Eastern Europe. The difference between temporary and permanent change distinguishes carnival from revolution. In Eastern Europe, China, and America there was a critique of social, political, and economic relations 'from below,' from the perspective of those who do not hold power – that is, from the perspective of everyday life. There is no critique from below in Mardi Gras and Gasparilla, where the Lords of Misrule are actually the cities' elite.

[. . .]

When entertainment is really free, when it gets out of hand, when there is no fixed calendrical conclusion, then the authorities get nervous. Such festivals reverberate through the population in unforseen ways. People in Beijing and around China thrilled to the whorling choreography of the students in Tiananmen Square, just as people throughout Eastern Europe took their cues from what was happening at the Berlin Wall. At these times, official leadership is no longer the focus of attention, no longer in control of the means of producing or controlling public celebrations. The power to produce public fun passes into the hands of new leaders, often ordinary people. The single-focus reviewing stand gives way to many diverse pockets of participation and leadership. Instead of prepackaged 'media opportunities,' not even the leaders themselves are sure of what's happening. Still, events take a theatrical turn. Effigies appear, as do homemade banners and posters; street theatre flourishes, soap box orators draw cheering crowds. Official leaders are cut down to size. If they show up, they run the risk of being mocked or chased away as Zhou, Nixon, and members of the GDR Politburo were. Official entertainment provides scripted fun contained within ritual frames, while unofficial festivity re-writes ritual, dissolving restrictive frames. When rituals are restaged as carnivals, the activity in the streets grows more free-flowing and loose, unpredictable in its outcome, if clear in its desires: to change the basis of social relations and/or state organization. On these occasions, the efficacious function of ritual is reassigned to entertainment.

The May 1970 Washington antiwar protest and the 1989 Tiananmen Square movement were enactments of the kind of society the students wanted to come into being. In America there was the feeling that anger and revulsion at the Kent State killings and the bombing of Cambodia had turned the tide of American public opinion against the Vietnam War. And with the end of the war would come a general restructuring. In China, the relative liberalism of Deng's regime seemed to open the way to big, fundamental changes. Many believed these festival theatres were in fact what they could not become – rehearsals of the near future. The American big chill and the dispirited Chinese I talked to in Shanghai in August 1990 (see Schechner 1991) reconfirmed this interpretation. After millenary hopes are dashed, people furl their banners, hunker down, and ride out history.

The popular street carnival-demonstration is actually a utopian mimesis whose focused, idealized, heated, magnified, and transparent clarity of consciousness dissolves once the show is over. But those involved in a festival of political desire too often deceive themselves into believing their utopian show will run forever. It is not only the tanks of Deng Xiaoping which enviously and with terrible clarity destroy the fun, but the only slightly longer process, when the revolution is successful, of postrevolutionary jockeying for power. This decay of festival into 'dirty politics,' the inevitable end to spontaneous communitas, is what the Chinese students now underground or in exile have learned, a lesson most American radicals of the 1960s and 1970s

RICHARD SCHECHNER

never studied. The carnival, more strongly than other forms of theatre, can act out a powerful critique of the status quo, but it cannot itself be what replaces the status quo.

Notes

1 Bristol is echoing ideas first enunciated early in the twentieth century by Arnold Van Gennep 1908 and Emile Durkheim 1915. See also Victor Turner 1967, 1969, 1974, 1977, 1982, and 1983 for his emendations to Van Gennep and Durkheim as well as his own theories regarding liminality, the ritual process, and antistructure.
2 See Turner 1977, 1982, and 1990 for distinctions between the liminal and the liminoid.

References

Bakhtin, Mikhail (1984) *Rabelais and His World*, Bloomington: Indiana University Press.
Baxandall, Lee (1969) 'Spectacles and scenarios: a dramaturgy of radical activity,' *TDR, The Drama Review* 13 (4): 52–71.
Bristol, Michael (1985) *Carnival and Theater*, London: Methuen.
Caillois, Roger (1959) *Man and the Sacred*, Glencoe Ill.: The Free Press.
Carlson, Marvin (1989) *Places of Performance*, Ithaca, NY: Cornell University Press.
Durkheim, Emile (1915) *The Elementary Forms of the Religious Life*, New York: Macmillan.
Esherick, Joseph W. and Wasserstrom Jeffrey N. (1990) 'Acting out democracy: political theater in modern China,' *Journal of Asian Studies* 49 (4): 835–66.
Harrison-Pepper, Sally (1990) *Drawing a Circle in the Square*, Jackson: University of Mississippi Press.
Mok, Chiu Yu and Harrison, J. Frank (eds) (1990) *Voices from Tiananmen Square*, Montreal and New York: Black Rose.
Rubin, Jerry (1970) *Do It!*, New York: Simon & Schuster.
Schechner, Richard (1974) 'From ritual to theatre and back: the structure/process of the efficacy–entertainment dyad,' *Educational Theatre Journal* 26 (4): 455–81.
—— (1988) *Performance Theory*, London and New York: Routledge.
—— (1991) 'Tales of a few cities,' *New Theatre Quarterly* 7 (28): 315–24.
Spence, Jonathan D. (1981) *The Gate of Heavenly Peace*, New York: Viking Penguin.
Turner, Victor (1967) *The Forest of Symbols*, Ithaca, NY: Cornell University Press.
—— (1969) *The Ritual Process*, Chicago: Aldine.

—— (1974) *Dramas, Fields, and Metaphors*, Ithaca, NY: Cornell University Press.

—— (1977) 'Variations on a theme of liminality,' in Sally F. Moore and Barbara Myerhoff (eds) *Secular Ritual*, Amsterdam: Van Gorcum.

—— (1982) *From Ritual to Theatre*, New York: PAJ Publications.

—— (1983) 'Body, brain, and culture,' *Zygon* 18 (3): 221–45.

—— (1990) 'Are there universals of performance in myth, ritual, and drama?' in Richard Schechner and Willa Appel (eds) *By Means of Performance*, Cambridge: Cambridge University Press.

Van Gennep, Arnold (1960) *The Rites of Passage*, Chicago: University of Chicago Press. First published 1908.

Chapter 26

Baz Kershaw

from THE CELEBRATORY PERFORMANCE OF JOHN FOX AND WELFARE STATE INTERNATIONAL

KERSHAW DESCRIBES A 'DOUBLE-EDGED' example of acting out utopia. Having settled down the road from Barrow, whose main industry is nuclear submarines, the deeply anti-war Welfare State International has struggled to devise artistic events that neither alienate local people nor compromise their own values. Here is a carnivalesque company forced to contend with the morning after and revealing the community-based direction that a number of European and US street theatres took in the aftermath of 1960s and 1970s activism.

Welfare State moves to Barrow-in-Furness

In 1983, at a time when most alternative theatre companies were running for ideological cover, Welfare State International began a seven-year project in Barrow. John Fox, founder (with Sue Gill and others) and artistic director of Welfare State, described the project's aim as:

> developing a concept of vernacular art whereby we respond continu-
> ally to local demand, producing plays, bands, dances, songs, ornaments
> and oratorios to order, so generating a social poetry of a high order
> within a very specific community context.

> (Fox 1987: 3)

This was a new departure for Welfare State, which for fifteen years had been mounting mostly short-term creative initiatives in settings as diverse as British inner-city housing estates and Japanese international theatre festivals.

The company was one of the original 'class of '68.' For the first five years of its life it was aligned at the performance art end of the alternative theatre spectrum, though it also included 'namings' and other secular ceremonies among its activities. As the 1970s progressed it evolved into a mobile creative community, travelling gypsy-like from gig to gig with its own caravan village, blurring the distinctions between art and life. Accordingly, its early policies were couched in semi-visionary counter-cultural terms, claiming, for example, to make 'art as a necessary way of offsetting cultural and organic death' (Coult and Kershaw 1990: 258). By the mid-1970s it had taken up a residency with Mid-Pennine Arts in Burnley, staging events which combined the wayward visual aesthetics of its earlier work with a populist appeal to the local community. Notable among these was the first *Parliament in Flames* (1976), a 'community bonfire' for November 5th which featured the destruction of a massive mock-up of the Houses of Parliament.

No one else was producing carnivalesque agit prop on this scale. [. . .] By the early 1980s Welfare State's work was predicated on an iconoclastic radical ideology, shaped by a deep opposition to the over-production and consumerism of the developed countries. At root the ideology rested on sympathy for the underdog, inspired by a primitive socialism – a collectivist, egalitarian utopianism that was not afraid to make grand, even visionary, claims for the healing power of creativity and the place of 'poetry' in a healthy culture. However, the anarchic edge to these ideas was honed by a pragmatism which produced, at the macro-level, an acute grasp of contemporary power structures, and, at the micro-level, an engagingly unpretentious commitment to local community activism (Fox 1988).

In the late 1970s and early 1980s Welfare State had tested this ideology through a series of large-scale epic models for radical performance in conservative contexts, which included shows such as *Tempest on Snake Island*[1] [. . .] These events were hugely successful and received considerable critical accolades. But John Fox has subsequently criticised them because:

> we were obliged to start from ART rather than from LIVING, to generate more product rather than process and work to rapid (and to an extent commercial) deadlines in strange lands. We could not allow ourselves to develop pieces organically over years or to respond to or follow up the longer term needs and rhythms of the host community, because essentially we were not part of any community.
>
> (Fox 1987: 1; White 1988: 203)

The desire to put down creative roots had led the company to settle in Ulverston, on the south coast of Cumbria, in 1979. By then it consisted of a core group of five employed full time, plus a network of fifty or so free-lance artists who were brought in for particular projects. By 1983, having set up a successful annual festival and lantern procession in their new home town, it made sense to extend the local residency to Barrow, fifteen miles down the road.

Barrow the community

Approach Barrow-in-Furness from any direction and you will be struck by one thing: looming over the town, like a featureless cathedral to an anony-mous god, the immense off-white hangar of the Devonshire Dock Hall. The town houses 70,000 people, and about 14,000 of them work for VSEL (Vickers Shipbuilding and Engineering Limited). This company owns the Hall, and inside it they are constructing Armageddon, in the shape of Britain's Trident-class nuclear submarines, able to deliver in one quick spurt more firepower than the whole of that used in the Second World War. The town is a remote place, and often seen by outsiders, such as the *Guardian*'s northern arts correspondent Robin Thornber, as a cultural desert (Thornber 1987a).

Hence, in 1983 the town was totally dependent for its future prosperity on the making of nuclear submarines. And in the year following the Falklands war, with the sinking of the Belgrano fresh in the memory, it seemed certain that submarines would remain central to the global balance of power. Against this backdrop, any challenge that the radicalism of Welfare State offered to the local and global hegemony would inevitably seem puny, a futile gesture in the face of overwhelming odds, less ideologically efficacious than a hiccup.

This analysis, though, ignores crucial aspects in the nature of Barrow as a community. Whilst it is true that the presence of VSEL held the town almost totally in thrall to the most cherished economic and political values of the capitalist status quo, it does not follow that Barrow's cultural and social networks were completely subjugated by the same nexus. In fact, Barrow has long traditions of vigorous grass-roots culture, of working-class organisation, and of civic independence reaching back to its Victorian heyday. In the mid-nineteenth century the place was a boom town, flooded with offcomers attracted to work in the rapidly expanding local industries of steel-making, mining, shipbuilding and shipping. [. . .] Poverty and drunkenness were offset by trade unionism, a strong local co-operative movement, and religious non-conformism. In the late-Victorian period this produced a strong civic authority, determined to make Barrow into an outstanding example of the self-made town. The pride and independence of these roots can still be seen in its magnificent town hall, opened in Victoria's Jubilee Year, 1887.

Almost 100 years later many traces of this history also could be found in the town's wide range of community organisations, which included several drama, music and opera groups. The local political scene was equally lively:

the borough council was Labour controlled, though the Member of Parliament was Conservative. However, the original industrial variety of the town had disappeared, so, whilst it had a moderately vigorous community life, in matters relating to employment the town was relatively, inevitably docile. This was reflected in a common attitude to the shipyard and its lethal products – what was the point in arguing about an enforced necessity, an accident of history? Such ideological resignation, coupled with high levels of technological and engineering skill, pushed the place towards being – in John Fox's words – a 'perfect Thatcherite town,' but how was a company with such radical objectives going to be received in such a town? What was the best kind of creative introduction?

A celluloid nightmare

Welfare State's opening gambit in Barrow was the production of a full-length 'community feature film', based on a playscript commissioned from Adrian Mitchell, *The Tragedy of King Real*, which in its turn derived from Shakespeare's *King Lear*. [. . .] About fifty local, mostly unemployed, young people were involved in the production [. . .] The world premiere of *King Real and the Hoodlums* (as the film was called) took place in the autumn of 1983, at Barrow's only cinema, the Astra, with all the silly razzmatazz of a feature film opening reproduced in satiric extravagance: glitzy limousines, red carpets, preening 'stars'.

The premiere showing of the film gave many Barrovians the chance to witness their daughters, sons, neighbours and friends ironically cavorting in the local landscape. And it was not a pretty sight, for they had transformed themselves into the 'Hoodlums', a kind of punk-medieval rabble in a wasted industrial junkyard, celebrating the crazy excesses of their loony monarch, King Real. And if that were not enough to send local sensibilities reeling, the film had a blatantly anti-nuclear story, which was bound to have an overtly subversive impact in Barrow. In fact, the 'politics' of *King Real* [. . .] were so radical for the context that Welfare State almost came unstuck at the very beginning of its residency in the town.

[. . .]

The exploding town hall

Four years after *King Real and the Hoodlums* was screened at the Astra, 15,000 Barrovians spent Sunday afternoon watching their town hall. Barrow Borough Council had invited Welfare State to effect a 'sculptural enhancement' of the building, to celebrate the centenary of its opening in Queen Victoria's Jubilee

Figure 26.1 Town Hall Tattoo, Barrow, England.

year. Robin Thornber described the event as 'not just an exceptional jollification but probably the biggest art work in Europe this year' (Thornber
1987b). Apart from its scale, *Town Hall Tattoo* was extraordinary for its integration of acceptable civic celebration, extravagantly anarchic imagery, and
a subtle radicalism which poked gentle and good-humoured fun at the very
values the event appeared to valorise. This was ironic agit prop on the grand
scale, heavily disguised as a straightforward carnivalesque party.

The six-hour entertainment included: a Victorian market; a forty-five-
minute town hall oratorio (composed and collaged from traditional songs by
Pete Moser, sung by a large Centenary Choir of Barrow people, accompanied
by the VSEL Works Band); a Queen Victoria lookalike competition; an official
opening of the town hall by the Mayor; a grand parade of wildly decorated
council vehicles, led by two astonishing Welfare State floats; a ten-foot
diameter three-tier exploding birthday cake; and the 'enhancement' of the
building itself. This spectacular transformation involved hundreds of coloured
'smokes' burning on the roofs and parapets, the stringing of four miles of
bunting in four minutes flat, a long series of exploding firecrackers and
maroons followed by panicking bureaucrats abseiling down from the roof,
and the flying of a giant pair of gaily fluttering Victorian bloomers from the
tower-top flagpole 160 feet above the heads of the huge crowd of spectators.
The witty effects, climaxing a long summer afternoon of fantasy, brought
loud cheers from the assembled Barrovians and crisply confirmed Welfare
State's claim to be Civic Magicians.

To get to this point of acceptance after the edgy start of *King Real* [. . .]
the company had realigned its approach to the town. Careful behind-the-
scenes negotiations with Barrow council gained support for a series of creative
projects, collectively called 'Town Hall Bonanza', which included cabaret-
style shows for the elderly, visual arts sessions in schools, a hand-made slide
workshop for children with learning difficulties, a writing group (with
Deborah Levy and Adrian Mitchell). Simultaneously, and crucially, Pete
Moser was working with an enthusiastic clutch of existing music organisations to forge the Barrow Centenary Choir. Considered in isolation, much
of this activity was little more than good-quality bread-and-butter community arts animation, deliberately calculated to appeal to the local authority
as a public relations exercise: Welfare State reaching the parts (and hearts?)
that officialdom could not. Inevitably, the project became ideologically
double-edged, as the company made accommodations to the authority in
order to gain support for grass-roots activity. This is an uncomfortable tactic
in most situations, but in Barrow it implied support (however reluctant and
guarded) for VSEL, as the council derived income from the shipyard.

All aspects of the project were inflected ambivalently by the context.
For example, the Centenary Choir drew on thirteen local choral and operatic
societies – potentially a great populist base for giving voice to any doubts
about the dominance of the shipyard and what it stands for. But the musical

backing for the choir was provided by the VSEL band, in effect making such voicing extremely problematic, if not impossible. In such conditions, how could the celebration encompass protest, how could the company be confident that the cheers of the crowd at the climax of *Town Hall Tattoo* might represent more than just a hegemonic letting off of mildly satirical steam? What guarantee could there be that the veiled radicalism of the event was taking root in the local networks of the community?

The interaction of the rhetorical and authenticating conventions of *Town Hall Tattoo* may have provided the framework needed for oppositional efficacy. The rhetorical conventions were all drawn from non-theatrical sources: a market to begin with [. . .]; an opening ceremony; an oratorio (but secular); a birthday party; a carnival parade; a daylight firework display coupled with quasi-military demonstration (the abseiling); the climatic flying of a 'flag.' Here was a mish mash of forms connected only by their provision of conventions for mass public behaviour. It made an appropriate structure for jollification and it stimulated a carnival atmosphere, an anything-goes-and-might-conceivably-happen expectancy. This is a typical Welfare State tactic, and it was used to open out the spectator's horizon of expectation, to encourage a positive response to the curious combinations of authenticating codes that the company's shows often employ.

Sometimes these codes are subtly understated, so subtly in fact that they can easily be missed. For example, the logo for the lead-up to *Tattoo*, prominently featured on thousands of booklets, leaflets and flyers, showed the town hall exploding with its main tower zooming up rocket-like, while two of the tower's side-pinnacles have broken away and are flying off in their own directions, for all the world like nuclear missiles. More overt critical use was made of another symbol of power, Queen Victoria. Her image and what she stands for were debunked several times. For example, the two main processional floats were satirically adapted from Barrow's coat of arms. The first represents a giant bee sitting on an arrow. The Lord Mayor of Fortune rides on the back of the bee, while the civic pest-control officer sits facing backwards beneath the bee's sting, which is pointing up at the second float. This takes the form of a grossly bloated elephant, an awesome but ugly symbol of the power of Empire, on top of which rides Queen Victoria herself. She is, of course, facing the sting and the pest-control officer. The witty images could be read as just an innocuous jab at the heritage of monarchy, politically irrelevant to the present – except 1987 was election year and Prime Minister Thatcher had only recently announced her view that Britain should return to Victorian values.

Even more obviously, at the climax of the show two giant puppets of the Lord of Fortune and Queen Victoria chase each other – like a monstrous Punch and Judy – around the high parapets of the town hall tower. As the firecrackers ignite and the town hall appears to burst into flames the puppets disappear, and out of the smoke the giant pair of pink bloomers slowly rise up the flagpole. The broad northern music-hall humour is double-edged, blowing a faintly sexist raspberry at authority. But if the final image is ambivalent in its detailed meaning, in broad terms it is fairly unambiguous: it is anti-hierarchical in a carnivalesque way, poking fun at power and pretension whatever its nature. John Fox maintains that the context of the comic image ensures it will become part of Barrovian mythology, undermining the presumption of authority every time anyone who saw the show glances up towards the town hall tower.

But there was a further strand to the spectacle which inflected it with a more specific and authentically subversive significance. The oratorio ended with the singing of the Barrow anthem, written by John Fox to music by Pete Moser, and it was short enough to be printed on 25,000 tiny ticker-tape slips which fluttered down from the roof of the town hall:

We sing to the stars, sing to the sea, sing to our neighbour's heart.
Hear the loving and the living. Rejoice!
Hear the loving and the living. Rejoice!
For the stranger is given a welcome, and hunger can't find the door
When the winds of July blow warmer and the children outlaw war.

The general ideological import is little more than broadly humanitarian. But of course the context of Barrow endowed it with a subtler oppositional meaning. When it is sung by the massed voices of many Barrovians within the framework of a show that has so clearly, if jokingly, attacked the idea of a centralised and individualised power structure – well then, maybe its subversiveness is just a little catching? Maybe it could carry just a little efficacious power on its own account? Perhaps by encouraging Barrow to deal more publicly – however indirectly – with the contradictions, paradoxes and ambivalences which derive from its dependence on VSEL, Welfare State was gently nudging the town towards a slightly more progressive ideological identity?

But perhaps, too, the company was operating too close to the heart of local power to take any really significant ideological risks at this stage of its residency. Maybe carnivalesque escapism had been the real order of the day. Yet one bit of serendipity symbolically signalled the potential efficacy of the company's presence in the town. At the climax of the show, as the town hall exploded, all the council's vehicles and all the fishing boats on Walney Sound hooted their horns and sirens. Ironically, the cacophony triggered the emergency alarms inside the Devonshire Dock Hall.

Note

1   Ed. Note: Ron Grimes wrote an excellent essay on this *Tempest* that took place in 1981 on Snake Island, a ferry ride from Toronto. The production

was a response to tension between modernized mainlanders and low-tech islanders. Grimes describes how WSI created a magical, sensorily engaging environment at the same time as demystifying its own technology, giving spectators the sense that they could make the magnificent puppets and masks themselves and in fact involving roughly 100 islanders in so doing. He points out the challenge and necessity of creating celebrations in which people retain their critical abilities:

> 'Tempest' is a good example of celebration-making, because it so thoroughly succeeded in generating spontaneous community, and, at the same time, provided for critical reflection on its own processes. In modern societies few activities can be as dangerous as unexamined public rites such as rallies, demonstrations, or festivals. If our head is lost, we risk being duped into complicity with commercial or political values we do not really hold. Yet if our head is not lost, celebration does not transpire . . .

WSI achieved this, in part, by not taking sides. Most of the images were multivocal and open to interpretation. Others were subtly utopian. Near the end, a 'technological boy' and 'woodland girl' were married. Then all danced, including the audience, suggesting an alternative to the animosity, but never a judgement as to who, in the conflict, was 'right' and who was 'wrong.'

References

Coult, Tony and Baz Kershaw (eds) (1990) *Engineers of the Imagination: The Welfare State Handbook*, (rev. edn), London: Methuen.

Fox, John (1987) 'Background Paper – How, Why and When Welfare State is working in Barrow-in-Furness', Ulverston, England: Welfare State International.

—— (1988) 'Between Wordsworth and Windscale' (an interview with Baz Kershaw), *Performance Magazine*, No. 54.

Thornber, Robin (1987a) 'Cultural desert blooms', *Guardian*, Saturday, July 11.

—— (1987b) 'Town Hall Tattoo', *Guardian*, Monday, July 13.

White, Mike (1988) 'Resources for a Journey of Hope: the Work of Welfare State International', *New Theatre Quarterly*, Vol. 4, No. 15.

PART FIVE

TRADITION

Introduction

THE PERFORMANCES IN THIS SECTION are grounded in traditional forms passed down over generations, often providing a cultural formulation of the values and behavior of people linked by a common past, present and aspiration for the future. Typically combining entertainment with education, such performances address themselves to whole communities. Already conceptualizing their audience as a united collective, a valuable pre-condition for social change, these performances take place in public by-ways where people tend to congregate. As radical street performance, they have been contemporized by filling their collectively meaningful form with current issues of group importance.

The paradox is that traditional performance's historical role is to conserve a culture over time, not to change it. In situations of colonization as described by L. Dale Byam and Ngũgĩ wa Thiong'o, when change is imposed from the outside, drawing on traditional performance can help keep a people intact, focusing on their own definition of themselves and their agenda. Quite often the performers come from the same community as the audience and the expressive practices, resulting in a kind of mirroring between them.

In other situations, such as that analyzed by Dwight Conquergood, those instigating the performance do not come from the same community as the intended audience but may recognize tradition's crucial role in what he calls continuity, stability and recreation of self and society. The difference between audience and performers in the work Mark Sussman investigates is mediated by a generically popular form, the circus, beautifully subverted here by its contemporary content.

Chapter 27

Dwight Conquergood

HEALTH THEATRE IN A HMONG REFUGEE CAMP

Performance, communication and culture

THE STREETS OF WHICH CONQUERGOOD writes are
in a Thai refugee camp, where Hmong people, forced from their mountain
home, eke out an existence. There the traditional cultural forms offer suste-
nance, continuity and a vehicle for learning how to adapt to wrenchingly
difficult and unfamiliar living conditions.

Ban Vinai refugee camp is located in an isolated, hilly region of northeast
Thailand. The camp has a population larger than any city in this remote
area, and surpasses even Loei, the provincial capital. All of the approximately 48,000 residents are crowded on to 400 acres of undeveloped land.
The camp space is intensively used because refugees are forbidden to go
outside of the camp without the express permission of the Thai camp
commander.

Ban Vinai is the largest gathering of Hmong in the world. The Hmong
refugees used to live in small mountaintop villages in northern Laos where
they tended animals and grew dry rice and corn in fields cleared from the
forest. When US forces withdrew from the area in 1975, Laos collapsed and
came under the rule of a government hostile to the Hmong who were viewed
as collaborators with the enemy. Almost overnight they were thrown into a
densely populated camp and had no time to develop adaptive cultural traditions, let alone garbage disposal systems. As a result of grossly inadequate
housing, latrines, and facilities for waste disposal, the camp has serious hygiene

and sanitation problems. Imported and simplistic health slogans would not work for Ban Vinai. What was needed was a programme that was sensitive to the refugees' history and the specific problems and constraints of the camp environment.

The refugee camp may lack many things – water, housing, sewage disposal system – but not performance. No matter where you go in the camp, at almost any hour of the day or night, you can simultaneously hear two or three performances, from simple storytelling and folksinging to the elaborate collective ritual performances for the dead.

A high level of cultural performance is characteristic of refugee camps in general. Since my work in Ban Vinai I have visited or lived for short periods of time in 11 refugee camps in Southeast Asia and the Middle East, not counting a shantytown for displaced people in Nigeria. In every one of them I was struck by the richness and frequency of performative expression. One explanation for this is that refugees have a lot of time on their hands to cultivate expressive traditions. But I think there are deeper psychological and cultural reasons for the high incidence of performance in the camps. Refugee camps are liminal zones where people displaced by trauma and crisis – usually war or famine – must try to regroup and salvage what is left of their lives. Their world has been shattered. They are in passage, no longer Laotian, certainly not Thai, and not quite sure where they will end up or what their lives will become. Betwixt and between worlds, suspended between past and future, they fall back on the performance of their traditions as an empowering way of securing continuity and some semblance of stability. Moreover, through performative flexibility they can play with new identities, new strategies for adaptation and survival. The playful creativity enables them to experiment with and invent a new 'camp culture' that is part affirmation of the past and part adaptive response to the exigencies of the present. Performance participates in the re-creation of self and society that emerges within refugee camps. Through its reflexive capacities, performance enables people to take stock of their situation and through this self-knowledge to cope better. There are good reasons why in the crucible of refugee crisis, performative behaviors intensify.

Developing popular theatre

In conjunction with Hmong refugees and a local Thai employee of the International Rescue Committee, I helped design and direct a health education campaign which used this wealth of performance. A refugee performance company was established to produce skits and scenarios. Drawing on Hmong folklore and using traditional communicative forms such as proverbs, story-telling, and folksinging, it was able to develop critical awareness about the various health problems in Ban Vinai.

There is always the danger, however, of appropriating performance and using it as an instrument of domination. I wanted no part of the puppet theatre approach used by some expatriates as simply another means to get refugees to do what bureaucrats think best for them. Instead, I hoped that performance could be used as a method for developing critical awareness as an essential part of the process of improving the health situation in the camp. My project was aligned with the popular theatre approach to development and political struggle that is being used with success throughout the third world, particularly Africa, Latin America, and Asia. This theatre movement frequently draws inspiration from Paulo Freire's fieldwork as documented in *Pedagogy of the Oppressed* (1986). Augusto Boal (1985) and Ross Kidd (1982, 1984) are perhaps the best-known names associated with the popular theatre, or people's theatre movement. Fortunately, a sizable body of literature is developing around this kind of third world theatre (Bustos 1984; Desai 1987; van Erven 1987; Eyoh 1986; Kaitaro 1979; Kidd and Byram 1978; Thiong'o 1981, 1983, 1986). In *Helping Health Workers Learn* (Werner and Bower 1982) – which is the companion volume to the widely distributed *Where There Is No Doctor: A Village Health Care Handbook* (Werner 1977) – there is an excellent chapter on politics, health, and performance entitled 'Ways to Get People Thinking and Acting: Village Theater and Puppet Shows.' This work perhaps more than any other inspired my efforts in Ban Vinai.

In popular theatre, the process of developing the performance is as important, if not more so, than its final presentation. The backstage processes of researching and developing culturally appropriate materials, the participatory involvement of the people are as significant as any explicit 'message' communicated in a skit or scenario. For popular theatre to work effectively as a tool of critical awareness and empowerment for oppressed peoples, it must be rooted in and begin with their cultural strengths. Of course, even before the Hmong became refugees, oral traditions and cultural performance were the primary ways of educating the young and promoting beliefs and values among adults. Instead of aesthetic distance and other concepts of elite theatre, popular theatre is contingent upon what Kenneth Burke calls rhetorical processes of 'identification' and 'consubstantiality' (1969: 19–23).

Health workers wanting to use popular theatre must become participant fieldworkers. Getting to know the culture is important not just as a technique for collecting appropriate materials and ideas to be worked into performances but as a way of earning the community's trust and respect. No matter how flashy and entertaining the health show, village people are wary of outsiders who drop in for a day or two and then leave. Refugees, even more than villagers, have good reason to be skeptical of officials who hold themselves at a distance. The Hmong have a proverb: 'To see a tiger is to die: to see an official is to become destitute' (Tapp 1986: 2). When a health worker gets involved, becomes part of the struggle, that speaks as forcefully as any line in a performance script. Ndumbe Eyoh said it clearly: 'There seems to be no other better way than associating fully with them, meeting them in the villages, joining them in their daily chores and sharing with them their lifestyles' (1986: 23). That is why it was crucial for me to live in the camp with the Hmong, although that was considered a great oddity by the other expatriate agency workers who commuted from Chiang Kham village, an hour's drive away. I hoped to break the pattern of importing the knowledge of 'experts' and distributing it to the refugees, who were expected to be grateful consumers. I wanted to help demonstrate to both expatriates and refugees that dialogue was possible.

Bartering health advice and practices with traditional healers was one of the methods that worked well for me and prevented the programme from being too one-sided. For example, early in my fieldwork I fell through a bridge and gashed my toe. Herbalists treated my wound with soothing poultices from a glossy-leaved plant. Within a week the wound had healed. Due to the camp conditions, I also suffered frequent intestinal disorders, and consulted women herbalists who gave me a root to chew that eased the problem.

I tried to engage in a dialogue through which each culture could benefit from the other. This was particularly important as refugees were accustomed to having expatriates undermine, even outrightly assault, their traditions.

The rabies parade

The first test was whether or not the Hmong would accept a popular theatre approach. Could we gather an audience? That test came earlier than I had planned when five rabid dogs rampaged through the camp biting children. It was proposed that IRC use its funds to buy a rabies vaccine and inoculate all the dogs in the camp. The vaccine was purchased and IRC personnel were at their stations ready with needles to vaccinate the dogs. No dogs arrived. The problem centered on communication. The Hmong were not boycotting the rabies programme. They simply were baffled by this strange procedure, or unaware of it. There was no effective way of getting the word out as to where, when and why dogs should be brought to the IRC stations for injections.

At that time, I had just arrived in the camp and was beginning to work with the newly recruited refugee performers/health workers. We had developed some characters based on stock figures in Hmong folklore and were designing and constructing costumes and masks. We were just starting to mesh as a group when the IRC director approached me and asked for help with the rabies vaccination project. Time was running out. The camp dogs would have to be vaccinated soon to prevent Ban Vinai having a serious rabies epidemic.

The performance company agreed on a grand, clamorous, eye-catching 'Rabies Parade' that would snake its way through all sections of the camp. The tiger costume – appliqued cotton fabric with a long rope tail – was

Figure 27.1 The tiger leads the Rabies Parade, Hmong refugee camp, 1985 (photo by Dwight Conquergood).

almost finished, so it was agreed that the tiger would be the lead figure in the parade. The tiger is a trickster in Hmong folklore and mythology. We knew the tiger would draw attention and inspire awe. The tiger would be followed by a nature-spirit, a ragged costume with long coloured strings for hair, that would sing and bang on a drum. That noise, we hoped, would reach people inside their huts and bring them out to see the commotion.

We agreed that the chicken, a feathered costume with a striking card-board mask that covered the entire head, would be the pivotal figure. After the dancing tiger and the clamorous nature-spirit got people's attention, the chicken would talk through a bullhorn and explain in terms the Hmong would understand, the seriousness of rabies and why it was important for every family to round up the dogs and bring them for injections. The chicken couched all this in an appeal to protect the children and then gave specific instructions for each neighborhood in the camp as to where and when they should bring the dogs. The chicken was chosen to be the leading speaker because in Hmong lore chickens have divinatory powers. They are frequently used as offerings in spirit ceremonies to lead the way to the sky kingdom. Hmong naturally associate the chicken with divination because, as was explained to me, 'Who is the one who knows first when the sun comes up every morning?'

In terms of its ability to gather an audience, the Rabies Parade was a huge success. However, the real test was whether or not the Hmong would bring their dogs to the vaccination stations. The next morning, on watch at the first station, I saw dogs come pouring in. We could not vaccinate them fast enough and by the end of a week we had vaccinated almost 500 dogs.

Incorporating feedback

We took advantage of the performance company's initial outing to elicit direct audience feedback as part of the process of testing, developing, and refining our concepts. Throughout the development of our health theatre programmes, we actively solicited feedback from Hmong elders. One elder critiqued the performers on three points: (1) the plain-clothed performers and stage managers should wear traditional Hmong clothes, and not Western-style T-shirts and trousers available in the camp through charity outlets; (2) the backup music for the dances should be authentic Hmong, not Thai or Western-influenced melodies; (3) the rhymed chants were a little off from the traditional Hmong prosody and so he taught the young performers the correct speech patterns.

Through other critiques we learned that a few people found the masks and the tiger scary and worried that some of the children's spirits might be scared away and they would fall sick. This was very serious. If one shaman attributed the sickness of one child to spirit-flight precipitated by the parade, the Ban Vinai health and performance company would be destroyed. No accusations came but we did decide to modify our staging techniques as a result of this feedback. Powerful characters like the tiger would no longer play directly to the audience. Instead, we would direct the energies of the tiger and other masked characters inside a circle, using an onstage focus. These dramatic characters would interact in an animated way with one another, but not directly confront the audience.

Mother Clean

We did not want to lose the power of open-form communication, so we needed a narrator character who could safely and directly address audiences. Proverbs are an important and popular communication form amongst the Hmong. We wanted to use a character who could recite health proverbs and tell stories and who would have a special rapport with small children. This led to the creation of our most successful character who became the symbol for the entire health communication programme: the beloved Mother Clean (Niam Tsev Huv), our cleanliness clown. She was the collective creation of the entire performance company. In fact, the performance company worked collectively on all phases of the performance process, from research for scenarios to composing songs and proverbs to costume construction. Except for the tiger's mask which I purchased in Loei, all of the costumes and props were handmade from local materials.

Once we had demonstrated that performance was an appropriate and successful way of communicating with the Hmong, we set to work on the environmental health problems of the camp. Instead of blaming the Hmong for the poor health conditions and issuing messages instructing them to change their behavior, we developed performances that would stimulate critical awareness about the camp environment, particularly how it differed from the Hmong mountain villages in Laos. Once their radically changed living conditions could be brought to consciousness through performance, the Hmong might understand the need for changing some of their habits to adapt to this altered situation.

Garbage

We mounted a series of performances focused on the problem of garbage in the camp. The first thing we had to do was problematize 'garbage.' In a traditional Hmong village, garbage was not the problem it was in Ban Vinai. If all disposable waste is organic, and you live in a small hamlet on a windswept mountain slope, then pitching waste out of the door is not a problem. It becomes instant feed for the household pigs or it biodegrades. In the context of a crowded refugee camp, however, this means of waste disposal has radically different consequences. We wanted to get this message across without demeaning the Hmong and suggesting that they were dirty.

Ban Vinai is notorious for the image of refugees relieving themselves in the open space. This act, so shocking to 'sophisticated' sensibilities, functions discursively as a sign of 'the primitive.' Before I left Bangkok en route to Ban Vinai, I heard stories about this behavior from other aid workers and came across this motif in written reports as well as oral anecdotes. This recurrent image is psychologically and rhetorically interesting for what it reveals about our discursive projections of the Other. My observations are that the Hmong are a very modest people. The act does not occur with the frequency the stories imply. However, you have only to spend three days and nights in the camp in order to understand the environmental circumstances that produce such behavior even occasionally. Living in the camp with the refugees and experiencing these environmental constraints and indignities was instructive for me.

Our 'Garbage Theme' month featured Mother Clean in one of our most successful scenarios. Drawing on the evil ogre character from Hmong folklore (poj ntxoog), we created an ugly Garbage Troll in soiled ragged clothes and a mask plastered with bits of garbage and dirt. The Garbage Troll would lumber into the centre of the playing space and begin dramatizing the behavior to be discouraged – peeling eggs and other food and throwing the waste on the ground, picking up dirty food from the ground and putting it into his mouth, and so forth. After a few minutes of this improvisation, the Tiger would charge on stage and rebuke the troll for such unseemly behaviour. The Tiger would growl and snarl and pounce at the impassive Troll, all the while making verbally explicit how bad this behavior was. The Tiger would give up and leave but then the Pig would run out on stage and fuss at the troll for his disgusting conduct. The young performer who played our Pig was a gifted clown and there would be much farcical business between the Pig and the Garbage Troll until the Troll drove the Pig away. Then the Chicken would follow suit and sagely admonish the Troll about the environmental consequences of his behavior and how he would make children sick by throwing garbage all about. The Troll would respond by throwing more garbage on the ground and at the Chicken, driving the latter away.

From a considerable distance, Mother Clean would slowly sweep toward the dirty Garbage Troll. The children forming a circle around the playing space would have to open up their ranks to permit Mother Clean's passage. They would call out, warning her to beware of the nasty Garbage Troll. But Mother Clean would be unaware of the danger; absorbed in sweet thoughts she would sing to herself and dance as daintily as her bulk would permit. The children in the audience would increase the volume of their warning cries until Mother Clean heard and caught sight of the Garbage Troll. Unafraid, slowly, triumphantly she would sweep toward the nasty Troll huddling in the dirt making menacing noises. She'd reach down, pull him up by his hands, then, in a moment of redemptive grace, remove his dirt face mask and wash his face and hands. Transformed, the Troll and Mother Clean danced as music was played from our battery-operated cassette player. Tiger, Pig, and Chicken rushed back on stage to dance and sing with Mother Clean and the redeemed Troll. Our refugee health workers, wearing sandwich-board posters with the health theme boldly lettered, would join the circle, and Mother Clean would slowly spell out and read the poster proverbs for those in the audience who were nonliterate. She would talk and invite comment and discussion about the theme.

Mother Clean would lovingly amplify the message of the proverb, pointing out that Ban Vinai is very different from the mountaintop villages in which the Hmong used to live. She exhorted a change in behavior without degrading the people whom she was trying to persuade, locating responsibility in the environmental circumstances. Everyone could agree that indeed Ban Vinai was very different from their former home. After establishing that premise, Mother Clean then could make the point about the need for adaptive response to this new situation.

This scenario was staged three or four times a week, each time in a different section of the camp. In this way we could reach most of the camp population in a month's time. Each day we would find a wide place in the road, or a clearing between houses, and use that empty space for the performance. One of the company members would walk around the area with a bullhorn announcing the performance. The performances were so popular that we sometimes had crowd control problems, with people pressing in so close that there was no room for the performers to move. One of the company members, usually the one who made the initial announcements over the bull-horn, would serve as 'house manager.' He would draw a large circle on the ground with a pointed stick and declare that area the players' space, off-limits to curious children. This strategy worked, except for the occasional dog that wandered on stage.

Over the next few years, Mother Clean became fully integrated into the culture of Camp Ban Vinai. Literacy textbooks produced in the camp print shop were illustrated with images of Mother Clean. Mother Clean hand puppets were made in the camp and used for entertainment and instruction. Mother Clean puzzles delighted children. The ultimate test was that Mother Clean had been invited by the Hmong leaders to perform at the New Year Festivities, the most important and elaborate celebration of Hmong culture.

In retrospect

As I critique my work in the camp I realize that I should have developed more consciousness-raising performances specifically for the expatriate health professionals. They needed to develop a critical awareness about health problems in the camp at least as much as did the Hmong. Directing most of the performances to the Hmong resulted in a one-sided communication campaign and subtly reinforced the prevailing notion that the Hmong were primarily responsible for the bad conditions.

The ideal is for the two cultures, refugees' and relief workers', to enter into a productive and mutually invigorating dialogue, with neither side dominating or winning out, but both replenishing one another. Intercultural performance can enable this kind of exchange.

Works cited

Boal, Augusto (1985) [1979] *Theater of the Oppressed*. Translated by Charles A. and Maria-Odila Leal McBride. New York: Theatre Communications Group.

Burke, Kenneth (1969) *A Rhetoric of Motives*. Berkeley: University of California Press.

Bustos, Nidia (1984) 'Mecate, the Nicaraguan Farm Worker's Theatre Movement.' *Adult Education and Development* 23 (September): 129–140.

Desai, Gaurav (1987) 'Popular Theatre, Participatory Research and Adult Education in Africa: A Preliminary Bibliography.' Unpublished manuscript, Northwestern University.

van Erven, Eugène (1987) 'Philippine Political Theatre and the Fall of Ferdinand Marcos.' *The Drama Review* 31, no. 2 (T114): 58–78.

Eyoh, H. Ndumbe (1986) *Hammocks to Bridges: Report of the Workshop on Theatre for Integrated Rural Development.* Yaounde, Cameroon: BET & Co.

Freire, Paulo (1986) [1970] *Pedagogy of the Oppressed.* New York: Continuum.

Kaitaro, Tsuno, ed. (1979) 'Theater as Struggle: Asian People's Drama.' *Ampo* 11, nos. 2–3 (special issue).

Kidd, Ross (1982) *The Popular Performing Arts, Non-formal Education and Social Change in the Third World: A Bibliography and Review Essay.* The Hague: Centre for the Study of Education in Developing Countries.

—— (1984) *From People's Theatre for Revolution to Popular Theatre for Reconstruction: Diary of a Zimbabwean Workshop.* The Hague: Centre for the Study of Education in Developing Countries.

Kidd, Ross, and Martin Byram (1978) *Popular Theatre and Participation in Development: Three Botswana Case Studies.* Gaborone, Botswana: Bosele Tshwaraganang Publications.

Tapp, Nicholas (1986) *The Hmong of Thailand: Opium People of the Golden Triangle.* Indigenous Peoples and Development Series Report No. 4. London: Anti-Slavery Society.

Thiong'o, Ngũgĩ wa (1981) *Detained: A Writer's Prison Diary.* London: Heinemann.

—— (1983) *Barrel of a Pen: Resistance to Repression in Neo-Colonial Kenya.* Trenton, NJ: Africa World Press.

—— (1986) *Decolonising the Mind: The Politics of Language in African Literature.* London: J. Currey.

Werner, David (1977) *Where There is No Doctor: A Village Health Care Handbook.* Palo Alto, CA: Hesperian Foundation.

Werner, David, and Bill Bower (1982) *Helping Health Workers Learn.* Palo Alto, CA: Hesperian Foundation.

Chapter 28

L. Dale Byam

COMMUNAL SPACE AND
PERFORMANCE IN AFRICA

THE NOTION OF TRADITIONAL PERFORMANCE as street theatre is not without irony. In post-colonial Africa, states Byam, the streets are the mark of European settlers, who built them to facilitate the movement of raw materials and goods for their own profit. There the spirit of street performance as public forum exists in indigenous forms that, having been pushed to the side during colonialism, are revived, reshaped and reintroduced.

The multi-dimensional character of African theatre prevents it from being pigeon-holed into generalities; but certainly in emerging from its own unique history, a phenomenon emerges. The underlying ritualistic beginnings is the nexus of this phenomenon. Here ritual is the event that draws the community together, reaffirms it and highlights the connection between man and god. The communal quality of ritual creates an implicit space central to the community's ethic – what South American community theatre artist, Augusto Boal, refers to as aesthetic space (Boal 1995: 18). In pre-colonial Africa people gathered for celebrations in a variety of outdoor venues: in the market-place, under a tree in front of the chief's home. Even within some of these spaces, portions were sometimes reserved for the privy of the most sacred. Such space was indeed a marketplace of community culture, brandished to ensure the preservation of a way of life. The particulars vary from one African country to another, but most relevant to our inquiry is how the notion of communal space complements African performance's unique evolution from purely ritualistic origins to diversification resulting from its encounter with the Western world.

Increased foreign presence in many African countries invalidated indigenous artistic expression forcing it underground and into the interior, sometimes under the rubric of secret orders. Still discernable is the characteristic impromptu involvement of the audience be it through ululation or verbal commentaries. Given the communal nature of theatre in Africa – as a meeting ground for ideas and for sharing community culture through performance – much of it is now presented in schools and community centers. In rural areas or sites where it still occupies a significant role in the community, nature provides the most convenient theatre in the form of the shade of a tree or the like. In contrast, European-styled theatres, replete with dialogue, stage design and costumes were established alongside European settlements. Legitimate theatre, according to the colonists, was performed indoors, in the colonist's constructed theatres, in the universities and only occasionally, under the supervision of Europeans, in the streets and communities of the indigenous population.

The notion of street theatre literally defies the logic of developing countries and is basically an inaccurate description; streets are perceived as by-ways erected to encourage European trade and connote tools of development and movement away from communalism. Seldom is African performance referred to in this manner. Michael Etherton, a British theatre historian, takes such liberties by defining street theatre, in the African context, as 'performance given in ad hoc situations, by the roadside, in the market place – wherever people congregate in the normal course of events' (Etherton 1982: 19). However, the definition proves to be problematic since such performances were *customarily* presented in public spaces in many parts of Africa.

During the colonial era, many forms of indigenous performance were outlawed. European drama as well as African adaptations became the center of cultural activity, catering to Europeans. Ironically, Africans filled the forced and expanding communal void by gravitating toward the missionary churches and schools for guidance and instruction. Missionary education nevertheless concertedly attempted to eradicate the notion of an African identity: The fundamental reason why the Christians were so keen to suppress African performing arts was that they realized cultural forms held the symbolic key to the religious and moral bases of indigenous societies (Kerr 1995: 18). Missionary schools encouraged students to do adaptations of European plays. European artists performed in newly built theatres and African ritual began to be perceived as a hedonistic and primitive form of expression. African performance was depleted of its spiritual content while adapting to European guidelines of theatre.

In Zambia, Kenya, Zimbabwe, South Africa, Namibia and other countries where European settlement territories were created, little theatres were constructed for the foreign communities and very much to the exclusion of the indigenous people. African artists resorted to the readily available performance spaces, in open air, while still lobbying for a place in the constructed theatres designed for the Europeans. This is not to imply that the communal open air space was inferior to the constructed theatres, but the latter occupied very central locations. In Zambia, these little theatres could be found close to the railway line. In Kenya, the National Theatre occupied a central space in the heart of the capital, Nairobi. During the nineteenth century the hub of cultural activity shifted from the rural communities to the towns and cities, another reason that indigenous performance assumed a lesser role as a form of African cultural expression. Nevertheless, attempts were often made to maintain its communal verve. The traveling theatres were responses to this displacement.

The traveling theatres, developed during the early 1900s, carried popular songs combined with folk tales and dramas into rural areas. They syncretized indigenous performance with the then-popular European and American styles. This type of theatre was often spearheaded by an individual who conceived the traveling theatre concept. In South Africa, Gibson Kente toured his popular musicals throughout the townships. In Ghana this occurred through the Concert Parties led by Bob Johnson and in Nigeria, through the Yoruba Traveling Theatre. The Yoruba Traveling Theatre has roots in the Alarinjo, itinerant performers who evolved from a religious order of pre-colonial masqueraders, the Egungun, who themselves began as court entertainers. Adedeji elaborates:

> Performances were enacted in any of the following places, depending on who had commanded the performance: court performance (the palace quadrangle or inner courtyard, or the piazza in front of the palace); Alagbaa's performance (the ode in front of the gabled frontage of his compound); lineage-heads, chiefs and other important persons (in the courtyard or the ode in front of the gabled frontage of the compound). No raised platform was necessary for any of these performances. An open space was all that was needed. A 'circle' was always formed by the spectators as they assembled round the open space (arena) to watch the show.
> (Ogunbiyi 1981: 237)

Herbert Ogunde, E. K. Ogunmola and Duro Ladipo were stellar examples of traveling theatre pioneers. Their performances brought music and drama that highlighted aspects of semi-urban African life to rural communities. People welcomed these theatre performances for their infectious music and, in some instances, the poking of fun at the government or some other aspect of African life.

The traveling theatre concept existed in many parts of Africa. Griots [ed. note: storytellers] often moved throughout villages and towns retelling myths and legends to those who stopped to listen or who invited them in, offering both bed and board. The style of the performances differed region-ally. Ogunde's work in Nigeria was often charged with political satire while Bob Johnson's work in Ghana conformed to a more vaudevillian style – both examples of African performance fused with European styles of theatre. However, as African cultural expression became more subjugated through colonialism, the theme of resistance surfaced in not only traveling theatres but all forms of performance, giving rise to the African political or protest theatre. And the theatre of resistance occurred in traditional and non-traditional places, in the communities and in the towns.

As post-colonial Africa continued to grapple with changing economic, social and political conditions, development agencies came to its assistance. Some relied on indigenous culture to absorb development messages through a blaming-the-victim strategy as had been done during colonialism. For example, health campaigns focused on the community's ignorance of European practices rather than missionary education and colonialism as the sources of underdevelopment. To this end many campaigns were undertaken to bring the development messages to the rural areas using local songs and stories. Often, government officials performed on the back of trucks or manipulated puppets with simple messages about hygiene or agriculture. As Graham-White recorded,

> In the Gold Coast a program was set up in 1948 which is still continuing. Teams of about fifteen tour, presenting short plays, perhaps twenty minutes long, which encourage literacy, good child care, sanitation, and cooperation, each play to be followed by a discussion. In a typical play a young man chooses a plain but literate girl as his wife rather than her beautiful sister – who thereupon enrolls in a literacy class.
> (Graham-White 1974: 65)

But though these performances were well received, they had little impact. For once the officials traveled on to other communities, the lessons were hardly implemented. Some development programs also experimented with radio campaigns to convey their messages to the growing population, but this technique relied on technology which was sorely lacking in rural areas.

Universities also participated in development programs. They sometimes contributed to the resuscitation of indigenous African theatre. The Makere University in Uganda under the tutelage of O'kot p'Bitek encouraged students to take a variety of plays into the community. Plays adapted to indigenous languages for rural communities attracted large groups of people. However, some university-based programs operated on the premise that the communities didn't have a theatre, perhaps assuming that only written plays provide a legacy for drama in the universe. This premise is immediately dismissed by consideration of the oral tradition that has withstood the absence of pen or paper in Africa.

Indeed, education played a large role in the development and the under-development of Africa. Formal education during colonialism imposed the format of the colonizers and excluded large numbers of African people. In the most rural areas, formal education was, traditionally, not confined to school buildings. Such structures were a function of the financial viability of a community. In the post-colonial era, aiming to make education available to all Africans, greater emphasis has been placed on the community's involve-ment in the process. Encouraged by the facility with which cultural activities aid education, development specialists began to consider theatre as a viable means of promoting development in Africa. Indeed it was a literacy educator, Ross Kidd, who first experimented with integrating theatre into the devel-opment process using Paulo Freire's work as the underlying foundation. This is known as Theatre For Development.

In 1973, the first Theatre For Development project was undertaken in Botswana by British and Canadian expatriate university personnel. The project was guided by what became the Theatre For Development format of plan-ning, investigating, story development, rehearsal, discussion and follow-up action. It involved the collaboration of extension workers and members of a rural community for the purpose of developing issue-based performances informed by community contact. Unfortunately, the performances were not shaped by the community but rather by extension workers who gath-ered the information. The audience, though attentive, reaped neither short- nor long-term rewards from the exercise. Still, the Botswana project had a domino effect; programs followed in Zambia, Zimbabwe, Nigeria, Malawi, Lesotho and other African countries. All pursued development as the ultimate goal, though the names, such as popular theatre, community theatre and Theatre For Development, were used interchangeably. The present day Theatre for Development movement in Africa has many view-points but its foundational objective is popular empowerment. However, this ideologicial premise has often been side-stepped by limiting community involvment in the interest of satisfying the time constraints of development programs.

Another Theatre For Development effort, though on a different ideo-logical footing, came by way of the Kamīrīīthū Cultural Center in Kenya. There, unrestricted by limitations of a development program, Ngũgĩ wa Thiong'o, a university teacher, Ngũgĩ wa Mĩriĩ, an adult educator, and the Kamīrīīthū community attempted the feat of popular empowerment through an adult literacy program. The Kamīrīīthū program was developed to address the problem of illiteracy in the community. The leaders of the program chose to explore the community's history as the foundation for this new learning. Out of this program came many stories that were regularly improvised. Performances occurred intermittently as the program revolutionized learning by acknowledging the issues of the peasants as the subject for literacy. The Kenyan peasants also actively participated in the development of the drama.

The collaboration resulted in a written play, *Ngeekha na Ndeenda*, and an open-air theatre constructed by the peasants for the performances:

> I saw with my own eyes peasants, some of whom had never once been inside a theatre in their lives, design and construct an open-air theatre complete with a raised stage, roofed dressing-rooms and stores and an auditorium with a seating capacity of more than a thousand persons.
>
> (Ngũgĩ 1981: 77)

Daily, as the participants rehearsed, the local people gathered and commented on the progress of the plays. That enthusiasm attracted other communities and unnerved the government who haltingly destroyed one of the few organic theatres to emerge in post-colonial Africa. [Ed. note: See Ngũgĩ's essay in this collection.]

Development, evidently, has many interpretations, many ambiguities. Such ambiguities are also to be found within the Theatre For Development movement, giving rise to contradictions amongst programs with similar names though dissimilar objectives. Kenya's lead provided the impetus for community-based Theatre For Development in Zimbabwe. In 1982, with Ngũgĩ wa Mĩriĩ forced into exile in Zimbabwe by the obdurate Kenyan government, communal theatre there took on an even wider scope. The Zimbabwean government supported the establishment of a national Community Based Theatre Project (CBPT) as a wing of an education agency known as the Zimbabwe Foundation for Education and Production (ZIMFEP). In 1989, the CBTP and its membership weaned themselves from government attachment and established an independent agency focused on community theatre. At present over 200 theatre companies operate under the umbrella of the Zimbabwe Association of Community Theatre (ZACT) and perform in a variety of communal spaces to address the issues of Zimbabwean people. During ZACT's national conventions when all companies converge for policy making and discussion, the artists take to the city streets to perform in shopping areas, marketplaces and bus terminals. This communal sharing can be equally effective in a pub, public stadium or refugee camp. ZACT finds aesthetic and political advantage in such spaces.

ZACT has become the contemporary prototype of Theatre For Development with a strong ideological foundation. Its process begins within the community where the artists train and work. The Community Theatre Process, a program designed by Ngũgĩ wa Mĩriĩ, is germane to the artist's development. During a typical training session where community theatre artists gather, a trainer presents the pyramid of class struggle – a class analysis of the position and role of the artist in society, placing those who own the means of production at the top of this pyramid. These include land and business owners. S/he places the unemployed, community theatre artists and organized labor at the bottom. In training the artists, the trainer provokes the participants to assess their position in society. Once this is determined, s/he asks, 'Can drama change the order of things?' Thus the final stage of training is to acquaint the artists with ways and means of using community theatre for education, development, conscientization and social change (Byam 1993).

To this end, ZACT performances often include a built-in mechanism for audience response and community action. For example, during a recent AIDS awareness campaign in Zimbabwe, ZACT artists were accompanied by health practitioners who offered further information on AIDS prevention and home care. Such work has arisen in the post-colonial stage of Zimbabwe's development as one means of combatting the miseducation that had been perpetuated under apartheid. In the post-independence stage, other theatres have also attempted to incorporate issue-based themes into their work with varying degrees of popular involvement throughout the process. In the case of the well-established Reps Theatre, run by whites in Zimbabwe, though the subjects addressed are sometimes issue-based, the process continues to exclude popular participation. ZACT is still left competing with established, European-funded theatres since all artists, despite their ideological leanings, compete for arts funding. Today ZACT struggles to gather the money necessary to create permanent structures to nurture this communal ideal while performing in a number of spaces both indoor and outdoors in the absence of its own performance venue. Its street work is a consequence of displacement and an ideology which aims to develop theatre with the community.

In spite of limitations, a unique phenomenon is emerging in Africa. ZACT's work has influenced the development of communal theatres in Botswana, Namibia and South Africa. ZACT artists now assist in the formation and development of community theatres throughout the southern region of Africa. There, the communal space has begun to defy a location and is emerging as a stream of consciousness.

References

Boal, Augusto (1995) *The Rainbow of Desire*, London: Routledge.

Byam, Dale (July–October, 1989; July–September, 1991; July–September 1993) Field Notes, ZACT Workshops and performances.

Etherton, Michael (1982) *The Development of African Drama*, London: Hutchinson.

Graham-White, Anthony (1974) *The Drama of Black Africa*, New York: Samuel French.

Jeyifo, B. (1984) *The Yoruba Traveling Theatre of Nigeria*, Nigeria: Nigeria Magazine.

Kerr, David (1995) *African Popular Theatre*, London: James Currey.

Kidd, Ross and Byram, Martin (1978) 'Popular Theatre: A Technique For Participatory Research,' Working Paper No. 5, Toronto: Participatory Research Group.

Ngũgĩ wa Thiong'o (1981) *Detained*, London: Heinemann.

Ogunbiyi, Yemi (1981) *Drama and Theatre In Nigeria: A Critical Source Book*, London: Pitman Press.

McCrimmon, Janet (1991) 'Evaluation Report on The Zact AIDS Awareness Play *Manyanya*,' ZACT/OXFAM.

Chapter 29

Ngũgĩ wa Thiong'o

from THE LANGUAGE OF
AFRICAN THEATRE

NGŨGĨ WA THIONG'O EMPHASIZES THE educational implication of traditional performance's orientation to process. Following a traditional model, he and villagers of Kamiriithu created an open-air theatre in which to meet, discuss, rehearse and perform. He contrasts the participatory process of 'open-air' theatre with the European model that only opens itself to the public at the end when the show is perfected.

Early one morning in 1976, a woman from Kamĩrĩĩthũ village came to my house and she went straight to the point: 'We hear you have a lot of education and that you write books. Why don't you and others of your kind give some of that education to the village? We don't want the whole amount; just a little of it, and a little of your time.' There was a youth centre in the village, she went on, and it was falling apart. It needed group effort to bring it back to life. Would I be willing to help? I said I would think about it. In those days, I was the chairman of the Literature Department at the University of Nairobi but I lived near Kamĩrĩĩthũ, Limuru, about thirty or so kilometres from the capital city. I used to drive to Nairobi and back daily except on Sundays. So Sunday was the best day to catch me at home. She came the second, the third and the fourth consecutive Sundays with the same request couched in virtually the same words. That was how I came to join others in what later was to be called Kamĩrĩĩthũ Community Education and Cultural Centre.

[. . .]

All the activities of the centre were to be linked – they would arise out of each other – while each being a self-contained programme. Thus *theatre*, as the central focus of our cultural programme, was going to provide follow-up material and activities for the new literates from the adult literacy programme, while at the same time providing the basis for polytechnic type activities in the material culture programme.

But why theatre in the village? Were we introducing something totally alien to the community as the Provincial Commissioner was later to claim?

[. . .]

Drama in pre-colonial Kenya was not [. . .] an isolated event: it was part and parcel of the rhythm of daily and seasonal life of the community. It was an activity among other activities, often drawing its energy from those other activities. It was also entertainment in the sense of involved enjoyment; it was moral instruction; and it was also a strict matter of life and death and communal survival. This drama was not performed in special buildings set aside for the purpose. It could take place anywhere – wherever there was an 'empty space', to borrow the phrase from Peter Brook. 'The empty space', among the people, was part of that tradition.[1]

It was the British colonialism which destroyed that tradition. The missionaries in their proselytising zeal saw many of these traditions as works of the devil. They had to be fought before the Bible could hold sway in the hearts of the natives. The colonial administration also collaborated. Any gathering of the natives needed a licence: colonialism feared its own biblical saying that where two or three gathered, God would hear their cry. Why should they allow God above, or the God within the natives to hear the cry of the people? Many of these ceremonies were banned: like the *Itu\u0129ka*, in 1925. But the ban reached massive proportions from 1952 to 1962 during the Mau Mau struggle when more than five people were deemed to constitute a public gathering and needed a licence. Both the missionaries and the colonial administration used the school system to destroy the concept of the 'empty space' among the people by trying to capture and confine it in government-supervised urban community halls, and schoolhalls, church buildings, and in actual theatre buildings with the proscenium stage. Between 1952 and 1962 'the empty space' was even confined behind barbed wire in prisons and detention camps where the political detainees and prisoners were encouraged to produce slavishly pro-colonial and anti-Mau Mau propaganda plays.

[. . .]

On looking back now, it is clear that Kenyan theatre in the early seventies was trying to break away from the imperialist colonial tradition whose symbols were the European-dominated Kenya National Theatre (albeit aided by the ruling regime), the Donovan Maule Theatre in Nairobi and other similar centres in the major towns.

Its main handicap was still its petty-bourgeois base in the schools and University Colleges, from where came the majority of its actors, directors and plays. Above all it was limited by the very imperialist tradition from which it was trying to break away. English was still accepted as the main medium of revolt and affirmation. Original scripts, even the most radical, were often written from the standpoints of the petty-bourgeoisie. And theatre was still confined within walls. Where it tried to break away from the confines of closed walls and curtains of a formal theatre building into rural and urban community halls, the assumption was still that theatre was to be taken to the people. People were to be given a taste of the treasures of the theatre. People had no traditions of theatre. The assumption that people were to be given theatre was of course in keeping with the government fiction that people were there to be given development particularly if they behaved themselves.

But it was imperialism that had stopped the free development of the national traditions of theatre rooted in the ritual and ceremonial practices of the peasantry. The real language of African theatre could only be found among the people – the peasantry in particular – in their life, history and struggles.

Kamĩrĩĩthũ then was not an aberration, but an attempt at reconnection with the broken roots of African civilisation and its traditions of theatre. In its very location in a village within the kind of social classes described above, Kamĩrĩĩthũ was the answer to the question of the real substance of a national theatre. Theatre is not a building. People make theatre. Their life is the very stuff of drama. Indeed Kamĩrĩĩthũ reconnected itself to the national tradition of the empty space, of language, of content and of form.

Necessity forced the issue.

For instance, there was an actual empty space at Kamĩrĩĩthũ. The four acres reserved for the Youth Centre had at that time, in 1977, only a falling-apart mud-walled barrack of four rooms which we used for adult literacy. The rest was grass. Nothing more. It was the peasants and workers from the village who built the stage: just a raised semi-circular platform backed by a semi-circular bamboo wall behind which was a small three-roomed house which served as the store and changing room. The stage and the auditorium – fixed long wooden seats arranged like stairs – were almost an extension of each other. It had no roof. It was an open air theatre with large empty spaces surrounding the stage and the auditorium. The flow of actors and people between the auditorium and the stage, and around the stage and the entire auditorium, was uninhibited. Behind the auditorium were some tall eucalyptus trees. Birds could watch performances from these or from the top of the outer bamboo fence. And during one performance some actors, unrehearsed, had the idea of climbing up the trees and joining the singing from up there. They were performing not only to those seated before them, but to whoever could now see them and hear them – the entire village of 10,000 people was their audience.

[. . .]

The use of English as my literary medium of expression, particularly in theatre and the novel, had always disturbed me. In a student's interview in Leeds in 1967 and in my book *Homecoming* (1969) I came back to the question. But I kept on hedging the issue. The possibility of using an African language stayed only in the realm of possibility until I came to Kamĩrĩĩthũ.

It was Kamĩrĩĩthũ which forced me to turn to Gĩkũyũ and hence into what for me has amounted to 'an epistemological break' with my past, particularly in the area of theatre. The question of audience settled the problem of language choice; and the language choice settled the question of audience. But our use of Gĩkũyũ had other consequences in relation to other theatre issues: content for instance; actors, auditioning and rehearsals, performances and reception; theatre as a language.

[. . .]

Now many of the workers and peasants in Kamĩrĩĩthũ had participated in the struggle for land and freedom either in the passive wing or in the active guerrilla wing. Many had been in the forests and the mountains, many in the colonial detention camps and prisons; while some had of course collaborated with the British enemy. Many had seen their houses burnt; their daughters raped by the British; their land taken away; their relatives killed. Indeed Kamĩrĩĩthũ itself was a product of that history of heroic struggle against colonialism and of the subsequent monumental betrayal into neocolonialism. The play [*Ngaahika Ndeenda*] was celebrating that history while showing the unity and continuity of that struggle. Here the choice of language was crucial. There was now no barrier between the content of their history and the linguistic medium of its expression. Because the play was written in a language they could understand the people could participate in all the subsequent discussions on the script. They discussed its content, its language and even the form. The process, particularly for Ngũgĩ wa Mĩrĩĩ, Kimai Gecaũ, and myself was one of continuous learning. Learning of our history. Learning of what obtains in factories. Learning of what goes on in farms and plantations. Learning our language, for the peasants were essentially the guardians of the language through years of use. And learning anew the elements of form of the African Theatre.

What are these elements of form?

First was song and dance. Song and dance as we have seen are central to nearly all the rituals celebrating rain, birth, the second birth, circumcision, marriage, funerals or to all ordinary ceremonies. Even daily speech among peasants is interspersed with song. It can be a line or two, a verse, or a whole song. What's important is that song and dance are not just decorations; they are an integral part of that conversation, that drinking session, that ritual, that ceremony. In *Ngaahika Ndeenda* we too tried to incorporate song and dance, as part of the structure and movement of the actors. The song arises from what has gone before and it leads to what follows.

The song and the dance become a continuation of the conversation and of the action.

[. . .]

The content of the play was asking many questions about the nature of Kenyan society and this generated ever more heated discussions on form and content during the entire period of the play's evolution. Sometimes these involved not just the actual participants but the ever widening circle of the audience.

Auditions and rehearsals for instance were in the open. I must say that this was initially forced on us by the empty space but it was also part of the growing conviction that a democratic participation even in the solution of artistic problems, however slow and chaotic it at times seemed, was producing results of a high artistic order and was forging a communal spirit in a community of artistic workers. PhDs from the university of Nairobi: PhDs from the university of the factory and the plantation: PhDs from Gorki's 'university of the streets' – each person's worth was judged by the scale of each person's contribution to the group effort. The open auditions and the rehearsals with everybody seeing all the elements that went into making a whole had the effect of demystifying the theatrical process.

In the theatre that I was used to in school and colleges and in amateur circles, the actors rehearsed more or less in secrecy and then sprung their finished perfection on an unsuspecting audience who were of course surprised into envious admiration: oh, what perfection, what talent, what inspired gifts – I certainly could never do such a thing! Such a theatre is part of the general bourgeois education system which practises education as a process of weakening people, of making them feel they cannot do this or that – oh, it must take such brains! – In other words education as a means of mystifying knowledge and hence reality. Education, far from giving people the confidence in their ability and capacities to overcome obstacles or to become masters of the laws governing external nature as human beings, tends to make them feel their inadequacies, their weaknesses and their incapacities in the face of reality; and their inability to do anything about the conditions governing their lives. They become more and more alienated from themselves and from their natural and social environment. Education as a process of alienation produces a gallery of active stars and an undifferentiated mass of grateful admirers. The Olympian gods of the Greek mythology or the dashing knights of the Middle Ages are reborn in the twentieth century as superstar politicians, scientists, sportsmen, actors, the handsome doers or heroes, with the ordinary people watching passively, gratefully, admiringly. Kamĩrĩĩthũ was the opposite of this. The Kamĩrĩĩthũ practice was part of education as a process of demystifying knowledge and hence reality. People could see how the actors evolved from the time they could hardly move their legs or say their lines to a time when they could talk and move about the stage as if they were born talking those lines or moving on that stage. Some people in fact were recruited into the acting team after they had intervened to show how such and such a character should be portrayed. The audience applauded them into continuing doing the part. Perfection was thus shown to be a process, a historical social process, but it was admired no less. On the contrary they identified with that perfection even more because it was a product of themselves and their collective contribution. It was a heightening of themselves as a community.

The research on the script of *Ngaahika Ndeenda*, the writing of the outline, the readings and the discussions of the outline, the auditions and rehearsals and the construction of the open-air theatre took in all about nine months – from January to September 1977. The readings, the discussions and the rehearsals were timed to keep in rhythm with the lives of the people. So these were set sometimes on Saturday afternoon but always on Sunday afternoons. Even Sunday afternoon was chosen so that Kamīrīīthū theatre would not interfere with church attendance in the mornings.

The results of all this effort to evolve an authentic language of African theatre were obvious when the play opened to a paying audience on 2 October 1977. Once again the performances were timed for Sunday afternoons. Evening would have been too cold for everybody. *Ngaahika Ndeenda* was an immediate success with people coming from afar, even in hired buses and taxis, to see the show. Theatre became what it had always been: part of a collective festival. Some people knew the lines almost as well as the actors and their joy was in seeing the variations by the actors on different occasions to different audiences. There was an identification with the characters. Some people called themselves by the names of their favourite peasant and worker characters like Kīgūūnda; Gīcaamba; Wangeci; Gathoni. But they also used the names of such characters as Kīoi, Nditika, Ikuua, and Ndugīre, to refer to those, in and outside the village, who had anti-people tendencies. The language of *Ngaahika Ndeenda* was becoming part of the people's daily vocabulary and frame of reference. There were some touching moments. I remember one Sunday when it rained and people rushed to the nearest shelters under the trees or under the roofs. When it stopped, and all the actors resumed, the auditorium was as full as before. The performance was interrupted about three times on that afternoon but the audience would not go away. The people's identification with Kamīrīīthū was now complete.

Later, they were driven away, not by the rain, not by any natural disaster, but by the authoritarian measures of an anti-people regime. On 16 November 1977 the Kenya government banned any further public performances of *Ngaahika Ndeenda* by the simple act of withdrawing the licence for any public 'gathering' at the centre. I myself was arrested on 31 December 1977 and spent the whole of 1978 in a maximum security prison, detained without even the doubtful benefit of a trial. They were attempting to stop the emergence of an authentic language of Kenyan theatre.

[. . .]

On Thursday 11 March 1982 the government outlawed Kamīrīīthū Community Education and Cultural Centre and banned all theatre activities in the entire area. An 'independent' Kenyan government had followed in the footsteps of its colonial predecessors: it banned all the peasant and worker basis for genuine national traditions in theatre. But this time, the neo-colonial regime overreached itself. On 12 March 1982 three truckloads of armed policemen were sent to Kamīrīīthū Community Education and Cultural Centre and razed the open-air theatre to the ground. By so doing it ensured the immortality of the Kamīrīīthū experiments and search for peasant/ worker-based language of African theatre.

A collective theatre, or what Boal has called a 'theatre of the oppressed', was produced by a range of factors: a content with which people could identify carried in a form which they could recognise and identify; their participation in its evolution through the research stages, that is by the collection of raw material like details of work conditions in farms and firms; the collection of old songs and dances like *Mūthīrīgū*, *Mūcūng'wa*, and *Mwomboko* and opera forms like *Gītiiro* etc; their participation, through discussion on the scripts and therefore on the content and form; through the public auditions and rehearsals; and of course through the performances. The real language of African theatre is to be found in the struggles of the oppressed, for it is out of those struggles that a new Africa is being born. The peasants and workers of Africa are making a tomorrow out of the present of toil and turmoil. The authentic language of African theatre should reflect this even as it is given birth by that very toil and turmoil. Such a theatre will find response in the hearts and lives of the participants; and even in the hearts of those living outside the immediate environment of its physical being and operation.

Note

1   I am indebted to Wasambo Were for the comparison between *The Empty Space* of Peter Brook's title, and the practice of African literature during a discussion I had with him on theatre in Kenya in London 1983.

Chapter 30

Yolanda Broyles-González

from EL TEATRO CAMPESINO AND THE MEXICAN POPULAR PERFORMANCE TRADITION

TEATRO CAMPESINO WAS CREATED DURING the Chicano, i.e. Mexican-American, Farmworkers' Movement by, for and with Chicano farmworkers. Early performances frequently took place at picket lines, on the dirt roads of California migrant camps and at union halls. In this excerpt, Broyles-González elucidates the Mexican popular cultural forms at the source of El Teatro Campesino and the Chicano theatre movement. Like traditional performance, popular forms cannot be attributed to individuals; that may be why, embedded in some of the most persistent, seemingly light-weight entertainments is a deep sense of the identity and world view of the people with less cultural and political clout who developed them. Here Broyles-González celebrates the carpa, or travelling tent show, grounded in the perspective of the Mexican working class, and the key contribution of actors who transmitted these forms.

The year 1965 marked the beginning of a widespread Chicano theater renaissance. In that year the celebrated Teatro Campesino came suddenly into existence, seemingly from out of nowhere. What is more, an entire Chicano theater movement exploded onto the cultural scene in a matter of months. Dozens of Chicano theater groups made their appearance across the Southwest and Midwest during the 1960s and 70s, performing, for the most part, within Chicano communities. Generated by the anger and hope of the progressive social movements of the time – such as the Civil Rights Movement, the

Anti-War Movement, the United Farm Workers' Movement, the Chicano Movement, and the Women's Movement – a widespread theatrical mobilization sought to affirm an alternative social vision with reliance on a distinctly Chicano aesthetic. Despite existing differences among Chicano theatrical groups they nonetheless manifested an astounding degree of similarity or common ground. Those commonalities were rooted not only in a common working-class social experience but in a common cultural heritage of performance forms. Kanellos, for example, at the time elaborated upon how 'all these groups incorporate folkloric material.' He furthermore points out that 'these theaters not only represent the world view of their *pueblo*, but often carry on traditional forms of acting, singing, and performing' (1978: 58).

Notwithstanding occasional references to 'traditional forms of acting,' the body of research on the Chicano theater renaissance and especially on El Teatro Campesino has focused almost entirely on aspects of its textuality, its topical nature, and on the conditions of its founding and evolution. El Teatro Campesino is characteristically viewed in and of itself, and not as a phenomenon which, like the mythical Phoenix, arose from the ashes of its own Mexican past. Wherever antecedents or a past are briefly named we invariably find Eurocentric references to the Italian *commedia dell'arte*, to the German playwright Brecht, or to Russian *Agitprop*.

In seeking to establish the origins of the Chicano theater movement as a whole, many researchers point to the Teatro Campesino ensemble. It is widely regarded as the theatrical fountainhead from which all inspiration and technique trickled down to other Chicano theaters. Critics' conceptualization of creativity usually narrows even further, crediting one individual and ignoring groups of people: Luis Valdez is seen as the omnipotent agent who variously 'brought,' 'introduced,' who 'wrote' for, who 'directed' the anonymous others. This top-down view of creation – related to the great man ideological construction of history – is symptomatic within dominant Western print culture which a priori conceptualizes theatrical (and other) production as the work of an *individual* male 'creative genius.' An alternative construction or model might well invert relations and reveal to us, for example, that the farmworkers introduced the acto form *to Luis Valdez* who subsequently made it his own.

A more far-reaching model for constructing our understanding of El Teatro Campesino and of the Chicano Theater movement is one which seeks out a commonality of origin within the Mexican popular performance tradition. Only these common older roots can account for the notable homogeneity of a Chicano theater movement which exploded onto the American scene from the *physical memory* of a dormant tradition. [. . .] Elements from that tradition abound within the performance activity of all groups within the Chicano theater renaissance and most certainly within El Teatro Campesino during the ensemble years: 1965–1980.[1] In establishing the vital linkages between El Teatro Campesino and expressive cultural practices from the Mexican popular performance tradition I do so not in the manner of an inventory or grouping of disparate or discrete elements. Instead, I seek to conceptualize those cultural practices as constituent parts of a larger unified field of interlocking cultural practices which I call Mexican oral culture or the popular performance tradition. What I posit here, in other words, is that the Mexican culture of orality (used here interchangeably with 'popular performance tradition') constitutes the conceptual bedrock from which a coherent understanding of seemingly disparate or unconsolidated surface manifestations of Chicano theater become possible. [. . .] It is my contention that the inordinate strength of El Teatro Campesino was not as much a function of innovation as of its reliance on tradition: its grounding in Mexican oral culture.

[. . .]

In seeking to characterize El Teatro Campesino, Luis Valdez kiddingly described El Teatro Campesino as 'somewhere between Brecht and Cantinflas' (1966: 55). A statement issued more in an effort to orient a non-Chicano audience (in this case *Ramparts* readers) was promptly taken at face value by many critics.[2] Critics avidly seized the European reference to Brecht – an influence I consider less than negligible – while discounting the Mexican reference and tradition.[3]

[. . .]

The name Cantinflas is virtually synonymous with a Mexican popular tradition of comedy associated in the past 200 years with the *carpa* or tent show. It is impossible to define the Mexican carpa as one thing, for it encompassed a field of diverse cultural performance practices popular among the poorest segments of the Mexican populace. The carpa's central association with the blood, sweat, and tears of the disenfranchised masses of Mexicans certainly accounts for the obscurity of its origins and evolution: it has not been the object of sustained scholarly research activity or documentation. Mexican playwright Emilio Carballido places the origins of the carpa in the 18th century, if not earlier: 'There is a popular tent theater which comes down to us since the Eighteenth Century, but more than likely even before that; it has given something of its vitriolic quality even to our elite political theater' (1988: 2; trans. Broyles-González).

The Mexican carpa and, more broadly speaking, the Mexican popular performance tradition has throughout history served as a counterhegemonic tool of the disenfranchised and oppressed. [. . . Its] periods of vigorous revival coincide with periods of social upheaval and popular distress. In 20th century Mexico the carpa experienced a major resurgence in connection with the Mexican Revolution and its aftermath. Among Chicanos in the United States its revival coincides with the global popular liberational movements of the 60s and 70s. The Mexican artist Covarrubias (1938: 596) describes the world of the carpa in the 1930s:

collapsible, barn-like carpas, show tents that were drawn on trucks and even mule carts from suburb to suburb and from village to village, quickly set up in the main square or out in the middle of the street, a presage of a coming fair. The carpa, a development of post-revolutionary Mexico and now a permanent institution, consists of a canvas tent, often walled by detachable wooden panels, a gaudy small stage with bizarre painted drops, lit by a single naked glaring electric bulb. The music is provided by a melancholy orchestra. . . . The 'house,' simply rows of home-made hard benches, is generally packed with a most colorful crowd, an amazing variety of types: workers, Mexican Apaches, soldiers, Indians from the country, proletarian women with babies, in their blue rebosos, side by side with overdressed city girls and white collared men of the middle class. Barkers go in and out, leaving the entrance curtain partly open to entice the customers, describing the excellences of Lupe la Veracruzana, tropical torch singer, the ludicrous skits of the mad comedian 'Chicote,' or the Rabelaisian humor of 'Conde Bobby.'

This same observer speaks to the socio-cultural importance of the rough, elemental, and hilariously ribald world of the carpa:

However crude, vulgar and tainted with bad taste they may be, they have created a style and a technique of the disconcerting mixture of rough slapstick and fine, biting satire that is characteristic of the Mexican humor. The very informality of these performances and the highly culti-vated art of improvisation give an intensity and a liveliness that is sadly lacking in other theatrical efforts.

(596).

[. . .]

The carpa continued with full force into the 1950s and early 60s, a resilience probably attributable to its native and working-class roots, as well as its ability to speak to the daily reality of Mexican workers in an enter-taining manner. This is the world of working-class performance inherited by El Teatro Campesino.

[. . .]

Prior to the establishment of the Teatro Campesino in 1965 César Chávez had been wanting to use a carpa as an organizing tool. As a child and young adult he had witnessed the power of carpa performances and was keenly aware of the value of humor as a vehicle of critique and mobilization. Chávez's strong reliance on Mexican cultural practices – the carpa and other more spiritual practices – to consolidate farmworkers politically was new in the annals of US labor unions. Chávez perceived a need to organize by means of a specific cultural language shared by the overwhelming majority of farmworkers:

I had the idea of using the carpa in the Farm Workers Union. I had seen carpas a lot in Mexicali, Tijuana, and Nogales. I wanted a carpa in the union for purposes of communication. With a carpa we could say difficult things to people without offending them. We could talk about people being cowards, for example. Instead of being offensive, it would be funny. Yet it could communicate union issues. When the Teatro Campesino was formed I gave the early characters their names: Don Sotaco, El Patroncito, El Coyote, etc.

(1993)

The intimate relationship between the Mexican carpa tradition, César Chávez, and the Teatro Campesino was referenced recently by Luis Valdez, who indicated: 'Without César, there would have been no Teatro Campesino' (Benavídez 1993).

One very important transmitter of the Mexican Rasquachi performance aesthetic of the *carpa* was the farmworker Felipe Cantú. Cantú worked with the earliest Teatro Campesino ensemble almost from its beginnings, until the Teatro separated from the Farm Workers Union in 1967. The eldest of the early Teatro formation (forty-four years old), Cantú came to be regarded as a maestro whose superb performance skills became legendary among all Teatro Campesino ensemble members. Ensemble member Olivia Chumacero later recalled: 'He is the funniest man I have ever met in my entire life' (1983). In a *Ramparts* article, Valdez referred to him as 'a comic genius' who 'made his talents apparent on the picket line, where lively dialogues between pickets on the road and scabs in the field inspired his Mexican wit. . . . He speaks no English, but his wild, extravagant Cantinflas-like comic style needs no words' (1966: 55). Teatro Campesino cofounder Agustín Lira referred to Felipe Cantú as 'the heart or soul of the *actos*' and described how other characters orbited around Cantú's Cantinflas-like underdog character, Don Sotaco:

To me, the most important person of the Teatro Campesino was Felipe. Not just personally, but talentwise. Of all the comedians who have been around and whom I've seen, whether they're Mexican comedians like Cantinflas, or comedians from Europe or other parts of the world, I still haven't seen anyone with the comedic talent of Felipe Cantú.

All he needed was the idea. He would take that idea and peel away everything it was NOT. Like making a statue. He took the rock and carved away everything that was not the character. He had a natural talent for getting into his characters. That's why, back then, Don Sotaco's personality was the heart − or the soul − of the actos. He was the victim and we moved around that character.

(1983; trans. Broyles-González)

Figure 30.1. In comic role reversal, the boss is played by the farm worker, Luis Valdez, and the esquirol, or scab, by Danny Valdez. In El Teatro Campesino's *Las Dos Caras del Patroncito* (photo by George Ballis).

Even the *Wall Street Journal* took note of the 'incisive comic shenanigans of Felipe Cantú' (O'Connor 1967).

What earned Felipe Cantú the title of maestro was that he transmitted a concrete working knowledge of community-validated performance skills to the Teatro Campesino. Luis Valdez describes Cantú's pivotal role within the Teatro: 'Felipe became the prototype of El Teatro Campesino. He established a level of performance that influenced the whole CHICANO THEATRE movement. Many of the techniques the Teatro learned on the road were assimilated by osmosis from Felipe. A lot of people don't realize the impact of one campesino' (1989).

Although Cantú's impact as an individual was indeed great, we can understand that impact fully only if we situate him within the broader performance tradition of which he formed a part and from which he emerged.

[. . .]

On numerous occasions Luis Valdez and other members of the Teatro Campesino ensemble have affirmed and reaffirmed their strong roots in the carpa tradition and the carpa aesthetic, usually referred to as the Rasquachi Aesthetic within the Teatro Campesino. [. . .] Valdez indicates: 'We evolved – in our own earthiness – characters that emerged from Cantinflas and the whole comic Mexican tradition of the carpa, the tent' (Broyles 1983: 38). It was particularly the performing family of El Circo Escalante that made a great impression on the young Valdez. The Escalantes were itinerant artists who at times lived from performance income and at other times from farm labor income. That was to become a model for the early Teatro Campesino.

Linguistic markers pointing to a relationship between El Teatro Campesino and the Mexican popular tradition also abound: the term 'carpa' appears in the titles of Teatro Campesino performance pieces such as the classic *La gran carpa de los Rasquachis*; another piece, for example, was entitled *Carpa Cantinflesca*. Like most Teatro Campesino pieces it is based in the Mexican performance style embodied by the great carpa comedian Cantinflas, particularly popular from the 1930s through the 50s and now legendary.

[. . .]

Cantinflas' mass appeal was due to many factors. Chief among them is the fact that his performance techniques and character were derived from the popular Mexican performance aesthetic and the plight of the underdog. His shabby attire was the standard poor-man attire of generations of comics. Cantinflas also enjoys the distinction of having brought those Mexican popular performance techniques of the carpa to the silver screen. Those techniques were not solely *his*, but based on the arsenal of popular performance techniques found (with variations) in all carpas and in all Mexican/Chicano communities into the late 50s. In other words, Cantinflas was but one very prominent and gifted representative from a tradition much larger than himself.

It is a popular performance tradition which has traditionally thrived in Mexicano working-class communities throughout Mexico and the US Southwest. The performance techniques, forms, language, style, characters, audience relationship, performance sites, and social relations of production of El Teatro Campesino emerge from that Mexicana/o *community* context and history – and not from Europe or from one individual.

[. . .]

Notes

1   Some of those elements have been enumerated by Nicolás Kanellos (1978), yet they are inventoried in piecemeal fashion and not conceptualized as a unified cultural field

2   Upon [Campesino actor] Felipe Cantú's death in 1989, Valdez once again issued a similar orientational statement concerning Cantú: 'He combined the styles of Brecht and Cantinflas' (Valdez 1989) [. . .] Brecht, however, cannot be regarded as a direct or indirect influence upon Cantú since, for one thing, Cantú's formation predated any entry of Brechtian influence into the Chicano theater movement – or even the existence of the movement. Furthermore, Cantú's formation precluded any exposure to print culture (such as Brecht): Cantú could not read. It might, in fact, be realistic to study the influence of the carpa upon Brecht: He resided in California during the heyday of the carpa (1941–1947).

3   Although the young Valdez certainly *read* Brecht and was in some way influenced by him, two facts speak to Brecht's very marginal influence: 1 The Teatro Campesino aesthetic *and* performance pieces were collectively generated from a farmworker collective ensemble steeped in the Mexican popular performance tradition and entirely unfamiliar with Brecht. In other words, they came from the Cantinflas tradition. 2. Much of what Brecht generated in the way of technique, theory, and plays came, in his own words, directly from popular culture traditions, which have affinities and resemblances world-wide, even though they originated and evolved entirely independent of each other. Common to many peoples, for example, is a comedic tradition. Many elements which critics immediately identify as 'Brechtian' are, in fact, native folk comedy techniques. Hence, many techniques of the Mexican comedian Cantinflas or the English Charlie Chaplin show a relationship to Brechtian theory, where in fact they predate Brecht and were certainly never influenced by him. What is more, Brecht never took credit for 'inventing' the techniques which scholars have come to identify solely with him. The much discussed and quoted *Verfremdungseffekt* (defamiliarization technique), for example, was nothing new or original with Brecht. Brecht himself refers to it as 'an ancient art technique, known in comedy, certain areas of popular culture and in the practice of Asiatic

theater.' (My translation of 'Der V-Effekt ist ein altes Kunstmittel, bekannt aus der Komödie, gewissen zweigen der Volkskunst und der Praxis des asiatischen Theaters.')

Although critics have quickly seized upon the reference to Brecht and other European sources (*commedia dell'arte*), Valdez himself was quick to see the European traditions in terms of the Mexican one. He reverses the relationship which critics falsely establish by indicating how very much like Cantinflas Brecht is, or how the harlequin echoes the popular Mexican performance tradition (represented by Cantinflas). In other words, Valdez will admit to parallels, but not readily to influence:

> . . . Then what Cantinflas was doing up there on the screen was a direct reflection of that audience. They identified with him. They reveled with him because he was dealing very directly in his humor – especially in his early movies – he was identifying with the low man on the totem pole, he was the victim of fate, and yet trying to survive in his own way, using his wits; outwitting the rich, outwitting the powerful, doing a double-talk that everybody knew was nonsense but it was imitative of education, it was imitative of being powerful. And so he became a very popular hero, and a magical hero to watch. There is some of that character, of the Cantinflas character, of the harlequin character in Brecht's work, here and there. Some of them are sometimes women. Mother Courage is a female Cantinflas, in her own way; if she is portrayed in a certain way, you can get that tragic-comic quality about her. Certainly some of the central figures in Brecht's anti-military plays, such as *Man is Man*, are Cantinflas types.
>
> I guess the closest way for American audiences to see that is in English music hall Chaplinesque terms. For me as a Chicano I saw that in Cantinflas terms. . . .
>
> I think Brecht derived the alienation effect from the ancient roots of the theater. To the extent that I am drawing from my own ancient roots, it is there too.

These quotations and a discussion of Brecht and El Teatro Campesino are found in Broyles (1983).

References

Benavídez, Max. 1993. 'César Chávez Nurtured Seeds of Art.' *Los Angeles Times* (28 April), section F, p. 1.

Broyles, Yolanda Julia. 1983. 'Brecht: The Intellectual Tramp. An Interview with Luis Valdez.' *Communications from the International Brecht Society* 12, no. 2: 33–44.

Carballido, Emilio. 1988. 'Editorial: El Eslabon.' Tramoya. *Cuaderno de Teatro*, new series 14–15: 2.

Chávez, César. 7 March 1993. Interview. La Paz.

Chumacero, Olivia. 19 January 1983. Interview. San Juan Bautista.

Covarrubias, Miguel. 1938. 'Slapstick and Venom: Politics, Tent Shows and Comedians.' *Theatre Arts Monthly* 22, no. 8: 587–596.

Kanellos, Nicolás. 1978. 'Folklore in Chicano Theater and Chicano Theater as Folklore.' *Journal of the Folklore Institute* 15, no. 1: 57–82.

Lira, Augustín. 22 March 1983. Interview. Fresno.

O'Connor, John. 1967. 'The Theater: Shades of the 30s.' *Wall Street Journal* (24 July).

Valdez, Luis. 1966. 'Theatre: El Teatro Campesino.' *Ramparts* (July): 55–56.

—— 1989. 'Felipe Cantú, Original Teatro Member, Dies April 26, 1989.' El Teatro: El Teatro Campesino Newsletter (15 May).

Chapter 31

Joi Barrios

THE TAUMBAYAN AS EPIC HERO, THE AUDIENCE AS COMMUNITY

THE CLOSE CONNECTION BETWEEN AN oppositional political movement and the revival of street performance in the Philippines between 1970 and 1990 parallels the same dual phenomenon elsewhere in the world. Barrios documents the rich indigenous forms that have served as vessels for activist street theatre, finding a through line in the recurrent positioning of the *taumbayan*, or masses, in the role of epic hero.

From 1970–1990, when the struggle for Philippine national democracy was strongest and the national cultural movement at its peak, theatre artists moved out of the confines of theatre buildings to perform in the streets. Influenced by Brecht, the Chinese cultural revolution, Augusto Boal and African theater, these artists used a variety of forms, among them puppetry, Japanese noh, religious plays, vaudeville, play-poems, improvisation, radio dramas and above all, the indigenous Philippine epic. Originally chanted by the *binukot*, a woman trained from childhood, they told of heroes who embarked on a search, courageously fought battles, died and in the end, were reunited with the beloved. Indigenous theatre, not unlike the political theatre of the late twentieth century, was performed by the community for the community.

This sense of community continued during the Spanish colonial period when religious plays were introduced. The *sinakulo* dramatized the life of Jesus Christ, the *salubong*, the meeting of Christ and the Virgin Mary and the *panunuluyan*, the search of Mary and Joseph for an inn. In these plays, the central figure, Jesus Christ, like the epic hero, journeyed to earth, struggled with temptation, died through crucifixion, rose from the dead and was reunited with the Father. Free performances were held in front of the chapel, at the town plaza or in the streets. People immediately accepted such plays and participated either by performing as a *panata*, or vow, or by contributing in cash or in kind to finance the productions.

However, it was also during the Spanish colonial period that theatre slowly moved inside theatre structures. These productions became dependent for financing on the producer who, to recoup investments, charged audiences. Theatre was no longer accessible to those who lived far from the theatre building or who could not afford to buy tickets.

In the spirit of 'bringing back a sense of community' and 'bringing theatre back to the people,' performers from the late 1960s through the 1990s moved to the streets. During this period people also took to the streets to stage protests. Theatre companies were commonly part of political organizations. For example, the theatre group *Panday Sining* (Molders of Art) began as the cultural arm of *Kabataang Makabayan* (Nationalist Youth). Through street theatre, these groups articulated issues such as the political dictatorship of Marcos, low wages and land reform. Numerous plays influenced by traditional religious theatre retained the epic structure of journey, death and rebirth. Tanghalang Bayan's *Ang Kalbaryo ni Juan de la Cruz* (*The Calvary of Juan de la Cruz*), 1970, a processional street performance, was staged during Holy Week. The Christ of the play was represented by the Filipino Juan, tormented by truncheon-wielding military men.

In 1972, President Ferdinand Marcos declared martial law to extend his presidential term. Some theatre artists responded with 'lightning plays,' performed in marketplaces. In a flash, actors coming from different points formed a tableau and shouted slogans against the Marcos dictatorship, expressing popular resentment of martial law. To elude arrest they left immediately, the performance lasting only one or two minutes. But because of intense militarization and the deployment of artists to other areas of work, few street plays were performed during the mid-1970s.

During the late 1970s, the national democratic movement started to regain its strength. Workers staged strikes for better wages, students held rallies against tuition increases. Street theatre became synonymous with political theatre. At the heart of each play was the issue; plot, form and production elements followed. Again, their structure was quite similar to the Philippine epic: exposition on the conditions of the main characters, usually workers or peasants; the 'journey' they embark on in Philippine society; the heightening of difficulties and oppression; a 'death' in the form of a seeming defeat in the struggle; and then, gathering strength from each other, 'resurrection' as they unite to face the enemy.

This structure is evident in UP Repertory Company's many plays using the dula-tula or play-poem form. In *Ang Kagila-gilalas na Pakikipagsapalaran*

Figure 31.1 Peryante performs a song-movement piece during a march against the Marcos dictatorship (photo by Donato Majia Alvarez).

ni Juan de la Cruz (*The Fantastic Adventures of Juan de la Cruz*), 1975, the lead character is citizen Juan who travels to different places in the city, from parks to moviehouses to restaurants, encountering various characters and problems. He is always restricted by signs: 'No Smoking, Boss,' 'No Parking,' 'Passes Not Honored Today,' 'Beware of Dogs,' 'Keep Off the Grass,' 'Your Credit is Good But We Need Cash,' 'Not Wanted Dead or Alive.' Juan finally decides to go to the countryside to join the armed struggle. The play was performed by one reader and two actors. One played the main character, and the other, known as Ms. Ellaneous (usually played by a woman, but sometimes, more hilariously, by a man), played all the others. The production thus needed only one microphone, which is all rallies usually had. Props and costumes were light so that actors could carry them if the rally was dispersed and they had to run from police. These plays served also as models for groups such as teachers, workers and journalists, to articulate their own problems and conditions.

Theatre artists found creative ways to articulate political issues before large groups and avoid arrest. In 1979, a group with no name joined a tuition protest, wearing red and black cloth masks similar to that of the movie character Zorro. They performed a movement play, the narration interpreted through gestures influenced by martial arts. Later groups used movement from the traditional martial dance *kuntao* and modern dance. In order to be visible to huge audiences, Dulaang Palanyag, known for its use of pantomime, wore black shirts and pants and painted their faces white. *Ang Babala ng Lawin* (*The Hawk's Warning*), directed and designed by Cris Gosalvez and performed in front of the US Embassy, used puppets to augment a small company. Narration read by one actor holding a microphone was interpreted by two puppets, a hawk and an eagle, representing the Philippines and the United States.

During student rallies, organizers would ask the assistance of street performers to attract fellow students. Thus, forms that used comedy and music were developed. For example vaudeville, popular during the 1930s and 1940s, was resurrected by Peryante in 1980. A barker invited passing students to watch the play. The group then performed songs, dances and comedy routines.

Peryante's most popular play, *Ilokula, ang Ilokanong Dracula* (*Ilocula, the Ilocano Dracula*), written and directed by Chris Millado, referred to then-President Marcos as a dracula hungry for the blood of the Filipino people. Ilocula, stricken by a mysterious illness, is attended by singing and dancing doctors: Dr. Bareta (then Finance Minister Cesar Virata) carrying gold coins, the two-headed monster Dr. Barrile (Defense Minister Enrile), Dr. Revolver (Chief of Staff General Ver) and Dr. Eric Baines (an American dentist in a television commercial, here representing American intervention). The doctors find out that Ilocula has 'eaten too much,' proving his greediness. In an operation, they recover body parts he has gobbled up: the worker's shoulders, the peasant's feet, the student's fist, the intellectual's brains, the artist's tongue. These body parts are reassembled, symbolizing the unity of the people. They rise up against Ilocula, defeating him, thus showing the will of the people. In *Ilocula*, as in many revolutionary plays, the epic hero who dies and is reborn is configured as the *taumbayan*, the people.

Traditional religious forms, familiar to most audiences, were also used to attract attention to contemporary issues. *Salubong sa Maynila* (*Meeting in Manila*), 1994, was drawn from the traditional *salubong* which reenacts the meeting of the Virgin Mary and the resurrected Christ. Performing on top of a truck, actors portrayed women dressed in black veils, shirts and pants with sad-looking masks made of brown paper. At the center stood the Virgin Mary, wearing the national Filipina costume. The script, recited by readers as the performers moved, included prayer chants and songs. The women, who at the beginning of the play were shown weeping because of poverty, war and the loss of their children, metamorphosed into warriors ready to fight for their country's liberation from poverty and colonialism. The play reinterpreted the Virgin Mary as the Mother Country and other female icons as strong women from whom female spectators could draw wisdom and determination.

Augusto Boal's image theatre proved to be an effective means to discuss the boycott campaign during the 1984 parliamentary elections. The play, performed in front of a department store, relied heavily on the participation of the audience. Actors presented three images of the political situation: the present, the ideal and a transitional image. Volunteers were then asked to change the images as they wished – adding or subtracting characters, changing their positions or acting the roles themselves. This way, the audience 'wrote' and 'performed' the play with the actors serving as facilitators for a discussion of issues.

Another popular form was the 'reenactment.' In 1985, the Artex Cultural Group reenacted the strike they staged the previous year. True to the incident, actors portrayed hired goons destroying their picket line, resulting in bloodshed. Performed by those who actually had participated in or witnessed the event and staged during the anniversary of the strike, the reenactment was like a ritual.

In 1986, the Marcoses were driven out of the country and Corazón Aquino was installed as president. But soon incidents like the massacre of peasants marching peacefully and the summary execution of labor leader Rolando Olalia and student activist Lean Alejandro led people back to the streets in protest.

Among the theatre groups that adapted new forms for new times was the Mindanao Council for People's Culture. They based *Bulawan* (*Gold*), 1986, on a two-person South African play that they had seen on videotape. The two characters, Kaloy and Poloy, are sitting on a rock (a chest actually), fishing in a river. Poloy catches a fish and finds a piece of gold inside it. They dig for more gold but find, instead, a book containing an advertisement urging them to listen to the radio station DXBB. The scene shifts to a rally. Poloy becomes a field reporter and Kaloy, a worker giving a speech; the chest becomes a radio station. They both become artists leading the masses singing and, later, police officers dispersing the rally. They then go back to being Kaloy and Poloy discussing the rally. The action then depicts issues such as militarization, elections, the influence of the Catholic church and poverty. The actors shift roles, portraying Cardinal Sin, supporters of President Aquino, knife-wielding vigilantes and trigger-happy military men. In the last scene, the actors turn back into Poloy and Kaloy. They realize that the real meaning of the 'gold' they are searching for lies in the dreams and aspirations of the people. In a split second, Poloy changes into a military man looking for Kaloy, and then reverts back to his original character, warning Kaloy of the danger. They agree to share the 'gold,' vowing to continue the struggle in the cities and the countryside.

The influence of the epic is evident. Poloy and Kaloy embark on a journey to search for gold; they engage in 'battle' through strikes and protest actions; the fight is stopped by a deity, in this case, someone 'saint-like' such as Aquino; there is a 'revelation' wherein they find that the problem is not just Marcos but the ruling elite; the 'hero dies' as the revolutionary movement seems to be dying; the 'hero is resurrected' as Poloy and Kaloy realize that the gold is in the aspirations of the people; the 'hero' goes home as the struggle continues; and the 'hero is married' because the people and the national democratic movement are one. The play was performed in 1986 when rallies were few and far between and street plays were scarce. It was some time before artists became critical of the Aquino government. The play pointed out the reality of the class struggle and the uselessness of a revolution that benefitted primarily the elite.

Bulawan used a variety of theatre forms to elicit two kinds of reactions. Satire, as in Brecht's 'epic theatre,' encouraged audiences to be critical and take action. Realism elicited sympathy for the poor and oppressed. Ordinary characters like Kaloy and Poloy were portrayed realistically and villains, like the fanatical vigilantes, absurd Cardinal and indecisive Aquino, were portrayed comically. As with most street plays, *Bulawan* was designed with mobility and versatility in mind. Actors wore T-shirts and traditional pants (*kantso*), changing character by using sunglasses (according to old people, a symbol of a person you cannot trust because you cannot see the eyes), putting on caps or adding costume parts. They used a *tubao* or traditional kerchief as a scarf, tie, towel, microphone and fishing rod. The chest transformed into rock, radio station, rally platform and army tank.

Philippine street performers regularly adapted to lack of financing, different venues, number of cast members available, time allotted for preparation, security measures and type of audience. Costumes were usually made from katsa or cheesecloth or the cheaper Filipino T-shirt known as *camisa de chino*. Props and masks were made of papier mâché. For improvised sound, tin cans and bamboo sticks were used. When only one microphone was available, a play had a double cast: a set of actors read the lines, another provided movements. When few actors were available or there was no time for preparation, playwrights wrote radio scripts that could be performed with only one rehearsal. Rally leaders or volunteers from the crowd were then asked to read from the script. The audience usually enjoyed seeing their leaders and friends as part of the performance.

Security measures were always taken into consideration. Masks served two purposes: to show character and to hide the actors' identity. In rallies and in long marches, actors used the 'buddy' system, memorized the numbers of human rights groups and called each other up later to ensure that everyone was safe. Specific audiences and the occasion determined the form to be used. For the generally apolitical student audiences, rock musicals and vaudeville plays were done. For huge gatherings such as Labor Day, workers' issues were tackled using songs, movement and slogans, agitating the crowd towards a rousing rendition of the 'Internationale.' In a play commemorating the death of a member of the New People's Army, the Japanese noh form was used, emphasizing grief and torment.

Still, of all Filipino street theatre forms, the most important is the epic, with its quest for freedom, struggle, death and rebirth. The epic hero is the *taumbayan*, the masses, with powers both magical and real, rising against the dictatorship and imperialism. At open-air venues where plays continue to be performed, the audience is a community united by political convictions. The street plays are rituals affirming the belief in victory, the destruction of the present social order and the birth of a new society characterized by freedom and equality.

Mark Sussman

A QUEER CIRCUS
Amok in New York

IN CONTRAST TO THE TRADITIONAL sources of other
case studies in this section, the circus does not count on identification
between performers and a broad audience. Rather, the circus makes a spectacle of its performers' differences. Circus Amok's members are gay and/or
avant garde, and the spectators for its street shows are whoever happen to
habituate the city parks. The form is, however, subverted. The very people
who might be labeled freaks, from bearded lady ringmaster to evening-gowned
male performers, are revealed to share many of the same concerns as their
urban spectators via the lively critique-as-circus that ensues.

Jennifer Miller is screaming. Three dancers on stilts, Tanya Gagne, Sarah
Johnson and Miller herself, burst through the magenta velour curtains in
giant flame-colored costumes and hurtle toward the audience. The crowd
sits, stands and sprawls in a half-circle, separated from the Circus Amok traveling ring by the foot-high painted plywood circular curb, its portable
backstage made by a quickly assembled steel scaffolding proscenium masked
by curtains and brightly painted canvas. Some adults have brought lawn chairs.
Kids, many of them attentive audience members throughout the day of stage
setup and performer warm-ups, press close to the edge, sometimes spilling
onto the stage floor. We are in the Williamsburg section of Brooklyn, in a
small, paved park beneath the entrance to the bridge to Manhattan. Miller
lets it out of her system: the tension and energy of expectation that has built

since parking the rented truck, unloading the scaffolding, stage floor, props and costumes, rehearsing bits, dealing with (usually electrical) emergencies and giving notes whenever a performer is free. The scream has become traditional in this, the third summer season of free, outdoor circuses in New York City parks and community gardens. She screams her transition from producer/director to performer and Bearded Ringmistress Extraordinaire.

It's a call to battle, or at least a call to satirical, political performance in the variety format of the free street circus – the trademark of this Bessie Award-winning troupe. Miller has been a mobile presence, shuttling between the avant-garde dance and performance world and the East Coast sideshow circuit. She travels easily in a given season between New York's historically experimental venues (Dance Theater Workshop, Performance Space 122 or La Mama, ETC) and Sideshows By the Seashore, which bills itself as the last remaining 'ten-in-one' sideshow attraction on the Coney Island boardwalk. Circus Amok mixes the aesthetics and verbal styles of these worlds, particularly in its relation to its audience and its occupation of public space, taking elements from popular traditions as well as from the avant-garde scene.

The traditional sideshow belongs to the commercial environment of carnival. Consisting of rides, games, food concessions and 'shows,' carnival is, in the words of Brooks McNamara, a mobile marketplace of popular entertainments and unusual attractions. Sideshows travel within a temporary city that occupies an empty lot, public park or other marginal public space for a limited time. The financial success of a sideshow depends on the virtuosity of the 'talker,' an oral poet who sells the attraction to an audience of passersby, usually speaking from the 'bally platform' outside the show (McNamara 1992: 9–19). The bally is a form of advertising, a linguistic performance in which the talker transforms distracted strollers and carnival-goers into an audience willing to pay the admission price for a variety show that cycles through a series of acts and then returns to the beginning in a day-long loop. The sideshow is possibly the most basic and disturbing form of solo performance, in which humans have, since colonial times, been displayed for being – ethnologically, physiologically or otherwise – different.

In summers, Miller's regular gig is performing Xenobia, her solo act that confronts Coney Island audiences ten times a day with a mix of fire-eating, machete-juggling and a monologue/rant that at once demystifies and displays her self: a woman with a beard who performs amazing stage tricks, shares the sideshow stage with the Human Blockhead, the Elastic Woman and the Illustrated Man *and* lives a normal life – much like any feminist, lesbian, performance artist and circus director, except with more facial hair and vocal politics. In a sense, Circus Amok is that too – a normal one-ring traveling circus with drag queen clowns, papier-mâché animals instead of live ones, concerns about the quality of everyday New York life and utopian visions of a world with less homophobia and more fashion accessories made from the finest recycled materials.

At the Coney Island Sideshow, Xenobia is one of the acts displayed on the 'inside,' and she takes firm control of the content of her act. Her beard is never simply an object of display; it functions as an occasion for thoughtful looking, a medium through which to show the fluidity and playfulness of having *any* gender – in this case, a queer femininity expressed through a heterogeneous mix of elements: flying machetes, consumed fire, improvised storytelling, circus tricks and the beard.

On a hot, sunny day in the Williamsburg section of Brooklyn (a neighborhood of Dominican, Salvadoran and Satmar Hasidic communities jammed in and around formerly industrial buildings) with an audience of local kids and adults craning their heads out of buildings above a small concrete park, Miller is both the 'outside talker' and part of the attraction. She shares the stage with a wildly creative and committed company, some of whom stretch and warm up on the mats in the ring during the hour before show time.

Circus Amok was born as 'The Ozone Show: A Circus of Environmental Destruction,' performed by The Stratospheric Circus Company at Performance Space 122 in October, 1989. It was, as Miller remembers it, 'just a show,' not a regularly performing company, although several of the original members – dancers/choreographers Jennifer Monson and Scott Heron and writer Sarah Shulman – still work with the circus in its present incarnation. Thriving despite the real economic downsizing of small arts groups in New York, Circus Amok is in its eighth year of reinventing the circus form, borrowing drag fantasy from Charles Ludlam's Theater of the Ridiculous, large-scale transformation and puppet-animal acts from Bread and Puppet Theater's Domestic Resurrection Circus, and the outdoor bally and verbal rhythm and repertoire from the Sideshow, as well as an acrobatic movement vocabulary from post-modern dance.

Since that first project, Miller has collaborated with a crew of performers, many of whom double as technicians and designers for theater and dance the rest of the year, most of whom she has trained in the traditional arts, lingo and folklore of the circus. It is a porous group that dwindles during the year, growing to its greatest force during the months of rehearsals and the performing weeks in June. The crew of performance freelancers who regularly choreograph, dance, write, design and teach includes Cathy Weis, Rick Murray, Karen Sherman, designer Alessandra Nichols, and band leader and Miller's onstage sidekick Jenny Romaine, as well as Heron, Monson, Gagne and Johnson. All accumulate circus, dance and musical skills during the downtime between performances, training regularly at Miller's Williamsburg loft, which functions as Circus studio, storage, office, construction and living space. They incorporate an eclectic mix of yoga and contact improvisation, breathing and relaxation, acrobatics, juggling and stilting. A broad, comic acting style serves in representing the slashing of the city budget by a maniacal, knife-throwing city planner, the Budget Butcher, or the distribution of wealth in American society by a juggling dance of flying folding chairs. Ideas for circus acts are generated through year-long discussion, then written by Miller herself or in collaboration with outside writers. In 1996, for instance, veteran San Francisco Mime Troupe playwright Steve Friedman contributed Miller's monologue, a meditation on the meaning of running amok – 'Amok is when it gets to you! when your blood boils! when the last straw has snapped!' – for the opening *charivari*, a parade around the ring in which each performer introduces a character in a short ambulatory tableau. As acts are conceived, musical scores are drawn from a broad range of popular styles. The band may switch from Macedonian dance music to a klezmer medley to an original tango by composer Terry Dame. The brass band does a walking parade around the neighborhood before each performance, attracting an audience and arriving back at the stage with an explosive percussion piece for the entrance of the stilters.

Miller's first scream from atop a tall set of stilts is a wake-up call, to the audience as much as to the rest of the cast, her final 'note' to tell the company to perform with spirit and to say what needs to be said about the political ecology and economy of New York with a healthy mix of outrage, humor and love. It is also an embodied recognition that *something* will go wrong before this show is over. And Miller delights in those unexpected moments, when a stilt strap is tied too loosely or when the leather straps, buckles and padlocked chains on the straightjacket are a *bit* too tight and the Escape Act – a miniature allegory of bondage transformed to freedom, according to Miller – is a bit long for comfort.

On the road with Circus Amok since 1989, Miller made a shift in 1993, when preparations began for the first free, outdoor summer circus. Previously, it had been an indoor affair, performed at New York's avant-garde venues, situated in the context of Performance Art. Taking it outdoors was a risk, a move that meant rethinking the finances, the message, the live band and the role of gay imagery. How would the blurring of genres play in the inner city of Brooklyn? How would the embodiment of family entertainment by a corps of queer bodies play in a community garden in Harlem? Would the Williamsburg audience read the campy fabulousness and drag aesthetics as a threat? What would the reception of a mostly white company be like next door to the housing projects of East New York in Brooklyn by an audience of color? Would the blend of styles and messages pass as a kind of normality within the frame of the circus ring, a space traditionally inhabited by 'freaks' in the first place?

A greater tension is magnified here: the safety of the avant-garde inhabiting its own turf – in New York, 'downtown' – versus the danger of touring experimental or explicitly political work to an audience that has not, necessarily, asked to see that work. The challenge was to learn – or relearn – how to perform for everyone, for a broader slice of the public sphere, and for kids and families. I am not suggesting that the culture of New York's avant-garde is entirely segregated from 'the public sphere.' In a real sense the indoor spaces

I have mentioned, and the audiences and touring networks they represent, were and are home territory for this group. Performing outdoors and for free, where the stage may at any moment cease to be the focus of an audience's interest, required an especially flexible theatrical form that could use spectacle, music and tricks to draw attention to the performers in the ring.

The answer was to trust the format and conventions of circus, bolstered by public references to a local news story or a slice of national politics. Herein is the safety in the circus form, and its risk. Based in the visual display of the trick or the crazy characterizations of clowns, enhanced by the joyful outness of the performers and smartly mixed with a healthy dose of political rage at the city's Powers That Be, Circus Amok is instantly understood by people of all ages and cultural backgrounds. The troupe balances danger with laughter, slipping its critique between the pies in the face and the surreal, scary and sometimes gender-bent characters of the *charivari*. Protected by the magic of the ring, this circus performs the ancient function of running amok: a burst of chaos into the everyday sphere in which a possessed person or crowd flies into a murderous, though temporary, frenzy.

The issue of class and racial differences between inner-city audiences and the currently all-white company initiates a long discussion with Miller. 'It feels shocking to perform as all whites for these audiences,' she says. And yet, 'it represents a reality in the world.' Miller talks about her training in sideshow and dance. 'When I grew up in circus, I barely saw people of color. It's a fairly segregated world and a fairly segregated art scene.' That is, of course, changing. The move outdoors was a step in the direction of confronting differences of race, class and sexuality in a public space on a hot summer day. 'George [Sanchez, fellow performer and longtime fan] calls it a "culture clash," ' Miller says. 'That's interesting, once it's recognized. And it's problematic.'

Literally a culture clash: the band crashes out a series of percussion breaks scored for drums, gongs, struck metal and conch shell, with the occasional horn blast. The stilters make circles, switch directions, kick, jump and stop, facing the audience as the band resolves into a final ta-da. Gagne and Johnson peel off the sides and exit, leaving Miller alone down center. She begins to look slightly alarmed, looks left and right, then wobbles on the stilts, bowing and thanking the audience for their applause. The stilts give way under her. The thank-yous turn into another scream as she topples backward into the arms of a waiting roustabout (part stagehand, part trick-spotter), who softens her landing onto the stage surface (a portable floor of plywood, athletic mats and a canvas mat cover between the performers and New York playground asphalt). Horns and drums blast amok in the band as Miller begins to flail helplessly. A stilter on the ground is like a fish flopping in a net. Two roustabouts assist, tearing off the extra-long costume and the stilt bindings. This takes some time and some work, only partially drawn out for comic effect. Miller smiles apologetically at the audience before executing as many pratfalls as she can possibly work in. Finally, she is up on her feet, micro-phone in hand, revealed as the show's Ringmaster in a strapless blue satin evening gown, her wild hair and formidable beard and mustache truly visible for the first time.

She welcomes the audience to the show, to their neighborhood and their park. 'Ladies and gentlemen, boys and girls. . . .' Pause, and then, a sly aside: '. . . and the rest of us!' This always gets a laugh, and the size of that laugh is often one gauge of that day's audience. Who else in the crowd is identifying as different, as a member of a group not covered by the Ringmaster's time-honored mode of address? This moment is different in Tompkins Square Park than in the South Bronx, a big laugh in Brooklyn's Prospect Park and maybe not as big a laugh in Van Cortlandt Park in Riverdale – though there is always somebody who acknowledges Miller's split-second estrangement-effect that, along with the beard and the evening gown, says it's okay to look, but don't forget to listen and to think about the bodies you're seeing in this ring and their agency as performers. What constitutes queer content here? The question comes as a comic jolt in the thick of things. Yet it persists as a puzzle. In its ontology, this circus presents bodies that crossdress and move in all kinds of same-sex combinations, though sexuality may rarely be the central issue. The effect is to naturalize the company's drag personae, with the circus ring as a theatrical buffer, giving these performers permission to change the law of the 'normal.'

She continues, warming up the audience, giving the ring of kids on the floor in the front rows a chance to answer back in chorus. 'How are ya doing today?' 'Fine,' they answer. 'I can't hear you!' 'FINE!' Here Miller does her favorite thing and improvises. She gets comfortable and studies the crowd, as the company backstage prepares for the opening *charivari*. 'But wait!' she cries. And then, a pause between each question, a crescendo culminating in panic and fear: 'Did you close the grate on the window before you left your apartment? Did you remember to turn off the stove? Is your house on fire?' The crowd catches on, by this point, and gasps in mock horror.

> Did your mother love you? Did your lover . . . leave you? Well these problems, they are small . . . for today is the day that the CIRCUS COMES TO TOWN!

The company bursts through the curtain accompanied by the band's French fanfare tune: Scotty Heron in a shocking red wig, high heels and garters, with makeup from an Edvard Munch painting, Rick Murray juggling balls in an evening dress with Karen Sherman standing on his shoulders, Sarah Johnson balancing an ax on her chin, Cathy Weis, waving a handkerchief, staggering under the weight of an aluminum backpack frame that suspends a steam iron inches in front of her nose. The company is introduced in this circular procession around the ring.

Figure 32.1 Circus Amok (photo by Kathryn Kirk).

After the *charivari*, the year's theme is introduced. In 1995, it was 'New York Ground Under,' an alternative history of the city. In 1996, the theme is money and its distribution, or lack thereof. The acts themselves, when overtly political, make visible the everyday distinctions of class. One act critiquing the Metropolitan Transit Authority's anti-panhandling advertising campaign takes verbatim dialogue (not to mention the very props themselves) from subway car placards that literally suspend thoughts, interior monologues printed inside cartoon bubbles, over the heads of seated subway riders, trans- forming them into silent, bourgeois subjects who take offense at the mere presence of a panhandler:

> Oh, please, don't come stand in front of me! What do I do?
> I'll pretend I'm reading my book.
> But, hey, it's my money! And how do I know what you're gonna spend it on? Sorry, no money from me!

Even for those who may agree with the sentiments expressed, the advertise- ment is psychologically invasive. The act ends with the clowns tearing the cardboard placards to shreds to the audience's cheers.

A new act for 1996, written by Sarah Shulman and entitled simply 'The Skit,' features a small troupe of workers engaged in a mechanical dance suggesting an abstract assembly line while, standing on stools over them, Miller and Karen Sherman shout commands:

> Work harder to get ahead! Work harder to get ahead!
> Work harder to get ahead! Harder! Harder! Harder!

To which the performers, running in place, reply

> We're working! We're working! We're not getting ahead!

They eventually protest, looking up meekly at Sherman, the towering authority figure,

> But he makes one hundred and seventy-nine times as much as we do!

The skit ends on a questioning note that stops just short of agit-prop. Karen Sherman's boss character *should* be asked to contribute his fair share to the common good. But, as she asks in the skit's final line, 'Who's gonna make me?' The question hangs there, as the players exit, repeating the question to the audience as much as to themselves. 'Who's gonna make him? Who *is* gonna make him? Are you . . .?'

In the 1996 'Adagio,' a slow, trancey act that fuses dance, lifting and acrobatics, three women (Sherman, Gagne and Johnson) perform lifts and combinations that recall the Barnum and Bailey 'strongman,' the muscly heavy lifter performing feats of strength. Here, the women lift each other in all kinds of difficult combinations. As they shift and sweat, with deadpan, focused expressions, they comment in low, calm voices, amplified by wireless microphones, on shifting tax policies for the rich, and the origins of the national debt. The act is quiet, sexy and political. The audience holds its breath and becomes silent at this point, taking in the complexity and beauty of the image along with the disembodied pieces of conversation.

It's a queer circus, amok in New York. But the queerness is presented and set aside. It is normalized, not made the central issue, as are the life of the city, the distribution of money and resources, the attitude of the politically powerful toward the working poor. Everyday life is parodically assaulted from this ring, a space traditionally occupied by 'freaks.' Queer signifying is visible to some, invisible to others, and for most of the audience, I suspect, just beneath the surface. Circus Amok presents two messages at once: an overt one, concerning the fairness of tax laws and the injustice of the removal of the urban social safety net; and a covert one, which shows (rather than tells) the range of genders and bodies that are possible despite *and* in the face of greater economic injustices, no matter what geographic, ethnic, religious or gender neighborhood one happens to inhabit. In realistic drag performance, the object being copied, 'man' or 'woman,' is stable. Circus Amok parodies the freaks of former times – the Double-Bodied Wonder, the Armless Girl, the Egyptian Giant, Barnum & Bailey's 'peerless prodigies of physical phenomena' – by substituting the freakishly normal.

In the 'Safety Net' act, an acrobatics display featuring a miniature trampoline, an airborne procession of characters representing various typical professions – a doctor, a chef, a businesswoman – spring and fly, landing on a gigantic soft mat labeled 'The Safety Net.' Miller interrupts, as 'budget cuts' intervene. 'I gotta show to run, here,' she yells, as the roustabouts remove the mat, the next jumper (a costumed mannequin) is prepared to hit the pavement, and the act continues, this time without the net.

The author wishes to thank Jennifer Miller for her patience and generosity during the research for this article and Jenny Romaine for the invitation to play in the band.

References

McNamara, Brooks (1992) ' "A Canvas City . . . Half as Old as Time": The Carnival as Entertainment' in *The County Fair Carnival: Where the Midway Meets the Grange*, Elmira, New York, Chemung County Historical Society.

Chapter 33

_____

John Bell

LOUDER THAN TRAFFIC
Bread and Puppet Parades

BREAD AND PUPPET WAS ONE of the seminal 60s counter-culture theaters that continues to survive because of a tight, hard focus on its work. Though Bell focuses here on the company's use of a traditional genre, the parade, Bread and Puppet has also taken to the streets of many continents in an impulse akin to agit-prop. Since the early 70s, the theater's annual Domestic Resurrection Circuses on its Vermont farm have presented both utopian and practical visions. Bread and Puppet witnesses and responds to events both here and abroad, attempting to integrate performance into the fabric of everyday life. Bell has both participated in and documented the company for over twenty years.

> I decided to take my painting and sculpture into the street and make a social event out of it, and out of that grew my puppet theater.
>
> Peter Schumann

31 October 1996, 7:30 P.M., New York City:

I am walking – or, more exactly, strutting – up Sixth Avenue towards Fourteenth Street, right in the middle of the six-lane thoroughfare, cradling my trombone in my hand. There are nine of us in the band: trumpet, accordion, clarinet, soprano saxophone, two trombones, tuba and bass drum. We are dressed in white shirts and pants, but wear a heterodoxy of odd hats and accessories on this chilly evening. Michael Romanyshyn, the leader of our ensemble, counts off the beat and we start playing 'Second Line,' an old New Orleans brass-band tune. The sidewalks, cordoned off from the street by blue Police Department sawhorses, are packed with thousands of people from the New York/New Jersey area. We kick off the beat, then layer in the melody, bobbing and dancing up the avenue. The Bread and Puppet Theater contingent of the annual Greenwich Village Halloween Parade stretches out on the street for five blocks.

The focus of the Bread and Puppet parade is a kind of snapshot reaction to the situation of the city under Mayor Rudolph Giuliani, whose pro-business, cost-cutting, patriarchal approach seeks to reverse the sense of government social responsibility which had been central to the United States since the 1930s. Quite specifically, the Bread and Puppet parade concentrates on the scores of community gardens created by New Yorkers on vacant city-owned lots, which Giuliani wants to auction off to commercial bidders.

Our organization of this event is not unlike other Bread and Puppet parades: it combines a selection of puppets, masks and banners from Bread and Puppet's large vocabulary of such images, the organizing and performing skills of a handful of experienced puppeteers, and scores of volunteers both excited about participating in a political theater event and willing to do intense, brief rehearsals immediately before the performance.

For three and a half decades the Bread and Puppet Theater has been communicating in the language of puppets, masks and images; sharing (with hundreds of volunteer performers who have worked with the theater around the world) a particular dialect of that language formed by founder Peter Schumann's artistic aesthetics and theatrical ideals. Of course, this language is not *sui generis*. In addition to Bread and Puppet design innovations it is informed by – and borrows from – many traditions. Our parades reflect those we've seen, studied or been part of: the massive, semi-chaotic Carnival parades of Basel, Switzerland; the intimate street buffoonery of the Catalan theater group Els Comediants; the straightforward determination of twentieth-century political street demonstrations; the boisterous music of New Orleans street bands; the turbulent serenity of Catholic processions of saints and relics; the pots-and-pans 'rough music' of street parades going back to the Middle Ages; the dances of lion and dragon puppets at Chinese New Year street celebrations; the modernist parades designed by Russian revolutionary artists in the 1920s; and the home-made color of patriotic summer parades in Vermont villages and cities.

Parade as political art form

Puppet theater is the theater of all means. Puppets and masks should be played in the street. They are louder than the traffic. They don't teach problems, but they scream and dance and hit others on the head and display life in its clearest terms. Puppet theater is an extension of sculpture. A professional sculptor doesn't have much to do but decorate libraries or schools. But to take sculpture to the streets, to tell a story with it, to make music and dances for it – that's what interests me.

Peter Schumann

Bread and Puppet Theater has been a distinct, unique presence in twentieth-century American theater because of its grounding in three consistent ideas: an embrace of puppet and mask theater as dramatic forms equal to or more expressive than realistic actors' theater; an explicit acceptance of political content as a possible and more often than not necessary element of performance;[1] and, not unrelated to the above, a persistent desire to operate as much as possible outside the strictures of commercial entertainment as defined by late twentieth-century American capitalism.

But there is also a fourth distinctive element in Bread and Puppet's work. In his extensive 1988 history of Bread and Puppet Theater, Stefan Brecht concludes that the parades which Peter Schumann created for 1960s street demonstrations were an original contribution to twentieth-century theater. While Schumann and his early collaborators in Bread and Puppet Theater 'came up with stationary agitational puppet shows that could be done by themselves or at rallies,' his 'main contribution' to these political events was 'the puppet parade,' through which he 'invented an art form' (Brecht 1988 vol. 1: 489). Of course, political street parades have a long pre-twentieth century history,[2] but Bread and Puppet parades during the anti-Vietnam War years were a particular contribution to American culture, a combination of the popular art forms of puppet theater and street demonstration with Schumann's sense of the possibilities of political art.

But for Bread and Puppet Theater the street parade as performance form outlasted its initial significance for the 1960s. Even after the Vietnam War ended in 1975, the Bread and Puppet Theater continued to perform parades as an important part of its theater. What have the twenty years since the end of the war meant for these parades as political street theater?

Bread and Puppet's move from New York City to rural Vermont in 1970 decisively changed the nature of the theater's parading. While participation in local and East Coast political demonstrations continued, these 'traditional' forms of Bread and Puppet parading were augmented by participation in the small community parades organized by local villages in the summer. These events transformed the character of Bread and Puppet parades, because the strident imagery of New York street protests had quite a different effect in Vermont villages such as Plainfield, where Bread and Puppet was first in residence at Goddard College. Bread and Puppet's first participation in Plainfield's Fourth of July parade was an eye-opening experience for Schumann, because many townspeople took offense at the stark

Figure 33.1 The Bread and Puppet Theater at the 1982 Anti-Nuclear March in New York City (photo by Keith Meyers).

images of war suggested by Bread and Puppet's Vietnamese women puppets and the soldiers pursuing them. Schumann did not, of course, subsequently eliminate political content from local Bread and Puppet parades, but a kind of accommodation was reached. A sense of how Bread and Puppet's political theater could interact with the local and patriotic functions of the village parades and subtly or not-so-subtly critique such patriotism began to characterize Schumann's work. In the mid-1970s, for example, Schumann began to experiment with stilt dancing, and one of the characters he invented was a copy of a traditional patriotic circus device: Uncle Sam on ten-foot-tall stilts. But while making use of this spectacular parading character, Schumann also critiqued it: across the band of his Uncle Sam top hat he painted dancing skeletons, which parade viewers could discern after their initial happy surprise to see the red, white and blue man on stilts. A fascinating relationship now exists between Bread and Puppet and Vermont villages: despite the fact that audiences know Bread and Puppet is apt to voice its political concerns, the theater's colorful puppets, stiltdancers and brass band are eagerly received.[3]

Bread and Puppet's participation in local community events and local politics has been an important complement to the international thematic and geographic scope of the theater's work since the early 1970s. The expanded context of the theater's work led Bread and Puppet to develop its parading techniques in four different ways:

1   as theatrical elements of parades and demonstrations planned by anti-war, anti-nuclear and Central American solidarity groups; for example, the 1982 Anti-Nuclear March in New York City, in which 1,000 volunteers (out of the estimated million who participated in the event) took part in Bread and Puppet's section of the parade (see Fig. 33.1);[4]
2   as elements in existing community parades which are not by definition 'political,' such as local Vermont parades or the Greenwich Village Halloween Parade;
3   as advertising devices to attract audiences to outdoor or indoor shows during Bread and Puppet tours; and
4   as short processional elements leading performers and audiences from one spot to another in such productions as *The Crucifixion and Resurrection of Archbishop Oscar Romero of El Salvador*, and *The Same Boat: The Passion of Chico Mendes*.[5]

What has developed then, since Schumann's innovation of the puppet parade as modern political art form, is the establishment of its currency as a live interruption of everyday public life, as a successful means of speaking out in a political fashion in ways which mass-communicated media cannot or will not do. The parade can reach large numbers of people directly, outside the bounds of mass-media, because it takes place in public space for a random audience, and because its processional nature makes greater use of public space than a stationary show.

Performing a city struggle

Bread and Puppet parades since the mid-1970s often choose to present themselves as narratives: presentations of political conflict which unfold through the juxtaposition of successive elements. Instead of simply presenting a series of hopefully powerful images, the parades create meaning through the images' juxtaposition – or, perhaps even better, through the images' active involvement with or against each other. This sense of the parade as a presentation of ambulatory conflict is an important feature of the Bread and Puppet element of the 1996 Halloween Parade, performed as a struggle between the city's community gardens and the political power structure bent on their elimination. To represent the gardens, Bread and Puppet combines life-size and over-life-size nature images with the actual presence of the community gardeners themselves. These are attacked along the parade route by an army of life-size and over-life-size skeletons, which, the parade shows by juxtaposition, are simply agents of the City, itself represented by life-size and over-life-size suited bureaucrats.

Leading the whole Bread and Puppet section is a twenty-foot-wide white cloth banner carried by two paraders and reading 'SAVE NEW YORK'S COMMUNITY GARDENS!' This is followed by the largest figure in the entire Greenwich Village Halloween Parade, a physical embodiment of those community gardens. It is a twenty-foot-tall brown papier-mâché head (its face reflecting a powerful enigmatic serenity) mounted on a set of rusted steel wheels. This Mother Earth puppet floats up Sixth Avenue prone, its huge brown papier-mâché hands reaching ahead, its chin gliding just above the pavement, and its white nylon body stretching out one hundred feet behind. This representation of the gardens is followed by a dozen Green Men: cardboard-masked figures of vegetation spirits inspired by the green men of European folk traditions.[6] Sound for the section is provided by a junk-instrument gamelan orchestra of musicians wearing three-foot by four-foot robes depicting giant yellow stalks of wheat. Sixty East Villagers follow, a group including gardeners and activists and artists concerned about the gardens. They are costumed as gardeners and carry rakes, shovels and hoes as well as placards naming the many gardens at risk.[7] All along the parade route the gardeners and Green Men are attacked by the Skeleton section which follows, attacks which are then beaten back by the Green Men.

The Skeleton section is led by thirty-five performers with cardboard skull masks and black-and-white skeleton costumes, whose aggressive chorus dances with wooden scythes were quickly rehearsed for an hour before the parade. Towering above and behind the human-sized skeletons are two eighteen-foot-tall skeleton puppets, each operated by three puppeteers. Attached to each bony rib cage is a sign: one reads 'DEVELOPMENT,' the other 'DESTRUCTION.' The two come together in a loose, gangly dance to the hot, loud and syncopated percussion ensemble of fourteen drummers. They play white plastic buckets (a loud and cheap alternative to 'real' drums), snaredrum style, with wooden dowels.

The section that follows defines New York City more generally, in an expanded critique of the Giuliani administration, which, the parade shows, is quite literally 'behind' the repeated attacks on the gardens. Six stiltdancers in skeleton masks carry six-foot-square flat cardboard buildings mounted to their backs, followed by a second twenty-foot-tall puppet, a featureless white-faced giant in a business suit (an unsettling figure named the Giant Butcher), mounted on two steel wheels and operated by a crew of six. Circling around this manifestation of civic authority are ten smaller life-size clones of the Giant Butcher, similarly clad in suits and wearing white and featureless head masks topped with black hats. This chorus dances around the Giant Butcher, each smaller Butcher holding a cardboard sign in their hands, painted with one of the following slogans critiquing current political mores and Mayor Giuliani's agenda for the city:

PRIVATIZE! PRIVATIZE! PRIVATIZE!

LESS ART, MORE BUSINESS!

WORKFARE, NOT UNIONS!

I ♥ DISNEY

MAKE NEW YORK SAFE FOR TOURISM

QUALITY OF LIFE

I ♥ SWEATSHOPS!

DOWNSIZE

OUTSOURCE

I ♥ RUPERT MURDOCH

Our brass band follows the butchers, making wild music for their nefarious agenda, and entertaining the audience at the same time. By mounting this parade, with the spirited participation of over a hundred New York volunteers and the community gardeners themselves, Bread and Puppet is able to bring the dire situation of the community gardens to the attention of thousands of spectators in an otherwise non-political event.

JOHN BELL

Puppet parades and the politics of the street

Street theater involves an appropriation of everyday public space for performance. The interruption of normal life created by a stationary street show or a moving parade is an obvious (and usually welcome) 'misuse' of the street's public space. But street performance is in fact a perfectly appropriate use of the thoroughfare, because of the formal attention it pays to the public nature of the street: its celebration of the street and, inevitably, those who happen to be walking on it. The innate politics of any street performance have to do with the definition of the street as a convenience and necessity provided by the state for its citizens. A parade celebrates the public nature of the entire street, repossessing it (momentarily) from the state and from productive use, redefining it as a performance space, and thus celebrating all those participating – paraders and pedestrians, performers and audience. The parade's festive, non-productive use of the street is always subtly or blatantly carnivalesque.

Parades and processions have traditionally incorporated puppets, masks, banners and signs in the festive use of civic space. These performing objects have always been central to European religious, regal and popular traditions. In the Middle Ages, processions with objects took the form of Lord Mayor's Pageants in London, Corpus Christi celebrations in Spain and in carnival performances across the entire European continent. Religious processions with statues and relics have characterized not only Christian traditions but earlier beliefs, for example in Greece, where processions with life-size and over-life-size figures predate the invention of tragedy in Athens. In the twentieth century, these parading techniques were adapted to modern needs: May Day celebrations in Europe and in New York's Union Square, revolutionary parades in 1920s Russia, and, for socio-commercial aims in the United States, the Tournament of Roses Parade in Pasadena and Macy's Thanksgiving Day Parade in New York. Bread and Puppet, as an American theater company led by a German-born director, has combined traditional puppet techniques (and those of its own invention) with a conscious sense of the parade as community ritual, an event which to be truly successful needs to reflect deeply felt social truths.

Parades and processions make more complete use of the street as performance site than do stationary street performances. They exploit not only the public nature of such sites and the possibility of reaching an undifferentiated audience which exists on the street, but also the physical length of the street and the possibilities of movement along it, which are in fact the essence of the street's spatial and public character. Moreover, puppets and other performing objects have a particular power on the street. If a full use of the street's potential involves movement down its length, what elements make the most sense to parade? While the bodies and voices of masses of performers have great theatrical potential in the massive space of the street, even more powerful are material objects which the performers can animate: statues, icons, fetishes, banners, signs and life-size or over-life-size puppets and masks. These, in combination with the performers' bodies, can immediately communicate with an assembled or random audience in the relatively short time during which parader and audience member connect.

Although parades are one of many performance forms used by Bread and Puppet Theater, in the 1987 documentary film *Brother Bread, Sister Puppet*, Peter Schumann speaks of their central importance, calling them 'our most radical statement on the simplicity and the publicness of the arts,' and defining them as '*the* basic form of theater.' The power of the parade, according to Schumann, has to do with its potential to reach a truly random audience:

> It's a defilation [Schumann says], a narrative defilation of added-on, contrasting images, with which you want to speak to a populace that didn't come for being instructed or for entertainment, but that finds itself there for whatever reason, and very often for no particular reason. . . . It's a kind of opportunity to make a giant show, to have this big avenue in front of you, available as a performing field, and these totally anarchic crowds that are milling [about] these streets as your audience. Very enjoyable stuff!
>
> (Farber 1992)

Schumann's sense of the parade's potential to reach a heterogeneous audience is, in one way, the most obvious antidote to the supposed vice of political theater: its tendency to 'preach to the converted.' Certainly this is what Schumann is thinking about above. But even if an audience is not swayed by the intensity of dramatic visualization inherent in puppet theater, the street parade represents a radical use of live public space in an age when ideology and politics saturate the mass-mediated forms of television, radio and film, and when public space itself is threatened by increasing privatization in such places as the shopping mall. In this sense, even if a political street parade is seen only by those who have come to see it, or does *not* persuade accidental audiences to, say, support New York's community gardens, it does assert a dissenting or critical voice; it bears witness.

In an interview made in the middle of the Vietnam War years, Peter Schumann was equivocal about the effects of political performance, an ambivalence that should temper one's sense of just how much is successfully conveyed to an audience in something like the 1996 Bread and Puppet section of the Village Halloween Parade. 'No one who does a play, or plays music, or gives a speech,' Schumann said in 1968, 'has any specific idea of what he wants to achieve with his audience. You say what you want to say and hope you're being understood. The consequences of your activities are pretty much out of your control'(Brown and Seitz 1986: 146–147). Schumann's statement could be taken as a wary resignation to a certain ineffectiveness of street theater, but I think it is, in fact, not. Instead, it represents Schumann's understanding of the ambiguity of meaning inherent in any form of art, and a sort of idealistic hope in the potential of puppet theater to jump the gap between performers and audience. In the years since 1968, Bread and Puppet has continued to use the form of the puppet parade to say what it wants to say, and hundreds of thousands of people have seen the images the theater has employed for that effect. In doing so, it performs the gesture of engaged thought and action, which Grace Paley, in a poem about Bread and Puppet, describes:

> Why not speak the truth directly? Just speak out! Speak up! Speak to! Why not?
>
> (Paley 1985: 7)

Notes

1 See, for example, Schumann's essay 'Puppetry and Politics' (Schumann 1986: 33), in which he writes:

> The arts are political, whether they like it or not. If they stay in their own realm, preoccupied with their proper problems, the arts support the status quo, which in itself is highly political. Or they scream and kick and participate in our century's struggle for liberation in whatever haphazard way they can, probably at the expense of some their sensitive craftsmanship, but definitely for their own soul's sake.

2 Ed. note: see especially Susan Davis. *Parades and Power*. Philadelphia: Temple University Press, 1986.

3 A local newspaper's account (N.A. 1986) is a typical example of how Bread and Puppet has woven itself into community rituals of northeastern Vermont:

> Hardwick's annual Spring Festival Parade just would not be the same without Bread and Puppet Theatre. The troupe had its own band as usual, which added to the festive atmosphere provided by school bands from Lamoille Union, Hazen Union and Greensboro, Hardwick, and Woodbury elementary schools.

4 See Bell 1982 and Brecht 1988 vol. 2: 631–644.

5 For an example of this form, see Bell 1989.

6 See Anderson 1990.

7 These volunteers for the Bread and Puppet Contingent of the parade were also members of Earth Celebrations, an East Village organization presenting

pageants and parades with puppets and music in support of the community gardens. The founder of the group, Felicia Young, created the organization after working with Bread and Puppet in Vermont.

References

Anderson, W. (1990) *Green Man: The Archetype of Our Oneness with the Earth*, San Francisco: HarperCollins.

Bell, John (1982) 'Fight Against the End of the World,' *Theater Work Magazine* 2.6: 20–27.

—— (1989) 'The Bread and Puppet Theater in Nicaragua,' *New Theatre Quarterly* 5.17: 8–22.

Brecht, Stefan (1988) *Peter Schumann's Bread and Puppet Theatre* (2 vols), New York: Routledge, Chapman and Hall.

Brown, H. and Seitz, J. (1986) 'With the Bread and Puppet Theatre: An Interview with Peter Schumann (1968),' in B. McNamara and J. Dolan (eds) *The Drama Review: Thirty Years of Commentary on the Avant-Garde*, Ann Arbor, Mich.: UMI Research Press.

Farber, J. (director) (1992) *Brother Bread, Sister Puppet* (16mm film and video-tape), Montpelier, Vermont: Cheap Cinematography Productions.

Gittelsohn, J. (1985) 'Schumann Made Theater a Social Event,' *Burlington Free Press* 27 March: 3D.

N.A. (1986) 'Spring Festival,' *The Hardwick [Vermont] Gazette* 27 May.

Paley, Grace (1985) 'Feelings in the Presence of the Sight and Sound of the Bread and Puppet Theater,' in S. Green *Bread and Puppet: Stories of Struggle and Faith from Central America*, Burlington, Vt.: Green Valley Film and Art.

Schumann, Peter (1986) 'Puppetry and Politics,' *American Theatre* November: 32–33.

Schumann, Peter and Schumann, E. (n.d.) *Short History of the Bread and Puppet Theater*, Glover, Vermont: Bread and Puppet Theater.

Chapter 34

Jan Cohen-Cruz

NOTES TOWARD AN UNWRITTEN HISTORY OF ANTI-APARTHEID STREET PERFORMANCE

IN THE SUMMER OF 1997 I traveled to South Africa, having received a New York University Research Challenge Fund grant to find or commission an essay on anti-apartheid street theatre. On the advice of Robert Sember, a South African living in New York, I began my trip in Grahamstown, home of a large annual festival.

The Meeting is the only street theatre piece on the official program of the Grahamstown Festival. A French company, Les Piétons, has joined with the Thesele Creative Society from Soweto (the Johannesburg township where, in 1976, students rioted at the advent of new laws forbidding instruction in their own language; a place where a history of resistant street performance might well be writ). *The Meeting* was created by the two companies during a month of living and working together. While the piece contains no overtly political content, members of the two groups answering questions at a press conference express how much they learned from one another through the collaboration. The performance is structured like a soccer game, perhaps the one context in which the two could meet on a level playing field. Occasionally the game erupts or transforms into a South African song or dance, a fight or romantic interlude. Incongruous images make brief appearances, such as the momentary presence of the referee in a tutu. The free performance, on a field near a township, has drawn an unusually mixed crowd of mostly white festival goers and black township dwellers. As soon as it ends, local children set up for a play they have made with a Grahamstown arts-in-education group. Within five minutes, the director, my daughter and I are the only white spectators left on the field. We watch the children enact, in open air, short scenes dealing with their lives, in their native language of Xhosa. But no one I meet at either show has information on street performance during apartheid.

My search is characterized by a series of false starts. At one extreme is this conversation with a local Rhodes University theatre instructor who intimates that street performance is not even a category of theatre:

> HIM: Theatre in South Africa is in a miserable state. It's still being used as a soapbox. No acting, no directing, no script. They might as well go speak from the street or write for the newspapers.

> ME: In the States there's been some very good art with a powerful message, at times strengthened by being played in the street. Strong statement and aesthetics have come together in some instances.

> HIM: If theatre here lasts that long. Critics write how wonderful these plays are just because a black man is standing on the stage. Audiences come. It's not art, it's bad theatre. Next time they go to a good film instead, like Bergman's *Fanny and Alexander*. We're sick of it here after ten years.

> ME: So for me maybe it's good.

> HIM: You'll be sick of it, too, after ten days.

The festival also offers a lecture series called The Winter School. I attend one on Black Economic Development by a successful black businessman, Saki Macozama. This moment, says Macozama, South Africa is between the acts. How will we undo the psychological ramifications of years of white control, like the idea that there is a racial dimension to aptitude, that blacks just don't have the right stuff? There's not enough recognition of what apartheid's effects have been and still are. Black roots, white fruit. Macozama asks us to imagine a marathon race in which the black runners have their arms tied down to their sides during the first three laps, then untied for the fourth. If they don't win, we must remember their roots.

I meet with Peter Larlham, a South African theatre historian who now teaches and directs in California. He advises me to find someone black who'd been part of performances around the funerals of anti-apartheid activists in the townships during the 1970s and 1980s. Peter believes that these were the most compelling instances of anti-apartheid street performance, as well as the least widely known, having been illegal to take part in, let alone document. There are few black people at this festival, to my naive surprise, and no one I meet has seen these funerals. So I go to the university library and search out accounts of township life of that period, novels that may include such descriptions, all the issues of the *South African Theatre Journal*. Coming up empty, I ask for help. A librarian sends me upstairs to the tiny office of a black man who also works there.

The man is 56 years old with gentle, sad eyes and a penchant for quoting Shakespeare. He is an anthropology student who grew up in a township. He was educated by the white man his family worked for who believed in equal schooling for everyone. He is a member of the ANC (African National Congress) and was involved in performances around the funerals of other anti-apartheid activists. I ask him if he would write about them for the book. He looks at me in disbelief. How could he possibly? You were there, I say. You are educated, you know how to write. He tells me about a friend who conducted the funerals and who now works as an auto mechanic in town. Perhaps I could talk to the two of them. I suggest that *he* talk to the friend, sensing that this is *his* essay to write, not mine. He agrees to think about it and talk with me tomorrow. The next day he shows me four handwritten pages that suggest a moving, clear article that could follow. He evokes his Xhosa tribe's traditional use of dance and song to prepare for battle and then, afterwards, to honor the dead. He sees these rituals as the root of performances at township funerals for slain warriors of anti-apartheid battles. I feel that I have found my writer.

But I am wrong. Back in the States in September, the agreed-upon deadline comes and goes and the essay does not arrive. I phone him at the library and he tells me he is under a lot of pressure, but it will be finished soon. Time passes. I call again and ask him to at least send me those original four pages he showed me in Grahamstown. He is always polite and agreeable, but he sends nothing. I call again with the idea of interviewing him but he is on leave from work. I have no other way to contact him.

Why didn't he send the essay? If he could do four pages from one day to the next, why did he not complete the essay in three months? I know he writes papers for his anthropology courses. I know he is very busy. I wonder if he did complete it but does not believe that what he wrote is good enough. I wonder if this is the fourth lap and his arms still feel tied down. I struggle with whether or not to use his name in this account. If I do, he may feel humiliated, though that is far from my intention. If I don't, am I not stealing his material, the very thing I was trying to avoid?

I can't bear this book appearing without something on anti-apartheid street performance. I contact a white South African scholar/activist. But his workload as a university professor is overwhelming. He and his colleagues struggle to find time for their own research much less for someone else's. I'm uncomfortable as an American writing it myself; in the early days of the women's movement, I felt that male essays on feminism were co-opting our territory. But I'm more uncomfortable leaving it out entirely. So I end this book with notes toward an as-yet unwritten history.

Black South African playwright Zakes Mda provides a useful framework for such a project in his distinction between the protest and resistant mode of political theatre:

> Protest Theatre disapprovingly depicts a situation of oppression, but does not go beyond that. It addresses itself to the oppressor, with the view of appealing to his or her conscience. [. . . I]t is a theatre of complaint, [. . .] of self-pity, of moralising, of mourning, and of hope-lessness. The leading practitioner of this political theatre was Athol Fugard whose plays [. . .] clearly protest against racial segregation by depicting its inhuman nature. But [. . .] the spirit of defiance that exists in the real life situation in the South Africa that we all know is non-existent in these works. The oppressed let oppression happen to them, and all they do is moan and complain about it, and devise ways to live with it.
>
> (Mda 1994: 8–9)

Addressed to the oppressor, these works could, of course, take place in theatre buildings. Perhaps Fugard's most radical act was integrating black and white actors in these segregated territories. Mda then identifies a Theatre for Resistance:

> In the mid-1970's black theatre practitioners went beyond protest, a position which was spearheaded by the Black Consciousness Movement of the time. [. . .] Theatre for Resistance addressed itself to the oppressed with the overt aim of rallying or of mobilising the oppressed to fight against oppression. [. . .] In the beginning Theatre for Resistance was performed at weddings and at funerals, at political rallies, in church and school halls in the townships, and in city venues such as the Market Theatre.
>
> (10–11)

Mda thus places these funerals within the early phase of an entire resistant aesthetic/strategy.

Another source for this as-yet unwritten history can be gleaned from white anti-apartheid novelist Andre Brink. He describes the role of a 'theatre of extremity' within the politically repressive atmosphere of South Africa in the late 1970s and 1980s:

> [A] veritable cultural explosion erupted in the country, communicating and amplifying the process of contestation in the most remote and deprived communities. And [especially black] theatre was central to this experience [. . .] because black theatre, often performed on a fly-by-night basis, hugely inventive in its means and mobile in its movements,

could literally flit from one venue to another, unfettered by formal
constraints of stage and lighting and auditorium. [. . .] Wherever an
empty space could be found or improvised a play could be performed;
by word of mouth an audience could assemble, within minutes, from
shacks and shanties and bushes and hideouts; and at the first intimation
of approaching police everybody, audience and actors, could disperse
just as quickly. Even so, inevitably, people were often arrested,
detained, beaten up or harassed. But far from discouraging them, most
of them were inspired by such persecution to feats of ever more daring
proportion.

Very little record of this 'theatre of extremity' has survived, as
both actors and audience would erase all evidence about the event as
soon as it was over; texts were almost never committed to paper: for
its efficacy this theatre relied exclusively on the immediacy and urgency
of the context.

(Brink 1996: 5)

Building on Brink, theatre scholars would do well to interview township
residents, many of whom would have participated as spectators or actors in
radical street performances of that period.

Mda uses the term 'reconciliation' to refer to the thrust of South African
politics, culture and art since Mandela's release from prison in 1990. Certainly
the centerpiece of this movement has been the highly controversial Truth
and Reconciliation Commission (TRC) hearings. Established in 1993 as the
white government gave way to Mandela and the ANC, this controversial
compromise consists of amnesty on a case-by-case basis in exchange for full
disclosure of politically mandated crimes of the apartheid era. These highly
emotional, televised hearings frequently feature confrontations between
families of the dead and their murderers. Some performance scholars are
looking at the TRC as performance. Others, like Mda, follow Coleen
Angove's definition of Theatre of Reconciliation as that which gives a perspective 'in which the reality of a polarised society is defied to present human
beings from all racial and cultural groups, communicating, sharing and understanding' (Angove 1992: 44).

Each of the three periods of anti-apartheid performance since the 1960s
has its own way of dealing with the dead. Fugard mourned them in the
protest phase; the black librarian and his colleagues used their funerals as
occasions to build energy and strengthen resolve during the period of resistance; the Truth and Reconciliation Commission hearings currently are a
means of remembering the dead, and, as Michael Ignatieff writes, re-estab-
lishing a moral order in South Africa by creating 'a public realm where truth
is truth and lies are lies, where actions are held accountable, where the state
is held to certain standards' (1997: 93). Ignatieff recounts Nason Ndwandwe's
efforts to find out what happened to his daughter Phila, an anti-apartheid

activist who was 'disappeared' in the 1980s. Because of the promise of amnesty, members of a police hit squad admitted responsibility for her death at the hearings. They then drove Ndwandwe and TRC investigators to the abandoned farm where she'd been shot, and exhumed her grave. Ndwandwe and his family cleansed her bloody bones and carried out other tasks so that at last she might go to her final resting place among her ancestors:

> They will visit every place to which Phila's bones were taken, including the Pietermaritzburg morgue and her new grave, so that her spirit can be gathered up from these places. While this is being done, Nason will keep silent. When they all get back to Umlazi [his home], they will slaughter a goat in his back yard, and a crate of beer will be brought out. Then Nason will resume speaking, and will celebrate the safe return of Phila's spirit to the ancestors.
>
> (Ignatieff 1997: 88)

How long will South Africa be 'between the acts,' a period character-ized by the heightening of everything: hopes, fears, crime, opportunities? An oft-repeated phrase these days is the gravy train, referring to people who take advantage of this transitional moment for individual gain. How critical that people see themselves as part of a great chain, beginning with their ancestors and stretching into a future where the fruits of the land may be shared by all. I'm struck by the role of performance in the township funerals and the post-TRC rituals alike to put individuals into the larger context of the community of the living and the dead. As Fats Waller sings, it'll have to do, until the real thing comes along.

References

Angove, Coleen (1992) 'Alternative Theatre: Reflecting a Multi-Racial South African Society?" *Theatre Research International* Vol. 17 No. 1, Spring: 39–45.

Brink, Andre (1996) 'Challenge and Response: The Changing Face of the Theatre in South Africa,' Salzberg Seminar, Session 340.

Ignatieff, Michael (1997) 'Digging Up the Dead,' *The New Yorker*, November 10: 84–93.

Macozama, Saki (1997) 'Black Economic Development,' The Winter School. Grahamstown Festival, South Africa, July 9.

Mda, Zakes (1994) 'The Role of Culture in the Process of Reconciliation,' Centre for the Study of Violence and Reconciliation, Seminar No. 9.

Index

Page numbers in italics refer to illustrations

London: Hyde Park 160, 161; Jubilee
Gardens 161, 162; Lord Mayor's
Pageants 278; Stock Exchange 160,
161
Loper, Steve 68–72
Lords of Misrule 198, 204
Los Angeles 39, 119; City Hall *40*, 41;
Sunset Boulevard 39
Lotto 139, 140
Lowe, Biba 41
luan (chaos) 204
Ludlam, Charles 264
Lunacharsky, A.V. 16, 17–18
Lupe la Veracruzana 248

Machine 36
McNamara, Brooks 263
Macozama, Saki 283
Macy's 92; Thanksgiving Parade 279
Madres de la Plaza de Mayo *see*
Mothers of the Plaza de Mayo
Madsen, Hunter 136
Makere University 233
Malawi 234
Malina, Judith 150–9
Malpede, Karen 65, 155
Malvinas, Islas *see* Islas Malvinas
La Mama 263
Mamet, David 198
Mancillas, Aida 87–8
Mandela, Nelson 286
Mao Zedong (Mao Tse-tung) 26, 30*n*,
199, 200, 201
March for Human Rights (Argentina)
79
marches 3, 79
Marcos, Ferdinand 256, *257*, 258,
259, 260
Marcos, Imelda 259
Mardi Gras 196, 198, 204
marijuana mailing 190–2
marketplaces 256
Marxism 9, 13, 17, 30
Mary, Virgin 79
masks 224, 225, 261, 272
masquerading 204
mass participation 20–1, 36–7

masses *see* working class
Mau Mau struggle 239
May Day, celebrations 18, 19–24, 278
Mda, Zakes 285, 286
media 41, 43, 48, 67, 105; *see also*
television
medieval plays 4
The Meeting 282–3
Mexicali 249
Mexico 86–9, 154, 180, 247–52
Meza, Fernan 148*n*
Mid-Pennine Arts 209
Millado, Chris 258
Miller, Arthur 198
Miller, Jennifer 262–70
Mindanao Council for People's Culture
259
minimal art 127–8
missionary schools 231, 233, 239
Mitchell, Adrian 213; *The Tragedy of
King Real* 211
Mojica, José 102
The Money Tower 155–6
Monson, Jennifer 264
Monteiasi 188
Montréal, AIDS conference 43
monumental propaganda 16–17
Moore, Harmonie 91
Moscow 17; May Day celebrations
(1919) 18, 19–21; Proletkult 20
Moser, Pete 213, 215
Mother Clean 225, 226–8
Motherfuckers 180
Mothers of the Plaza de Mayo 3, 51,
74–85, *75*
Mucho, Bessie Mae 91, 97
Munch, Edvard 267
Munich, beer-hall *putsch* 172
mural art 144
Murray, Rick 264, 267
museums 146–7
music 28, 94, 95, 103–10, 182,
185–7, *187*, 213–14, 271–2, 276
Muslims 108
*My Calling (Card) Number One: A Reactive
Guerrilla Performance for Dinners and
Cocktail Parties* 130–2

INDEX